CITIZENS APART

CITIZENS APART

A Portrait of the Palestinians in Israel

AMINA MINNS

NADIA HIJAB

I.B.Tauris & Co Ltd
Publishers
London · New York

Published in 1990 by
I.B.Tauris & Co Ltd
110 Gloucester Avenue
London NW1 8JA

175 Fifth Avenue
New York
NY 10010

In the United States of America,
and Canada distributed by
St Matin's Press
175 Fifth Avenue
New York 10010

956.74054
m i N
c . 1

British Library Cataloguing in Publication Data

Minns, Amina
  Citizens apart: a portrait of the Palestinians in Israel. –
  (Society and culture in the Middle East).
  1. Israel. Palestinian Arabs. Social conditions
  I. Title II. Hijab, Nadia III. Series
  305.89275694
ISBN 1–85043–204–X 3 4. 5 0

6/91
Printed in Great Britain by
Redwood Press Limited, Melksham, Wiltshire

For Khalil, who looked life in the eye,
who loved his country, to death

CONTENTS

PREFACE

The year 1948 marks the consciousness of Palestinians everywhere, but perhaps most of all those who have, in many ways, been paid the least attention: the Palestinians in Israel. Theirs is a dramatic story. Almost overnight, they were transformed from a majority in their own country to a minority. Isolated from their fellow Arabs, they were forced to live, work and study in an alien system.

Somehow, 'Israel's minorities', as Israeli officialdom looks upon the Palestinians, have survived, and the majority have done so as Palestinians. Even more worrying for Israeli Jews, their numbers have quadrupled since Israel was created, growing from the 150,000 or so that remained after 1948, when they constituted 11 per cent of the population, to nearly 700,000, or about 17 per cent of the population.

The Palestinians who have undergone the experience of 'Israelization', as opposed to the experience of exile or of later Israeli occupation, certainly remain part of the same people. Yet, in some ways, they seem a little different. As the notes from our first field trip for this book, in 1987, put it,

> The strongest first impression was the difference between the ones 'on the outside' and those 'on the inside'. The ones on the inside seem more subdued. They are also more prickly; they immediately assume you're attacking them if you make a comment. The ones asked about this impression agreed and said, 'It's because we have been culturally and mentally colonized.'

However, had the first field trip taken place in 1989 instead of

1987, the results might have been different: with each passing
day, the Palestinians in Israel are becoming more self-confident
and sure-footed. If the first major challenge to the Zionist take-
over of Palestine came from the Palestinians in exile, and the
second main challenge came from the Palestinians under Israeli
occupation in the West Bank and Gaza, then the third is likely
to come from the Palestinians in Israel. What final shape this
challenge will take is not yet clear; at the present time it takes
the form of a struggle, largely from within the system, for equal
rights with Israeli Jews.

There is a growing body of literature on the subject of the
Palestinians in Israel, but it is tiny compared with the volumes
on Palestinians in exile and under occupation. In this book, we
hope to bring the story of the Israeli Palestinians to a wider
audience. Although there are a handful of personal accounts by
Palestinians in Israel, the bulk of the writing has been on
political issues.

Moreover, very little has been written about the institutions
and voluntary groups that have been established at the grass-
roots level during the last 15 years by many Palestinians to
serve their community, which has suffered from discrimination
and official neglect over the last four decades. The process of
setting up these associations was an affirmation of Palestinian
Arab identity, and at the same time a reinforcement of that
identity through the collective experience of community service.
(In the decade leading up to the intifada, a similar process took
place in the West Bank and, to a lesser extent, Gaza.)

This book attempts to offer insights into the lives of
Palestinians in present-day Israel, and to examine how many of
them are preserving and developing their identity through
institutions. The second of these aims, we hope to cover in part
one. The political development of the Palestinians in Israel is
reviewed in chapter 1, 'Surviving'; the Palestinian efforts to save
what was left of their resource base is examined in chapter 2,
'Preserving'; Palestinian activism to alleviate the social fall-out
of discrimination, as it manifested itself in areas such as poor
education, drug abuse among young people, and lack of
economic opportunities, is described in chapter 3, 'Serving';
chapter 4, 'Reversing?', examines the attempts by the Israeli
Jewish authorities to halt the growing assertiveness of the

Palestinian community. In part two, the 'Portrait of the '48 Palestinians' (i.e. the Palestinians who remained following the creation of the State of Israel in 1948) is painted through the stories of some of the people who have themselves been active in institution building for Palestinians in Israel.

The material presented here is largely drawn from four field trips, each about a month long, conducted between 1987 and 1989. The first two trips involved wide-ranging surveys of the institutions that existed and that were being developed by the Palestinians, collecting material published by the associations, as well as conducting interviews with key members. These field trips covered several exclusively Arab towns and villages, including Nazareth, Umm al-Fahem, Taybeh, Sakhneen, Ailaboun, Majd al-Kroum, Mi'iliya, Musmus, Yarka, Baqa El Gharbeya, Kufr Kenna, Shafa Amr, Beersheba, Laqqiya, as well as mixed Arab–Jewish towns such as Jaffa, Acre, Haifa, Lydda, and Ramleh. As a result, we focused on five institution builders and their extended families, whose stories could give a sense of what life in Israel was like for Palestinians. The second two field trips consisted largely of extended interviews with members of these five families, whose stories are given in part two.

Naturally, the five institution builders all have a strong sense of Palestinian identity. Although they belong to different religious groups – Muslim, Christian, and Druze – their nationalism is secular. They identify themselves primarily as Arabs and Palestinians, with their religious identity coming later. The families also represent a cross-section of village, town and Bedouin life, and there is a range of ages to reflect the change across generations. As they seek to build institutions, there are some steps forward and some backwards. Pseudonyms are used in part two, and some details have been omitted in order to protect the identities of the story-tellers. For the same reason, we have also sometimes avoided names in part one.

The two parts of the book naturally complement each other, but it is possible to read each as a self-contained unit – certainly the most vibrant account of life in Israel for a Palestinian is to be found in part two, in which people tell their stories. We do not claim to be presenting a portrait of all Palestinians living in Israel: just as there are many who affirm their identity and demand their rights, there are many others who are content to work within the system, or who accept their situation as it is. In both parts one and two, we have focused on those Palestinians, rapidly increasing in number, who challenge the Israeli system to accept them as Palestinians and as equals.

When referring to the Israeli Palestinians, we will generally use the term ''48 Palestinians'. It is in common use among Palestinians everywhere to refer to their compatriots in Israel. Indeed, when they refer to their home country, many '48 Palestinians avoid using the word 'Israel'. When returning from abroad, they are likely to say, 'I'm going back to *al-bilad* (the country)'. We will also use the term Israeli Jews whenever necessary to avoid confusion (the Jewish state currently separates its citizens by defining them on their identity cards as Jews or Arabs).

During our work on this book, we received much moral and material support which we would like to acknowledge. Ms Hasna Mikdashi and Dr Nabil Shaath encouraged us to think about the project and gave us invaluable assistance in the early stages of research. Later research would not have been possible without the generous support of Mr Abdul Mohsen Qattan, as well as that of the Diana Tamari Sabbagh Foundation.

Of the many people who assisted with advice and with background material and documents, mention must be made, first and foremost, of Dr George T. Abed and Dr Khalil Nakhleh, who were particularly helpful in this respect. They have developed special expertise on Palestinian development, which is reflected in the Welfare Association, the institution they run as Director-General and Programme Director respectively. Established by a group of Palestinian businessmen and academics in 1983, the Welfare Association is one of the leading Palestinian development agencies in Europe, and we are grateful for the many instances where its specialized knowledge provided guidance.

We would also like to thank the following for their encouragement and support: Dr Adel Afifi, Ms Julia Helou, John and Sue Haycock, and Mr Ian Williams whose keen eye was of great help in the first part. We owe a debt of gratitude to Ayman, Emtiaz and Raja, George and Mona, and Ziad and Maysa.

Finally, there are many '48 Palestinians to thank, especially those who allowed us to use their stories. Often, advice and assistance blossomed into friendship. We cannot mention them by name, as this would doubtless make their lives more difficult than they already are, but we owe them a real debt of gratitude. Perhaps the publication of their story will help, in part, to repay this debt.

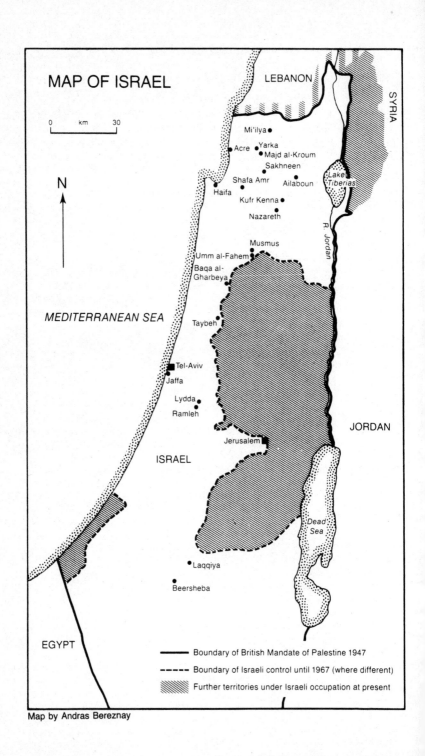

MAP OF ISRAEL

0   km   30

N

LEBANON

SYRIA

Mi'ilya ●

Acre ● Yarka ●
Majd al-Kroum ●
Sakhneen ●

Shafa Amr ● Ailaboun ●

Haifa ●
Kufr Kenna ●

Nazareth ●

Lake Tiberias

R. Jordan

MEDITERRANEAN SEA

Musmus ●

Umm al-Fahem ●
Baqa al-Gharbeya ●

Taybeh ●

Tel-Aviv ■
Jaffa ●

Lydda ●
Ramleh ●

Jerusalem ●

JORDAN

ISRAEL

Dead Sea

● Laqqiya

● Beersheba

EGYPT

―――――― Boundary of British Mandate of Palestine 1947

------- Boundary of Israeli control until 1967 (where different)

▨▨▨ Further territories under Israeli occupation at present

Map by Andras Bereznay

PART ONE
Identity Through Institutions

No one knows the Jewish mentality the way we Palestinians in the '48 area know it. Between the pressures we are putting on the authorities here, and the uprising in the West Bank and Gaza, they will be obliged to recognize us as a people.

Amer, teacher

1
Surviving

The stone that was neglected by the builders has become, truly, the corner-stone.

Salim Jubran

The political and social development of the '48 Palestinians falls into two broad phases: before and after 1967. The first phase was a period of fragmentation and isolation; the second a time of regrouping and of finding a political voice. It is hard to imagine just how difficult the early years were. Then, the '48 Palestinians had practically no relations with their fellow Arabs. The radio was their main source of both political news and news about their families. Even Arabic-language books and magazines were available only to a handful of Palestinians. Arab attitudes towards the '48 Palestinians were mixed. On the one hand, they were often lauded by other Arabs for remaining steadfast; yet, on the other, they were looked upon with suspicion because they dealt with the Israelis. As one '48 Palestinian put it, 'Some Arabs we meet abroad refuse to speak to us. They consider us traitors because we carry Israeli passports, even though we tell them we are Palestinians, not Israelis.'

The pre-1967 days were the days of Israeli military rule, which lasted from the end of 1948 until 1966. Palestinian towns and villages were declared 'closed areas' and 'security zones', and permits were needed to move outside these areas (a few years before it was completely lifted, military rule was eased somewhat to allow more freedom of movement, and to allow the Israeli Jewish economy – then booming – to tap the reserves of cheap Palestinian labour).

Isolated from the rest of the Arab world and from each other, many '48 Palestinians passionately espoused a pan-Arab

3

philosophy before 1967. However, that ideal was tarnished by the Arab defeat in the June 1967 war, during which Israel occupied the West Bank, which had been held by Jordan since 1948; Gaza, which had been held by Egypt; the Egyptian Sinai Peninsula; and the Syrian Golan Heights. As Emad, a 48-year-old teacher from Nazareth recalled,

> Like most of my generation, I identified with Nasser's goals, with pan-Arabism. I believed in his speeches, and I believed every word that I heard on Cairo radio. The Arab world was going to bring us freedom. It was no longer just the dream of the older generation, it was becoming a reality. And then came '67. It was a trauma for me and for all our people.

The 1967 war marked a turning point for '48 Palestinians like Emad:

> It radically changed my way of thinking because it made me confront the reality of my people's situation: we were alone, and we had to struggle on our own. We had to rid ourselves of our fears and we had to become self-reliant. I was a Palestinian with an identity and fate separate from the rest of the Arab world.

Yet, although many began to distinguish between their specific Palestinian identity and a general Arab one, the '48 Palestinians automatically use the word 'Arab' when they speak of something that is theirs, as opposed to 'Jewish'. And although there is bitterness about the 1967 defeat, little of it is directed against the late President Gamal Abdel-Nasser. Indeed, many people still have his picture on their walls.

The 1967 war had other results as well. After Israel's capture of the West Bank, contact became possible across the 'Green Line' – the dividing line between Israel and Jordan after the 1948 war (Israel has no fixed borders as yet). The '48 Palestinians could meet once more with their compatriots in the West Bank and Gaza, and with their families in exile, to exchange information and ideas. More recently, several '48 Palestinians became teachers at West Bank universities (although the Israeli occupation authorities made sure they had only one-year renewable contracts), and others studied in West Bank institutions. Some of the '48 Palestinians are still going through a process of rediscovery. About three years ago the al-Hadaf cultural club in Umm al-Fahem took a group of women on a day trip to the West Bank; they were pleasantly surprised to discover, as they put it, that the people there were not 'savages' as they had been led to believe by Israeli propaganda.

Before the intifada broke out on 9 December 1987, the '48 Palestinians had mixed views about the West Bankers and Gazans. The following is a sample: 'They are nothing but uneducated traders and peasants, who come to our region and trade with the Israelis'; 'They have a better Arab educational system and better research facilities'; 'They are not real fighters. It's just a bunch of kids who throw stones at the soldiers. This won't solve anything'; 'We have tremendous respect for them. We learn a lot from them, and they learn from us too.'

Following the uprising, the '48 Palestinians' pride and respect in their compatriots under occupation swelled: 'We must support our brothers in the West Bank and Gaza. Their struggle is our struggle.' Many village and townspeople formed committees to collect money and goods to support the intifada. On 21 December, a 'Day of Peace' (*yawm al-salam*) was observed by the majority of '48 Palestinians to show solidarity for those under occupation. Huge demonstrations were held. In Nazareth, they boasted: 'You should have seen our demonstration on yawm al-salam in support of the West Bank and Gaza. It was the biggest, most impressive and most successful demonstration in the country.'

In Jaffa, the people said, 'You should have seen the demonstration we had in support of our brothers. It was the biggest and most impressive. No one has seen anything like it.' In fact, whatever '48 town or village one visited in early 1988, the story was the same – theirs was the biggest demonstration in support of the Palestinians under occupation. While it was not surprising that there was a large turn-out in a politicized place like Nazareth, it was significant that the yawm al-salam demonstrations drew large crowds in hitherto fairly unpolitical places like the mixed cities of Lydda and Jaffa. It revealed the extent of the change that has taken place among the '48 Palestinians.

An observer of the Lydda and Jaffa demonstrations reported that

> People turned up spontaneously, including women and children. In fact, the ones who shouted and cheered the loudest were the women. Some even wanted to throw stones. They were far stronger than the men, and the rougher the police were with them, the stronger they resisted. Six girls were arrested, and the old traditional men were aghast when they heard about it. They went to plead with the police for their release, saying that it was against Arab values for girls to spend the night away from home. The girls were eventually freed. Can you imagine, they even arrested a five-year-old boy?

The '48 Palestinians had to work for many years before they reached a critical mass of political consciousness that enabled them to organize demonstrations like these, or to call strikes that paralysed the entire Arab sector in Israel for their rights in education or health. As the late Emile Touma (1985) put it, the day after the creation of Israel, 'all traditional Arab national activists, the known intellectuals and the professionals had left the country, and the Arab national minority of 150,000 was largely composed of peasants, workers and the middle class. Under the circumstances, the question is: how did this small Palestinian Arab minority survive?' The rest of this chapter will highlight the major milestones on this road to political mobilization and consciousness.

Pre-1967 political trends
Two main independent Palestinian political trends existed in the first decades after the creation of Israel. The first was the Israeli Communist Party, most of whose members were Arab. The strictly pro-Soviet party, which had existed before 1948, enjoyed legal status mostly because it had a Jewish membership. It believed in fighting for Palestinian rights within the Israeli system. The second was the Arab nationalists, who were not organized into a political party. Some of them established the pro-Nasserite al-Ard (The Land) movement in the early

1960s, but they were not granted legal status. The al-Ard members refused to accept the system that had been imposed on the Palestinians, although their charter recognized the UN partition plan of 1947. As a result, they were unable to organize openly as the Communists were.

These were the two non-Zionist political trends. At the same time, the Israeli Jewish political establishment ran Arab lists alongside their own lists for national elections. Through a judicious use of carrot and stick these candidates, who were largely drawn from the traditional leadership based on the extended family (*hamula*), managed to draw about 75 per cent of the Arab vote in the early years. The Arabs effectively functioned as a vote bank for the Israeli Labour Party, which in those years was the perennial government of the state.

These two broad non-Zionist trends remain in existence today. By 1965, the Israeli Communist Party, by then renamed Rakah, or the New Communist List, attracted 23 per cent of the Arab vote. In 1975, allied with the independent Graduates' League as the Nazareth Democratic Front, the Communists took over the Nazareth municipal council (the Democratic Front included the Merchants and Craftsmen's Movement and the League of High-school Students). It was a major turning point in '48 Palestinian affairs. A little later, Rakah allied itself with other non-Zionist forces to become the Democratic Front for Peace and Equality (often known simply as the Front, or Jabha).

The Communists are frequently criticized for being too 'moderate', and for compromising Palestinian interests in order to retain their legal status. Certainly, people who had lost homes and land were unable to see the advantage of remaining loyal to the state or working within the Israeli system that uprooted and oppressed them. However, the Communists' ability to organize legally, and most importantly to publish in Arabic, was a key factor in maintaining the '48 Palestinians' identity and awareness during the first two decades. The Haifa-based paper *al-Ittihad* (Union), edited by the brilliant Palestinian writer Emile Habibi, and the literary magazine *al-Jadid*, were for many years the only material available to the '48 Palestinians in their own language.

As Abed, a 46-year-old poet put it,

My awareness started at an early age because my father, who was a merchant, worked with the Communists. The Communists tried to change people's attitudes by going to villages and lecturing about nationalism. They played a big role in stirring up nationalist feelings. But it was only at the end of my secondary school that communism really began to influence my thinking. The influence was not just political, but also literary. I began to write poetry around 1955. It was about the land and the peasants. All those who wrote poetry in those days did so with political connotations.

Aref, a doctor, recalled,

I remember as a child I used to attend some of the secret meetings my father had with other Communists. At the age of 13 I went to summer camp in Moscow, which opened my eyes to many things. Then my awareness developed further when I went to the Orthodox school in Haifa. To me, Haifa was the centre of Arab nationalism, and I learned a great deal about our cause there.

The Palestinians in the Communist Party could work and publish legally, but the Arab nationalists continued to be harassed. As Jiryis describes it,

By the end of the first decade of Israel's existence, the summer of 1958, that [nationalist] opposition had taken distinct shape in the form of a political organisation ('The Arab Front', later the 'Popular Front'), whose declared objective was to combat the repressive policy of the state to its Arab citizens. Although that front was later to split, even this split was by no means useful to the Israelis, for it led to the rise of a new organisation with an Arab nationalist colouring (Al-Ard, or 'The Land Movement'). In the end, the authorities could only deal with Al-Ard by issuing a military edict ordering its dissolution. (1979, p. 32)

There was a short-lived popular front between the Communists and the Arab nationalists, before they settled into the mutual antipathy which continues to the present day. In 1959, the al-Ard group began to publish a newspaper, which was closed by 1960 (they were still able, through a legal loophole, to publish individual issues, each one carrying a different first name, but linked by a common last name). The group formed a political party in the mid-1960s, but this was banned within a few days. Al-Ard leaders, like Saleh Baransi and Mansour Kardosh, were harassed and Baransi, for example, spent ten years in gaol.

The beliefs behind al-Ard, resurfaced in the Umm al-Fahem-based movement, Abna' al-Balad (Sons of the Country), which made its appearance as an electoral list for municipal elections. Although Abna' al-Balad members rejected participation in Israeli national elections (as al-Ard had done earlier), they did take part in municipal ballots.

Pre-1967 personal trends
Perhaps the most difficult obstacle to raising political awareness for both nationalists and Communists was the nature of *al-nakba* (the catastrophe), as Palestinians refer to the loss of Palestine in 1948. For the most part it was suffered individually and not as a collective experience. At the time, the Palestinians, fragmented, dispersed and isolated, lacked an overall view of the national implications of their catastrophe, as well as the means to articulate a nation-wide response. The shock of defeat left the generation that was aged in their thirties and forties in 1948 with a sense of fear and impotence. This fear, and consequent passivity, was transferred to their children, although not on a lasting basis. By the time the children were in their thirties and forties, this generation was aware enough to develop a mechanism of response.

There is something of a schism between the generations of '48 Palestinians, with the younger generation adopting an accusatory tone to their elders. 'They did nothing. They sat back and let it all happen, and waited for the world to solve the problem for them', is a frequent complaint.

Not everyone, however, is unsympathetic to the older generation. Amer, a 46-year-old teacher whose family were forced to leave their village for Nazareth said,

It is true that when I was young, my awareness about our dilemma was very limited. The old people did not talk about it out of fear and ignorance. But I never condemned them, and I still don't. On the contrary, as my awareness developed, I sympathized and felt deeply for what they had lost and for how much they had suffered. The fact that they did not fight was not really their fault; they did not have the means.

The older generation is hurt by accusations of passivity, and feel pride in the activism of the younger Palestinians. One group of old men responded to their criticisms saying:

The young do not know what it was like to be brutally robbed of our land and homes. They do not know what it was like to live under military rule, forbidden to move from place to place without permission. We struggled in our own way, by resisting the police and soldiers, by singing nationalist songs at weddings and festivities, by listening to the national poets. The younger generation's awareness has developed as a result of our own experiences. We did not have what they have today. Conditions and convictions have changed, and so have the methods of struggle.

Describing his experiences with his parents, Emad, the 48-year-old teacher from Nazareth, recalled:

My father owned land in Ma'loul,* growing olives and maize. When the troubles started in '48, they went to Nazareth, hoping things would settle down. But this was not to be. As a young boy, I listened to my grandfather reminisce about his land and home, and I used to hear him rant and rave against the Jews for what they had done. My grandfather did not seem to be crippled by fear the way my father was. My father was constantly warning us not to complain out loud, to be wary of the authorities and of collaborators.

  Although my father's generation had witnessed the invasion, the expropriation and the massacres, they were defeatists. They could not conceive of struggling on their

* Ma'loul was one of the villages destroyed after Palestine became Israel. Its former inhabitants visit it once a year, to commemorate their links with the land. This ceremony is the subject of a short documentary by Michel Khleifi, 'Ma'loul celebrates its destruction' (*Ma'loul tahtafil fi damariha*).

own, because they had neither the education nor the know-
how. At first, that fear was passed on to my generation.
There was so much fear around, that no one dared utter the
word 'Palestinian'. No one even dared carry *al-Ittihad* openly
in the street as they do today. They were likely to be stopped
by the soldiers and questioned just for carrying that paper.

My generation was the transitional one. Today's generation also suffers, but differently. On the one hand, they have
advantages we did not have; although the Arab educational
system is by no means equal to the Jewish one, my children
have better facilities than I ever had. Moreover, I give them
what my parents did not give me: awareness and encouragement about their identity as Palestinians, and about their
heritage. They have access to several newspapers, books and
TV which keeps them informed about the fate of Palestinians
outside. They have material comforts I never had. On the
other side, their aspirations are higher. They leave secondary
school and are faced with the pain of the outside world –
discrimination, lack of job opportunities, humiliation, une-
qual rights. But they are not overcome by fear, they do not
retreat in silence. They ask, 'Why did we end up like this?'
And they become more ardent to fight for their rights and
identity.

This view was reinforced by Nidal, a 41-year-old municipality officer, who said,

The young people today are much stronger because they are
Palestinian from the minute they are born. They are also able
to do things we couldn't. For example, they can challenge
their teachers when they are taught subjects that negate their
identity. In my days, this was inconceivable. We would have
been punished severely not just by the teachers, but also by
our parents. Today, we have cultural centres where we
encourage Palestinian plays, music, poetry – all of which we
did not do in the past not only because we did not dare, but
also because we did not have the means.

Unsurprisingly, some of today's Palestinian pupils refuse to
celebrate Israel's Independence Day. One teacher recalled that
an eight-year-old boy had called her a liar when she tried to

teach them about Independence Day. She said with a smile, 'I wasn't angry when he told me that. On the contrary, I wanted to kiss him'.

Post-1967 political trends
In 1977, the Democratic Front for Peace and Equality (DFPE) was established at the initiative of Rakah (the Communist Party); it included the Black Panthers (headed by Charlie Biton), and some of the heads of Arab municipal councils.

According to Jiryis, Rakah's decision to broaden its base by allying itself with non-communists was brought on as a result of the increasing number of Arabs who were not voting in the Knesset. In the 7th Knesset in 1969 16 per cent of all Arabs entitled to vote did not do so; in the 8th Knesset in 1973 20 per cent did not; and by the 9th Knesset in 1977 the figure was 24.5 per cent. Jiryis noted that 'Rakah has re-examined its earlier policies, and changed one of them by now agreeing to form coalitions with other nationalist groups which possess influence in the Arab street' (1979, p. 42). The Democratic Front contested the local government elections in November 1978 and won the presidency of several Arab councils.

Meanwhile, the beliefs espoused by the al-Ard movement, as noted earlier, resurfaced in Abna' al-Balad, formed by Muhammad Kiwan in the early 1970s in the form of an electoral list in Umm al-Fahem. As Jiryis pointed out, the various organizations formed by Abna' al-Balad in different villages did not attempt to unite organizationally to avoid being disbanded, as al-Ard had been in the mid-1960s. Whereas al-Ard had emphasized Arab unity, Abna' al-Balad emphasized Palestinian identity. While the Communists called for activism within the legal framework, Abna' al-Balad argued against it, and did not vote in the general elections for the Knesset. However, there were internal differences of opinion about the position the movement should take *vis-à-vis* the state, and about participation in Knesset elections, which led to splits in the movement. As al-Ard members had been before them, Abna' al-Balad activists were often placed under administrative detention (imprisonment without trial) or town arrest. Their newspaper, *al-Raya*, was closed after the intifada, having only been published for a couple of years.

As nationalist trends strengthened, the Israeli Zionist parties stopped using Arab lists, and included Arab candidates in the Israeli Jewish party lists. But by the 1980s, these only attracted some 40 per cent of the Arab vote, compared with the 75 per cent of previous years.

The major turning point in the political development of the '48 Palestinians occurred in 1975–6. Rakah's success, headed by Palestinian poet Tawfik Zayyad, in winning the Nazareth municipal council in December 1975 was followed shortly afterwards by Land Day. Land Day was organized by Rakah and the Committee for the Defence of Arab Land (which had been set up by Arab municipal council leaders). It was the first major protest by Palestinians against Jewish confiscation of Arab land; this time, the state planned to take over 20,000 *dunums* (4 dunums = 1 acre) from the village of Sakhneen, and 3,000 from the village of Kufr Qassem.

Indeed, some saw the Israeli authorities' move to confiscate further Arab land as a response to the Communist take-over of the Nazareth municipality in 1975 – a move which, in the Israeli view, necessitated stronger control of the Galilee where the Arabs accounted for about half the population. However, the Israeli reaction radicalized the '48 Palestinians even further. During the demonstration, on 30 March 1976, six Arabs were killed, and many were arrested. Ever since, Land Day has been commemorated annually by Palestinians everywhere. It is one of the 'official holidays' marked by the Palestinian government-in-exile, the PLO, making this the first historic day presented by the '48 Palestinians to the rest of their people.

Jiryis recalled,

As a result of the turmoil on that day, the Israeli government once more reviewed its policies toward the Arabs in Israel and decided in late May 1976 to pursue a policy of 'incorporating' the Arabs inside Israeli society and state activity as a whole 'on the basis of full and equal citizenship and through consideration of their religious and cultural uniqueness'. The heads of the councils refused to accept that decision, and a delegation representing them met with Prime Minister Rabin at the end of that same month. The delegation protested against the decision and, at the end of June, submitted a memorandum requesting that the 'reality of the Arab national identity' be taken into account. (1979, p. 39)

This was an indication of the radicalization of the Regional Committee of Heads of Arab Local Councils, a network of the heads of elected Arab municipalities in Israel (there are now four Arab municipalities and 55 elected local councils). According to al-Haj (1988), the network took some years in forming. In the early years, it was, ironically, supported by the Jewish state, who tried to persuade hesitant mayors to join. Of course, most of the councils were then run by representatives of the traditional family groupings, the hamula, in a hangover from the period of military rule.

The Regional Committee met on the eve of the first Land Day strike in March 1976, according to *al-Qabas* (international edition 23 January 1989) but due to pressures from the authorities, only five council heads voted in favour of the strike (including, of course, the key instigator, Nazareth mayor Tawfik Zayyad). The huge turn-out on Land Day showed where the '48 Palestinians thought their interests lay. By the 1980s many councils were in the control of the Democratic Front and other independent Palestinian figures – the Regional Committee began to be called the 'real parliament of the Palestinians in Israel'. It has formed specialized committees – on land, health, social conditions, education, mixed cities – and marshals a wide array of forces representing the '48 Palestinians' needs. It should be noted that only about half the Arab villages which should have elected representatives have them; were all Arab villages to have elected councils today, the Committee would be immeasurably strengthened (which is doubtless one reason why many villages continue to lack them).

The municipal leaders' network has continued to function very effectively, even though it is represented by members of diverse political persuasions, including communists, nationalists, Islamists, traditionalists, and Zionist-associated members. According to Rouhana,

The committe gained the respect of the Arab public through its show of unity despite deep political divisions within its

ranks. The committee has earned the status of national
leadership because it represents daily concerns . . . No other
authority, including the Israeli government, enjoys such
status within the Arab community. (1989, p. 54)

Earlier, Jiryis had noted that the Regional Committee

established an Arab 'organisation' that the Israeli authorities, with their traditional and visible sensitivity toward the
rise of any Arab nationalist organisation in Israel, would still
find difficult to tamper with. This is not only because the
municipalities and local councils are legally established
bodies, but also because they are essential to the proper daily
administration of Arab towns and villages, and the authorities must necessarily cooperate with them. (1979, p. 39)

By 1987, the Regional Committee was escalating the protests
against discrimination in social and economic fields. A one-day
strike was called by the Arab local councils on 5 May to protest
low budgets. Ibrahim Nimr Hussein, the head of the Regional
Committee, said the one-day strike was 'the opening shot in a
campaign to press the Israeli authorities to honour pledges on
housing development, better educational facilities, and
increased municipal budgets' (al-Fajr, 10 May 1987).

Hard on the heels of the 5 May strike, a 'Day of Equality'
strike was called on 24 June 1987, and was almost universally
observed. This was the biggest protest the '48 Palestinians had
yet made against the social and economic conditions they lived
in. On 1 September, an all-out strike was called to protest
conditions in schools. The radicalization of the Palestinians in
Israel was proceeding very quickly. Indeed, had the intifada not
erupted when it did, a furious clash of wills between the Arab
minority and the Jewish majority would probably have taken
place. As it was, the intifada diverted the attention of the '48
Palestinians by placing support for Palestinians under occupation at the top of their list of priorities. This was reflected in the
21 December 1987 strike and demonstrations of Yawm al-Salam
in support of the intifada. Still, regular strikes continued to
protest their own conditions. For example, a one-day strike was
called on 6 October 1988 to protest plans to merge four town
councils into two, losing two mayors and already meagre funds.

In addition to the formation of the Regional Committee, the 1970s and early 1980s saw other political developments among the '48 Palestinians. The influence of the Palestinian national movement had grown ever since the PLO had established its credentials in 1968. By the 1980s, Palestinian issues and developments, as well as PLO activities, outside Israel were widely reported in the Israeli Arab press. Moreover, the different political parties were openly vying to show that they had PLO blessing. However, they were careful to do so as Israeli citizens who believed, along with many Israeli Jews, in a two-state solution to the Israeli–Arab conflict, with a Palestine alongside Israel. The '48 Palestinians would still, in the event of such a solution, be Israeli citizens, albeit with a Palestinian identity.

By the second half of the 1980s, there were strong links between '48 Palestinian political and social activists and their compatriots in the West Bank, Gaza, and the diaspora. For example, in 1987 the annual conference of Non-Governmental Organizations on the question of Palestine, held in Geneva under the auspices of the United Nations, was remarkable for the large number of both Palestinians and Jews from Israel in attendance. They mingled with close to a thousand other people: Palestinians from the occupied territories and in exile, other Arabs, and European and American supporters of the Palestinian cause. The conference's opening ceremony was addressed by none other than PLO leader Yasser Arafat.

The 1980s also saw the establishment of new political parties and trends. Muhammad Miari, one of the founders of al-Ard, formed the Progressive Movement with the retired Israeli Jewish general Matti Peled. They ran for national elections in 1984 as the Progressive List for Peace (PLP), and both leaders were elected.

The PLP had a similar political outlook to the Democratic Front, but without the communist ideology. Those who had backed the formation of the PLP hoped that this would attract non-voting Arabs who were alienated by communism. However, the Communists were very bitter about the support given by the PLO to the Progressive List, which undercut the position of the Democratic Front. Outlining the PLP's approach, Miari told the *Journal of Palestine Studies* (vol. XIV, no. 1):

We have a two-fold role to play. First, we must struggle for national and civic equality within Israel. Second, we must participate in the process of finding a just solution to the Palestinian problem, that is, the complete withdrawal [of Israel] to the 1967 borders and the establishment of a Palestinian state.

He said that the Progressive List had previously collaborated with the Democratic Front, but now they wanted to reach out to the non-voting '48 Palestinians through giving 'our struggle a distinctly Palestinian colour and identity rather than having it submerged in the overall democratic struggle'.

Given the Palestinian turn in Israeli political events, the Jewish state soon felt the need to reaffirm its control, through amendment no. 7, 1985, to the Israeli Basic Law: 'A list of candidates shall not participate in the elections for the Knesset if its aims or actions, expressly or implicitly, point to one of the following: (1) Denial of the existence of the State of Israel as the state of the Jewish people . . .' The Knesset refused proposals by Arab MKs (members of the Knesset) that it should refer to the 'state of the Jewish people and its Arab citizens', or restrict the amendment to the 'denial of the existence of the state of Israel' (Rouhana, 1989, p. 51).

Just as the PLP was formed in time for the 1984 national elections, so the Arab Democratic Party was formed in time for the 1988 national elections, after Abdel Wahhab Darawsheh broke away from the Labour Party in protest against Israeli Jewish policy in the occupied territories after the outbreak of the intifada. It is likely that Darawsheh followed rather than led the '48 Palestinian popular mood. Since the Israeli repression in the occupied territories was being co-ordinated by Defence Minister Yitzhak Rabin of the Labour Party, Darawsheh's position in the same party had become somewhat untenable.

The Arab Democratic Party won one seat in the 1988 national elections. In an interview with the London-based Arabic daily *al-Hayat* (18 August 1989) Darawsheh commented, with new-found insight, that the Arabs did not carry the political weight they should because of the

lack of co-ordination between Arab parties. The result was that the Democratic Front for Peace and Equality got four seats instead of five, and the Progressive Movement went down from two seats to one. The Arab loss was great due to internal splits and different political and material pressure by the Israeli authorities, so that 40 per cent of the Arabs voted for Zionist parties, and around 30 per cent did not vote.

The Arab Democratic Party received 27,000 votes – 9,000 short of a second seat in Israel's system of proportional representation.

Interestingly, in August 1989 Darawsheh led a delegation from his party to Cairo to meet with members of the ruling National Democratic Party and other Egyptian officials. As he told *al-Hayat*:

> We believe Egypt, with its special position and national stands, is of major importance to us as Palestinians inside Israel . . . Through Egypt, we are trying to break the siege and open the doors of the Arab world . . . After all, we are an inseparable part of the Palestinian people and of the Arab world, and we are proud of our Arabness and our heritage. It does not make sense that there should be a siege imposed on us, in which the Arab countries take part, and it is not rational that this siege should continue as though we were illegitimate children of the Arab world.

Indeed, one of the major changes in the political environment of the post-1967 era was the signing of the peace treaty between Egypt and Israel. Although there is a sense of deep betrayal concerning the Camp David accords of 1978 among many '48 Palestinians, thousands of them have taken the opportunity to visit Egypt. Not only is it cheaper to shop there, but, as one put it, 'Some of us have travelled to Europe, but to be able to go to an Arab country is totally different. It is as if we have come out of exile.'

But while some welcomed the end of their isolation, others looked inward for solutions. At the close of the 1980s, the most potent new force to burst on the political scene was the Islamic movement, which won several municipal councils in the 1989 local elections, to the consternation of the other Arab parties. The fundamentalists reached people through a simple slogan:

Islam is the answer. As one of their leaders summed up, 'The only way we can fight injustice and obtain our rights as Palestinians is through Islam. We must teach Palestinians to be good Muslims.'

As throughout the Arab world, the fundamentalists' strong point is organization at the grass-roots level and the provision of needed services. As religious organizations, they have some degree of protection against legal harassment. This combination of the practical and the religious makes a powerful formula for successful organization. In Umm al-Fahem, for example, where the Rabitat al-Islamiya (the Islamic League) was founded in 1985, they set up three bookshops, with a 10 per cent discount on books; computer courses; a clinic where they only charged six shekels (£1 = I£3 approx.); 11 mosques with space for kindergartens; cultural clubs; sports clubs where they played 'Islamic football' (in which the players were not allowed to shout or curse, and the games were stopped when it was time for prayer). They also lent people funds for commercial enterprises. The Umm al-Fahem Islamists were one of the first Palestinian voluntary groups to do anything about the drug problem by forming the Committee of Mercy in September 1987, which opened a drug centre and clinic with three doctors and two nurses. As in other parts of the Middle East, the Islamic movement in Israel receives heavy financial support from its co-religionists in the Gulf.

On the regional level, the fundamentalists take part in the Regional Committee of Heads of Arab Local Councils, but, at the local level, they are often in conflict with other groups. According to the July–August edition of *al-Hadaf* (the newsletter published by the Umm al-Fahem cultural club of the same name), an example occurred during the 10 June 1989 day of protest against discrimination called by the Regional Committee. The rally held at Umm al-Fahem on this occasion was addressed by the Labour Party, Mapam, the Progressive List for Peace, the Arab Democratic Party, and the local Islamic movement. 'According to the Democratic Front for Peace and Equality (Hadash) sources in Umm al-Fahem, they and the Abna' Balad Village movement did not participate as scheduled in the demonstration due to a disagreement with the local Islamic movement, who did not want women to participate.'

The Islamic movement took over Umm al-Fahem's town council during the municipal elections of 28 February 1989, unseating the Democratic Front. In an article in the 13 March 1989 edition of *al-Fajr*, Umm al-Fahem's defeated mayor, Hashim Mahamid, blamed the authorities for giving Umm al-Fahem a development budget 10 per cent of that of a comparable Jewish town, and said the Islamic bloc had unfairly attacked the municipal council for failing to develop the town. The new mayor, the 30-year-old bearded Shaikh Ra'ed Mahajneh, a University of Hebron graduate, said, 'Our dialogue with Umm al-Fahem residents is through work. They trusted us and expressed it by backing the Islamic bloc. They distrusted other groups for failing to ensure progress and development in the town.'

In fact, under Mahamid the town council did have some achievements to show, such as a completed sewer system for the first time in the town's history (indeed, they could claim credit for raising Umm al-Fahem's status from a village to a town). But Mahamid admitted that the Front had not lobbied hard enough: 'They [the Islamists] used 700 vehicles in bringing voters to the ballot box, while because of our inaccurate estimation of their resources, we only used 40 vehicles.'

Al-Fajr quoted a 38-year-old carpenter who voted for the Islamic bloc as saying, 'I backed the Islamic bloc for what they have done during the last ten years.' He cited the type of projects mentioned earlier, adding, 'They also built houses for needy families and assisted those whose illegally constructed houses had been demolished by the Israeli authorities.'

The sniping between the various '48 Palestinian parties and movements often takes place on the pages of the Arabic press and in leaflets. Following the Land Day commemoration of March 1988, one of the Islamic movement leaders, Shaikh Abdullah Nimr Darwish, criticized the Democratic Front in the 8 April 1988 edition of *Sunnara*:

This kind of madness, a madness inspired by the desire for hegemony and greatness, feeds on outbidding others and on lies . . . This megalomania affected the Front from the first; it increased when the Progressive movement began to challenge them in the Knesset; and reached its peak when the Islamic movement took its position amongst our Arab and Muslim masses in this land.

Salem Jubran, the editor of *al-Ittihad* retorted on 18 April 1988 that the Israeli authorities were trying to weaken the Communist Party. Thus, he said, after the Lebanon invasion of 1982, the Progressive List for Peace had appeared, and after the intifada, Abdel Wahhab Darawsheh broke away from the Labour Party. He cast doubts on the role of *Sunnara*, 'which only criticized councils headed by communists or Democratic Front people . . . but we were able to foil all such tricks in the past and to emerge all the stronger'.

Abna' al-Balad and the communists also lost no opportunity to score points against one another. There was, for example, the piece in the 3 July 1988 edition of *al-Ittihad*, written more in sorrow than in anger, about an incident when Abna' al-Balad youths tried to paste posters on the Beit al-Sadaka (House of Friendship) in Nazareth, and were asked politely by the communist youth not to use all the space and not to cover their posters. A fist fight broke out, but the conflict was peacefully and amicably resolved that night, according to *al-Ittihad*; yet the communist youth were dumbfounded the next day to see Abna' al-Balad distribute 'thousands' of leaflets giving totally false information about the incident. The leaflet 'was also published in *Raya* and *Sunnara* (and by the way, congratulations on this very "national" unity)', *al-Ittihad* commented sarcastically.

In a more reasoned reflection on the lessons to be learned from the municipal elections, Democratic Front MK Tewfik Toubi wrote in the 20 February 1989 edition of *al-Ittihad*:

> Summing up the results of the elections, the Democratic Front for Peace and Equality kept its strength in general. It lost the leadership in a number of councils, like the town of Umm al-Fahem, and the villages of Taybeh, Arraba, Tiraan and Ailaboun, but on the other hand candidates supported by the Front won the leadership of the councils in Sakhneen, Ba'ana, Kawkab, Kufr Manda and Beit Jann.

He stressed that since the main enemy remained the policies of the state, the Front should continue to work with all Arab forces, including those who cast their votes for the Islamic movement. He noted that Mahamid's vote had dropped by only a little, from 28 per cent in 1983 to 22.8 per cent in 1989, and that the voters had been split by Abna' al-Balad's decision to field a candidate. As for Nazareth, the Islamic movement got six seats on the municipal council, whereas the Front received 10 out of 19 (as opposed to 11 out of 17 during the previous elections). Likud, Labour and Abna' al-Balad got no seats, while the Progressive List dropped from four to two.

Although he criticized the Islamic movement for its personal attacks on Zayyad and Mahamid, he concluded:

> We call on the supporters of the Islamic movement to collaborate on the shared interests of all Arab citizens; to liberate Islamic *waqf* [charitable trusts]; to respect the right of the Muslim masses to handle their religious affairs themselves through their elected bodies; and to struggle against the authorities' threats to take action against the Islamic movement, which harms the rights of citizens.

In spite of Toubi's call (he has since resigned from the Knesset), it is not unlikely that the future elections may see some form of alliance between Abna' al-Balad and the Democratic Front against the Islamists. Certainly Abna' al-Balad were suffering from the victory of the fundamentalists in Umm al-Fahem. The *al-Hadaf* newsletter of March 1989 commented,

> The Islamic movement seeks to establish a homogeneous Muslim Community in which there can be no separation between private and public. It hopes to achieve this either by spreading its ideas to each individual member of society, or by using the apparatus of the state to impose the code of behaviour on the people. Since it does not see Islamic revolution as an immediate possibility inside Israel, in Umm al-Fahem it is working according to the first method. It has begun segregation between male and female at all levels of education, and has even gone to the point of hiring buses to take girls to the secondary school separately from the boys. At the other end of the educational ladder, Muslim kindergartens have been established where children are raised according to the ideology of the movement. The

Islamic movement is determined to make sure that women
do not escape their responsibilities as wives and mothers.
They organize lectures for women in Mosques.

In its Newsletter no. 12, *al-Hadaf* reported that things had got
worse:

> Many clerks and teachers at Umm al-Fahem's secondary
> school have faced the sack since the Islamic movement took
> control of the town council in municipal elections last
> February. Shortly after their victory two teachers had their
> working hours reduced despite legal stipulations against such
> action in the course of the school year. Then the council
> sacked two part-time history teachers and appointed one of
> their followers in their place . . . More recent cases include
> two women teachers sacked for refusing to dress in a way the
> fundamentalist authorities consider appropriate, and another
> woman teacher sacked during her pregnancy – though the
> motives here again appear to be ones of religious observance
> rather than anti-woman discrimination as such since her
> replacement was observant but also pregnant.

By the close of the 1980s then, the '48 Palestinians did not
form a single, unified political bloc, but they were certainly far
more politicized and well organized than at any time during the
previous forty years. In the November 1988 national elections,
there was a 75.6 per cent Arab turn-out, compared to 79 per
cent nationally, which was higher than the 72 per cent Arab
turn-out in 1984. The Arab vote for the non-Zionist parties –
the Democratic Front for Peace and Equality, the Progressive
List for Peace, and the Arab Democratic Party – rose from 52
per cent in 1984 to 60 per cent in 1988; whereas the vote for
Zionist parties – Likud, Labour, Mapam, the Citizens' Rights
Movement, and the National Religious Party – fell from 48 per
cent to 40 per cent. There was a striking swing among the
Bedouin, who were late-comers to Palestinian activism: only 46
per cent supported Zionist lists as opposed to 90 per cent in
1984.
  In spite of the animosity between the various Palestinian
forces, some political analysts like Rouhana see a form of
'consensus' on basic issues. The common grounds are: the

right of Arabs as equal citizens in Israel; cancellation of regulations for expropriation of land; an Arab–Israeli peace settlement based on withdrawal from the territories occupied in 1967; a Palestinian state that included Arab Jerusalem; the PLO as the sole legitimate representative for peace negotiations; and co-operation with the forces of peace in Jewish society.

At any rate, by the end of the 1980s the situation was so different from that of thirty or forty years earlier that the Israeli Jewish authorities showed signs of panic. For example, on the first Land Day ceremonies after the intifada, in March 1988, *al-Ittihad* was banned from publication for one week – an unusual move given that this sort of treatment was usually reserved for Abna' al-Balad and other radicals.

Post-1967 personal trends
As the political trends developed, many questions faced Palestinians on the personal level, particularly regarding their identity, and their relations with their co-citizens, the Israeli Jews. A survey by Rouhana (1989) in 1982 showed that in a systematic, national sample of the adult population, excluding Druze and Bedouin, 68 per cent chose the term Palestinian Arab or Palestinian to describe their collective identity; 6.1 per cent chose Palestinian Israeli; 18.2 per cent chose Israeli Arab; 6.9 per cent chose Arab; and only 0.5 per cent chose Israeli. Issues of identity and the future were raised both in private discussion and in public debate.

For instance, as the 1980s came to a close, a debate was held on the 'Arabs in Israel and their role in the Israeli–Palestinian conflict' by the Arraba al-Mustaqbal Association (Arraba of the Future: one of the dozens of new cultural clubs set up by the '48 Palestinians). Dr Sharif Kenaaneh, head of Birzeit University's Research Centre on the West Bank (and himself a '48 Palestinian from Arraba), wondered why the Palestinians of Israel should be considered any less Palestinian than the Palestinians outside. He summed up: 'First, I did not become Israeli by choice or by my own free will. Second, there is no Palestinian state for me to choose between going there or staying in Israel. Third, I am 100 per cent Palestinian, and my cause has not yet been solved.'

The editor of *al-Ittihad*, Salem Jubran, argued:

We take part in the Palestinian struggle by staying put, by struggling for equality, by holding on to our land, by our national commitment, by interacting and co-operating with Jewish advocates of peace, and by working to establish a Palestinian state alongside Israel. This important place is valued by the Palestinian people at large, headed by the PLO. The stone that was neglected by the builders has become, truly, the corner-stone.

In an interview with the *Journal of Palestine Studies*, Muhammad Miari of the Progressive List for Peace felt his options were clear: 'When a Palestinian state is established, we will ask for the right to carry two passports: the Israeli passport, which will grant us residency rights on our land, and the Palestinian passport in keeping with our ethnic and national affiliation' (vol. XIV, no. 1).

The late Palestinian educator Dr Sami Mar'i had also tackled the question, 'What if there is peace?', in an article in the *Journal of Palestine Studies* (1985). He answered his own question by saying, 'The Israeli consensus as to the treatment of Arab citizens may well be shattered under conditions of peace.' Further, as the Arab world would no longer be Israel's enemy, the Palestinians would be able to raise funds to improve their lot substantially. They would also be able to improve the quality and relevance of their education, and the Israeli Jews would not be able to argue against this.

At such a time, they [the Arabs] cannot be labelled a 'fifth column' or a security risk, neither will they be subjected – as they are at present – to the Emergency (Defence) Regulations which were initiated in Palestine by the British colonialist rule in 1945, and maintained in force by Israel since 1948.

As for the identity of the '48 Palestinians, he said, 'The Arabs in Israel are simultaneously an integral part of the Palestinian Arab people, on the one hand, and a group which maintains Israeli citizenship, on the other.'

Most '48 Palestinians believe that the uprising will eventually bring about an independent Palestinian state in the West Bank and Gaza. But not one of the interviewees for this book had any intention of moving to live there. As one man commented, only half-jokingly, 'We are the real Palestinians. We don't want the *Ashkenazy** Palestinians to come and rule over us.' And another said,

> When I was 18, I believed we could have an independent state here [in present-day Israel], but now I know that this is not realistic. The Jews are here to stay. However, an independent Palestinian state in the West Bank and Gaza is feasible, and I believe in it as a result of the uprising. But I would not necessarily go to live there. If we obtain equal rights here, if we can become ministers and prime ministers, then I would not move to the new state.

A 30-year-old doctor from Ramleh declared:

> I wouldn't leave my hometown to live in the new state. I don't agree with people, for example Abna' al Balad, who refuse to recognize the existence of Israel. It's a miserable reality which we have to accept. If we don't, it gives the Jews a good excuse to expel us from our homeland. What we in the '48 region have to do is to fight non-violently for equal rights. Some Jews ask me whether, if there was a Palestinian state and peace, I would accept military service in the Israeli army. What answer can I give? At the moment, there is no answer. But I think it's a question that should be put to all Palestinians, not just here but all over the world.

Some, like 46-year-old Amer, the teacher from Nazareth, are hopeful:

> No one knows the Jewish mentality the way we Palestinians in the '48 area know it. Between the pressures we are putting on the authorities here, and the uprising in the West Bank and Gaza, they will be obliged to recognize us as a people. They can no longer be ostriches.

However, the bulk of the Israeli Jewish political establishment continues to reject out of hand the prospect of a Palestinian state in the West Bank and Gaza as a settlement of

---

* The Western Jews, among whom Zionism originated. They emigrated to Palestine earlier than the Sephardim, or Oriental Jews, and are resented by the latter for their dominance in the economic and political sphere.

the Arab–Israeli conflict. At the same time, showing signs of schizophrenia, they are concerned that, when a Palestinian state is set up, the '48 Palestinians in Galilee will insist on becoming part of it. For instance, Ehud Olmert, Prime Minister Yitzhak Shamir's Arab affairs adviser, told the *New York Times* (18 June 1989),

> My professional advisers tell me that on the day the idea of a Palestinian state starts gaining legitimacy, the Arabs inside Israel will start campaigning for autonomy, and then they will ask to be integrated into the Palestinian state. We've got a real problem here. It's a national emergency.

After the intifada began, Eli Reches of the Dayan Centre at Tel Aviv University told the *Jerusalem Post* (13 April 1988) that, since the '1947–48 file' had been reopened, 'The events in the West Bank and Gaza have led more Israelis, Jews and Arabs alike, to reconsider the 1947 partition plan as a possible solution' (which would give Galilee to the Palestinian state). Nevertheless, he felt that the quiet tone of demonstrations on Land Day of March 1988 was a good sign,

> It's evidence that you can't erase forty years of Jewish–Arab coexistence in Israel in one hour. Alongside the process of Palestinianization, there exists the parallel process of Israelization. The major trend of the political struggle is still within the bounds of the law, and within the parliamentary system.

Certainly the intifada has unsettled the Israeli Palestinians. As the head of the Follow-up Committee on Arab Education and lecturer at Haifa University Majid al-Haj put it, in the 16 June 1989 edition of the *Jerusalem Post* (reprinted in *al-Hadaf* Newsletter, July–August 89), 'We are now standing on the Green Line. Before the intifada it was not so easy to balance the two components of our identity, but it was possible. But the intifada has heightened the confrontation between them.'

In contrast to Reches, he explained the calmness of the Palestinian demonstrations on Land Day of 1988 as signifying that they were going through a process of introspection. He saw the tension between their identity as Palestinians and as Israeli citizens becoming even greater. 'It is an increasing problem for

Arabs to find a balance between the national component and
the citizenship component. We are on a double periphery.' On
the one hand, he noted, Israeli Arabs were not participating
directly in the intifada. On the other hand, they faced economic
problems at home, exacerbated by wide-scale unemployment.
'Perhaps most damaging is the current hostile atmosphere . . .
in which cries of "death to the Arabs" and calls for transfer of
Arabs from the Galilee to the centre of the country or out of
Israel altogether are becoming commonplace.'

The key question for '48 Palestinians is what shape Israel
itself should take once a Palestinian state is formed. As Jiryis
wrote in 1979, 'The problem of the Arabs in Israel is not new.
It represents the continuation since the creation of Israel of a
curious state of affairs in which neither party has in any way
accepted the other.' The inability of the Jewish state to cope
with the presence of Arabs as citizens entitled to equality and
recognition was reflected in the amendment to the Basic Law in
1985 quoted above, that candidates would not be able to
participate in elections if they denied the 'existence of the State
of Israel as the state of the Jewish people'. Significantly, an
Arab proposal that this should read the 'state of the Jewish
people and its Arab citizens' was rejected. The Jews can still
only conceive of Israel as the Jewish state; the Arab citizens of
Israel cannot.

This is becoming the central issue. As Rouhana wrote,

> Recent developments in the Palestinian arena – to which
> Palestinians in Israel are very sensitive – indicate that the
> gamut of solutions advocated by Palestinians includes
> partition in one form or another, which means these Arabs
> will remain citizens of Israel no matter what political solution
> is reached. If so, their present identity as 'Palestinians in
> Israel' will not be sufficient; more pressure will be brought to
> bear on the Israeli system to make the proper modifications
> to accommodate its Palestinian citizens. This will require a
> reformulation of Israel as a nation-state, one that is based on
> Israeliness (for all citizens of Israel) and not Jewishness
> (inclusive of all Jewish citizens of other states and exclusive
> of non-Jewish citizens of Israel). But only if this reformula-
> tion is actively demanded by the Arab minority will Israel be

forced to face the absurdity – for its Arab citizens – of the present arrangement. (1989, p. 46)

This line of argument was earlier articulated by the Israeli Palestinian writer Anton Shammas, who stunned the reading public in Israel by writing his first novel, *Arabesques*, in Hebrew, using the language, some said, more eloquently than many Jews. In a lengthy piece in the *New York Review of Books*, entitled 'The morning after a Palestinian state', Shammas argued that both Israel and the new Palestine would have to become the state of their citizens. After opening its doors to all those Palestinians who wished to return for a fixed period, the Palestinian state should then apply the same immigration rules to Palestinians as to others seeking to reside there. The same applied to Israel, which should no longer accept unlimited immigration of Jews. Israel, he insisted, had yet to be born. So far, there were only Jews and Arabs in Israel (as marked on their ID cards), not Israeli citizens. Not until it became a real democracy for all its citizens, instead of the 'Jewish state' in which Jews got priority, would Israel begin to exist.

Only the '48 Palestinians can lobby for change of the present Israeli system. There is some time to go before they learn to bury the hatchet of opposing political views and work together on national issues. Yet, certainly, as Rouhana put it, 'The Arabs in Israel have grown to the point where they can no longer be ignored by either Israelis or Palestinians.'

It is perhaps not far-fetched to imagine a time when the diverse political forces learn how to network on national issues just as the Regional Committee of Heads of Arab Local Councils does on social and economic issues. They could then, in conjunction with some Israeli Jewish parties, become strong enough to push through change on their status as citizens of Israel. It is not inconceivable that they could also have the strength to push a peace process through the Knesset that would lead to the establishment of a Palestinian state and an end to the torment of Palestinians under occupation and in exile. At such a time, the '48 Palestinians could truly become the corner-stone of such a state, through being, and remaining, active citizens of Israel.

2

Preserving

It is time for them to practice justice, if only a little. Those who wish to live in peace must cease their discrimination, if only a little.

League of Jaffa Arabs

During the period when Arab towns and villages were under Israeli military rule, from December 1948 until 1966, the '48 Palestinians lost the bulk of what was most precious to them, their land. As Touma (1985) noted, the 'Israel Land Administration gradually seized over one million dunums of land belonging to Israel's Arab citizens, reducing Arab land ownership to an average of one dunum per head, whereas during the British Mandate period the average had been sixteen dunums per head'. Land confiscation continues to this day, although not on such a large scale (the Arabs simply do not have that much land left). It was accompanied by measures to break up Arab population concentrations, by building Jewish settlements in strategic areas. For the first two decades, there was little the Arabs were able to do to stop the wholesale take-over of their land, as we shall see below. But, as will be seen later in the chapter, after 1976 and Land Day, they began fighting to preserve what little remained.

In confiscating Palestinian land, the Jewish state made use of a series of laws, beginning with the British Emergency Regulations passed during the mandate. Perhaps the most devilish law in this respect was the Absentee's Property Law of 1950, which transferred the property of absentees to a Custodian. 'Absentee property' included that of the 700,000 Palestinian refugees who were forced to flee during the 1948 war when Palestine became Israel, as well as that of some 30,000 people who had fled from one place to another within Israel. The Custodian could then sell property to the Development Authority, set up in 1950, which was only entitled to transfer such lands to the state. In 1953, all the property remaining in the possession of the Custodian was transferred to the Development Authority (see Edge, 1988, for a concise account).

The authorities also used legislation which designated Palestinian towns and villages as 'closed areas' or 'security zones' under military rule, which meant that Palestinian farmers were unable to reach their lands to cultivate them. The thousands who did try to do so were taken to court and fined. When the land fell into disuse, it could be taken over by the state under the Emergency Regulations, Cultivation of Waste Lands (1948).

In a detailed study, Nakkara wrote:

> These laws and regulations resulted in the transfer by the Custodian ... of Arab absentees' properties and the properties of so-called present-absentees, citizens of the State of Israel, to the Development Authority. More than 4,500,000 dunums of cultivable land, out of a total area of 16,324,000 dunums (including most of the Negev lands) of abandoned Arab property, were transferred in this way. (1985, p. 18)

Further, under the Land Acquisition Law of 1953, the Minister of Finance simply certified that any 'closed area' or 'waste' land which was not in possession of its owners on 1 April 1952, or which had been used for essential development between 14 May 1948 and 1 April 1952 became vested in the Development Authority. In Nakkara's words: 'The Minister of Finance issued 465 such certificates in 1953 and 1954, requisitioning 1,225,174 dunums of Arab lands, including dozens of entire Arab villages made vacant by military action, and large tracts of land of other inhabited villages' (1985, p. 19).

The Arabs protested the laws, but the cards were stacked against them. For example, in 1954 the High Court rejected a petition by an Arab landowner challenging the 'acquisition' of his land by the Israeli Development Authority. This precedent-setting case meant that the Minister of Finance's decisions were no longer subject to judicial recourse. At the time, the laws were heavily criticized by Jews as well. Nakkara quotes the editor of *Maariv* who wrote on 25 December 1953 (p. 24):

> All those who took part in the robbery gather in the Knesset ... The land was taken ... by the departments of government, by Mapai and Mapam and the religious parties – all of them. They say: 'We are used to this land and we don't want the courts to disturb us and stop us farming it. Come, let us make a law . . .' The law is not so naive as to be swayed by the [wishes] of the Arabs. It changes the rights to their property without involving them in the process. It even grants the Arab owners compensation without their receiving it.

(It is worth recalling here that the 1945 Emergency Regulations were also heavily criticized by Jews after they were passed by the British, when they applied to Arab and Jew alike. 'The Emergency Regulations abolish the rights of the individual and grant unlimited power to the administration', declared Dr Moshe Dunkelblum, later a Supreme Court judge in Israel. 'Even in Nazi Germany there were no such laws', said Dr Jacov Shappira, later Minister of Justice. This did not stop the new Jewish state from maintaining these laws to use, first against the Palestinians in Israel, and then against Palestinians under occupation in the West Bank and Gaza.)

Not only was much of their land lost to them, but the '48 Palestinians could never hope to buy it back or lease it one day, even though they were citizens of the state. According to the state's 'Basic Law: Israel Lands', Jewish property is inalienable; it can only be sold to another Jew, and only Jewish labour can be employed on it. The second part of this tenet began to be ignored in the 1960s, when Arab labour was needed. But the state constantly kept a sharp look-out to stop the land it had acquired from being re-acquired by Arabs. According to Zureik, it became apparent in the mid-1960s that many settlers were gravitating to urban centres and leasing land to Arabs. 'This propelled the authorities to pass in 1967 the Agricultural

Settlement Law to halt the danger of Palestinian Arab repossession of their land' (1976, p. 42).

The battle for Galilee
In spite of the massive land take-over and settlement drive, the Galilee in particular remained heavily populated by Arabs, who comprised about half the region's population. This has been a source of worry for the Jewish state from the start. As Nazareth's mayor Tawfik Zayyad put it in 1976, 'Ben Gurion, Israel's first premier, toured the Galilee and declared in racist anger, "Whoever tours the Galilee gets the feeling that it is not part of Israel." For the majority of the inhabitants are Arabs' (p. 97).

A different version of this story was reported in the 12 June 1988 edition of *al-Fajr*:

> Ben Gurion made a tour of the Galilee and, as he was crossing the road between Acre and Suffrad, he saw Arab villages and asked their names. He was told that these were Majd al-Krum, Makir, Deir Asad and Rama. Ben Gurion is reported to have replied, 'Am I travelling in Syria?' and immediately ordered that the settlement of Karmiel be built in the area.

Various programmes to 'Judaize' Galilee were promoted over the years. As Jiryis wrote of an early Israeli plan,

> Initially described as the 'Judaization of Galilee' project, it was later described as the 'Development of Galilee' project. The object was to cut up the heavy Arab population concentration in that region and thus to facilitate domination over it. To execute this plan, more Arab land was expropriated. Three new cities were built. The first was Upper Nazareth, near Nazareth ... The second city was Carmiel, established on the main Acre–Safad road ... The third was Ma'alot, near Tarshiha, in Western Galilee. From 1957 and until the outbreak of the June War in 1967, the Israeli authorities made strenuous efforts to strengthen these cities and expand their population. Little was accomplished in this regard, and it became evident that these cities, instead of giving a Jewish character to that region, were to some

extent becoming Arab population centres, since large
numbers of Arabs went to work in them, dominating the
labour and professional work force. (1979, p. 45)

Spurred on by the Communist take-over of the Nazareth
municipality in 1975 and the Land Day demonstrations in 1976,
the Jewish state paid more attention to the 'problem' of the
bulky Palestinian presence. Such thinking surfaced in the
Koenig Memorandum in 1976. This recommended several
measures to contain the Arab population, including faster
settlement of the Galilee. Yisrael Koenig had for 13 years been
governor of the Northern District, where about half the '48
Palestinians live, and was well-informed about the situation in
Galilee.

Zayyad wrote angrily in 1976:

This is a racist document presented by its author as a work
program for the Israeli authorities concerning the Arab
population. Listed below are a number of the major ideas
from this document: 1. It describes the Arab mentality as
oriental, Levantine, superficial and backward. 2. ... [it
recommends] tightening the use of strong control against
them by the police, the army and the prisons . . . 4. It would
establish a special intelligence system to spy on the leaders
. . . 5. It would impose severe measures against student
leaders, and close the door to the universities in the face of
Arab students, putting obstacles in the way of their general
education, meanwhile facilitating the emigration of Arab
youth from the country and forbidding their return . . . 7. It
would advocate imposing stiff taxes and fines on the Arab
population that would deprive them of their financial
freedom and rob them of the economic energy to raise their
standard of living . . . (pp. 96–7)

The calls to Judaize the Galilee continued into the 1980s, an
indication that success eluded the Jewish state. For example, in
an article in the *Jerusalem Post* (2 June 1986) D'vora Ben Shaul
declared,

Israel is a Jewish state but in some vast areas of the country,
Jews are a minority. In mountainous Galilee a scant 20 per
cent of the total population is Jewish and in the entire region

from the Jezreel Valley to the Lebanese border, Jews comprise a bare 51 per cent of the population . . . Unless Galilee receives priority for Jewish settlement and for national endeavour we may, within a few years, find the region's majority population demanding their 'rights' as Palestinians.

In an earlier piece (15 May 1988), Ya'cov Friedler referred to the failure of the settlements set up to contain the Galilee Palestinians:

The 30 look-out settlements set up since 1979 were intended to bring more Jews to Galilee where the Jewish and Arab populations are practically equal. They were also designed to serve as Jewish look-out posts over the Arabs and to create a line of settlements to contain the expansion of the Arab villages. Now hundreds of thousands of olive trees, planted by the villagers, are containing the look-outs.

The Jewish 'concern' about a Palestinian 'demographic bomb' or about the 'demographic dilemma' posed by the rapidly expanding Arab population of Israel, worries the '48 Palestinians. So do the calls, by Rabbi Meir Kahane and others, for their voluntary or involuntary 'transfer' from one part of Israel to another, or out of Israel altogether.

Many Arabs feel that such views are the reason for claims that the '48 Palestinians are increasingly engaging in anti-state activity, particularly since the intifada. They have been accused of throwing stones and petrol bombs; of flying the Palestinian flag; and of being behind the spate of fires in Israeli forests in the summer of 1988. The *New York Times* quoted Abdel Wahhab Darawsheh as commenting, 'They want us to be more violent. All this talk helps them justify their ideology that no Arabs can be trusted' (18 June 1989).

Earlier, the March 1988 *al-Hadaf* newsletter argued that stories of Palestinians raising flags, throwing petrol bombs and so on are 'hugely exaggerated':

Take the piece in Ha'aretz. There is no library in Umm al-Fahem for a flag to be painted on, and there is no flag on the municipality building. The only 'flags' to be seen in the town are some crude graffiti consisting of three quickly scribbled

black horizontal lines and a black triangle – without a trace
of green or red. Hardly the people's republic of Umm al-
Fahem which Ha'aretz is trying to portray.

The newsletter continued:

> There is a strong feeling in Umm al-Fahem that the
> exaggerated reports are a sign that the authorities are
> planning to do something in Wadi Ara which they want to
> justify to the Israeli public in advance by convincing them
> that the town and surrounding villages are no-go areas. We
> cannot ignore the possibility that the government is prepar-
> ing the way for the reintroduction of military rule, as
> demanded in the Knesset in December. In the meantime the
> Housing Minister David Levy and Settlement Department
> head Matti Drobles have announced that three new
> settlements are to be established in the Wadi Ara area. One
> is to be at the Megiddo Junction at the head of the valley; the
> other two 'near Umm al-Fahem'. They are to add to the
> string of sparsely populated settlements which already lie
> along the hills on both sides of the valley, fully equipped with
> complete telephone systems, sewage lines and newly surfaced
> roads – unlike the Palestinian communities over which they
> keep silent watch.

Control through development
The alienation of the Palestinian Arabs from their land was also
pursued through the development of Jewish areas and the
deliberate non-development of Arab ones, in Galilee and
elsewhere. By 1978, as Elrazik, Amin and Davis noted,

> There is not a single Arab village in Israel which is classified
> as a development settlement, and thus there is not a single
> Arab village which is entitled to the enormous concessions
> that are offered by the government to investors wishing to
> establish firms and plants in the area. This privilege is
> reserved exclusively for Jewish settlement.

They continued, giving an example from the Galilee
settlement drive:

A typical case in point is the Deir al-Asad, Bina and Nahf area. The lands of these three villages were confiscated in 1962–3 for the purpose of the establishment of the exclusively Jewish city of Carmiel. Carmiel is classified as a development township (class A). The government has undertaken to establish a sophisticated and high advanced industrial infrastructure (the Carmiel Industrial Park) in Carmiel. Investors in Carmiel obtain considerable support in establishing their firms there, and corporations are encouraged through generous subsidies and tax concessions to transfer their plants from the central regions of the country's coastal plain to Carmiel. Similarly, the government offers prospective settlers in the new town generous loans and grants, and subsidised apartments for sale and rent, etc. These privileges are, however, reserved for Carmiel alone. The neighbouring Arab villages are, of course, not classified as development settlements. Furthermore, no Arab investor is allowed to establish a plant in Carmiel, nor are Arabs able to purchase apartments in the city. Although the population of these three villages exceeds that of Carmiel, the villages of Deir al-Asad, Bina and Nahf have not yet been electrified, thirty years after the establishment of the Jewish state. (p. 37)

Zayyad expostulated further:

Let us examine the bitter facts: vast territories which have been expropriated, and which were cultivated until the time of their confiscation, are still without cultivation because of lack of 'Jewish' manpower. It is deemed preferable to have them uncultivated than to return them to their Arab owners. In all the Arab towns and villages there is absolutely no industry. Nazareth with a population of 45,000 and the largest all-Arab city in Israel, has not a single factory. The factories which existed in Nazareth during the British Mandate were liquidated during the early years of the State of Israel. In the all-Jewish city of Upper Nazareth which has a population of 16,000, there are tens of factories, some of which are regarded as the largest in their field of production, such as textiles, food industry, and car assembly plants. Land was confiscated from Arab Nazareth to construct a Jewish city so that Arab Nazareth would be converted, with the

passage of time, into a neglected quarter of the Jewish city.
(p. 98)

The Palestinians were of course excluded from the benefits of
large development agencies like the Jewish National Fund,
which targeted Jews alone. Deprived of land and development,
the vast majority of Palestinian workers turned into commuters
for wage labour. As Zayyad noted,

> The picture in the Arab villages is even worse. About 60,000
> Arab workers, from a total of 80,000, travel each morning
> from their towns and villages to work in Jewish cities and
> settlements, returning home in the evening. These workers
> regard their towns and villages as nothing but places of
> residence. Their only prosperous 'industry' is the creation
> and supply of manpower.

Since the bulk of '48 Palestinians live in villages, Makhoul
described their case as one 'of proletarianization without
urbanization in which industrial workers are essential daily
commuters between residential rural spaces and urban work-
places' (1982, p. 77). She quoted a 1974 survey to show how
recent the Palestinian 'proletariat' was: of 23,100 sons employed
as skilled workers in industry, construction and transport, in
91.7 per cent of cases their fathers did not perform such labour
categories; only 8 per cent of the 9,000 sons working in
agriculture had fathers who were not farmers.

Describing such Palestinian industry as existed, Khalidi
wrote in 1984:

> By 1974, at the most optimistic estimate, there were only 59
> manufacturing enterprises in Arab regions with some degree
> of Arab ownership. Most employed under 30 workers, though
> a few others employed between 150–200 workers each, in
> marble and metal works; at best only a fifth of the Arab
> industrial employed was found in these enterprises. These
> plants mostly produce clothing and textiles, with some recent
> expansion into small chemical industry, and food processing.
> Generally, these plants in Arab regions are branches of larger
> Israeli concerns. Additionally, Arab villages are dotted with
> small carpentry, blacksmithing, sewing, car repair and other
> workshops. (p. 68)

In many cases where Jewish subcontracting existed in Arab areas, it had been set up to be close to non-mobile cheap labour, primarily Palestinian women. Khalidi added, 'An exhaustive search of a list of the top 5,000 registered businesses in Israel in 1982 failed to identify a single firm with Arab ownership or in an Arab region.'

The first steps to staying put
Given this state of affairs, in which every avenue towards self-reliant development seemed blocked, how did the '48 Palestinians manage to preserve what was left to them of their resource base? They began to mobilize slowly in the 1970s, but it was only really in the 1980s that the community began to be an effective force, and the struggle to retain some control over resources began in earnest.

At this point, the '48 Palestinians felt the need to define the problems that confronted them on their own terms – using their own data and analysis of the situation, rather than relying on Jewish sources. So it was that a spate of conferences were held on different issues: the first regional conference on education in the Arab sector was convened in 1984; on health, in 1986; on social and economic conditions, in 1987; and on agriculture, in 1988. The conferences were usually convened by the Regional Committee of Heads of Arab Local Councils, in co-ordination with one or more voluntary associations (land and other property are covered in this chapter, while chapter 3 concentrates on Palestinian groups active on social issues).

The first conference on agriculture in the Arab sector, held in the village of Ibillin in October 1988, focused attention on the problems of land, water and farmers. The voluntary group involved in organizing this conference was the Nazareth-based Regional Committee for Defence of Arab Land, which was set up in 1975 at the initiative of the Regional Committee of Heads of Local Arab Councils, and which played a major part in organizing the Land Day demonstrations of March 1976. Headed by the Revd Shehadeh Shehadeh, the Land Defence Committee had worked over the years to encourage villagers to resist threats to their land from the authorities, hired lawyers to defend people, and fought against racism (it took part in several

demonstrations to stop the extremist Rabbi Meir Kahane from
going into Arab villages to urge the population to leave).

In going about its activities, the committee co-operated with
a range of Palestinian political forces, from the Democratic
Front of Peace and Equality to Abna' al-Balad, as well as with
several voluntary groups. It monitored the land situation in the
Arab sector, in itself a full-time job: according to a leaflet the
committee published in September 1987, there were over thirty
'legal' means to expropriate Arab land.

For the agriculture conference, the committee organized
several studies, and five subcommittees were formed to cover
different areas: tobacco and olives, fruits and vegetables, cattle
and poultry, co-operatives and statistics. Pre-conference meetings were held in various villages to raise awareness.

Farmers from 43 Arab villages turned out when the
conference convened in October 1988 in the village of Ibillin,
along with the heads and members of various local councils (see
also *Tanmiya*, December 1988). A paper by Elias Kassis, the
head of Rama's local council, noted that in 1948 the Arabs had
owned 140,000 of the 150,000 dunums planted with olive trees;
most of the land had been lost on the grounds that it belonged
to 'absentees'. Even the unexpropriated land was interfered
with. For example, Kassis complained of the restrictions placed
on what olive farmers could plant: they could not, for example,
plant Syrian olives, which yielded between 25 and 38 per cent
oil, but were restricted to varieties which produced only 7 to 8
per cent oil.

Muhammad Mansour from Tireh noted that the most serious
problem facing fruit and vegetable growers was their restricted
access to irrigation. Arab farmers were only entitled to 5,000
cubic metres a year for five dunums, whereas Jewish farmers
were entitled to between 800 and 1,200 metres per dunum,
without restrictions on the size of land. Arab farmers needed
licences to grow potatoes, carrots, onions, and peppers. The fact
that they found these difficult to get was shown by the absence
of Arab potato growers. Tobacco farmers complained that their
production was undercut by imports.

In addition to restrictions on what they could grow, the '48
Palestinians' title to their land remained insecure. The Majd al-
Kroum council head, Muhammad Mannae, noted that Arab

towns and villages continued to lose land through re-zoning procedures, and that Jewish local authorities had the power to confiscate land for public purposes, without the need to compensate owners. To consolidate its work, the conference established a Follow-up Committee, along the lines of those established by the conferences on other social and economic issues in the Arab sector.

As on the land, so on the sea. By the 1980s Palestinian fishermen were beginning to organize, in the face of the serious danger of losing the little access they had left to the Mediterranean. In October 1986, in the mixed Arab–Jewish city of Jaffa, the 270 Palestinian fishermen were confined to a quarter of the port area: the Israeli authorities wanted to 'develop' the rest by building a private dock. As one Jaffa fisherman told *al-Fajr* (21 November 1986), 'On that day, while we were returning from fishing, we were astonished to see a large number of Israeli policemen and border guards. The Israeli forces came from land and sea; it was as if they were reoccupying the port.' According to *al-Fajr*, the operation took place despite a High Court order obtained by the fishermen banning the port administration from carrying out any development work there.

Suspecting the authorities of seeking to 'develop' the Arabs out of Jaffa altogether, the newly formed Arab fishermen's committee complained that the Jewish fishermen were helped to buy boats and nets by the Ministry of Agriculture, whereas the Arabs were not. Nevertheless, the number of Jewish fishermen continued to drop. The Arabs believed that the 'real reason is that Jews have greater opportunities than us for work'. As one Jaffa fisherman told *al-Fajr*, 'People think fishing is a good and profitable job. But in fact this is not true at all, fishing is full of risks and difficulties.' Much manual work is still required on the boats, which have to be manned by crews of four to six as they cannot afford to buy modern fishing equipment. The fishermen are also unhappy with the low prices for their fish, which they sell to Israeli companies and to merchants from Gaza.

The Palestinian fishermen in the Arab–Jewish city of Acre were better organized than their Jaffa colleagues, having formed the Acre Fishermen's Association to lobby for their rights in 1987. There are about eighty licensed fishermen, but probably more fishing without licences. They too are restricted to an increasingly narrow area of the port, and are prevented from fishing on the open seas for security reasons. They are often fined for fishing in forbidden zones, but they insist these are not clearly marked. As in Jaffa, the authorities plan to turn the rest of the port over to berthing space and facilities for luxury yachts. The fishermen fear that the tourists will force them away. They have already had complaints that the smell of fish puts off tourists; some of their stands have been burned over the years; and the storehouse where they kept their nets and equipment was closed by the Acre Development Company. Their list of demands include: access to running water and electricity outlets; expansion of the port area; allocation of part of the port area for the repair and maintenance of equipment; permission to sell fish directly; and an office for the association.

Putting the authorities' behaviour in context was an article in *al-Ittihad* on 12 September 1987, entitled 'O Acre Arabs, beware of the new danger!' It linked the harassment of the fishermen with the moves against Acre Arabs as a whole, deducing that the ultimate aim was to clear Acre of its Arab inhabitants. It quoted a (Jewish) member of Acre's municipal council as warning that the Arabs would become a majority in Acre within eight years, which made it urgent to stop Jewish migration from the city.

Be it ever so humble

The '48 Palestinian determination to stay put is very evident in the Arab–Jewish mixed cities of Acre, Jaffa, Haifa, Lydda and Ramleh. Before 1948, the Arabs accounted for 62.5 per cent of the total population of these five cities. By 1983, they accounted for 7.1 per cent of the total (around 47,000 people). While this was a drastic reduction, it was still higher than none, and the Arabs wanted to keep it that way in the face of persistent Jewish efforts to erase their presence from these historic towns.

In the mixed cities, the Arabs lived in quarters (some called them ghettos) that had been allowed to deteriorate so badly that they presented both physical dangers, because of the extent of disrepair of the buildings, streets and facilities, and the social ills of juvenile delinquency, unemployment and drug abuse. The Israeli authorities often used the argument that the houses were unfit to suggest that the Arabs should move out altogether. However, the Palestinians insisted that the houses could be repaired with a little investment of time and effort. Failing the necessary investment from the municipalities, they formed committees to carry out the repairs themselves.

In Acre, Arabs, numbering over 10,000, accounted for some 30 per cent of the total population by the 1980s. Changes to the external structures of the old city quarter were mostly forbidden so as to preserve its 'character', and conditions were indeed poor. On 9 June 1988 *al-Ittihad* described one family's housing problems in the words of the wife:

> We were sitting at home drinking coffee, some of my neighbours and I. They had come to help me remove the furniture so that the house could be whitewashed before Easter. Suddenly, a stone fell down, and we were dumb-founded; after a few moments, another fell, and we moved into the next room. We heard a horrifying rattle and in seconds the whole roof fell down on the furniture and everything.

To help such families, the '48 Palestinians in Acre formed committees, known as Lejan al-Ahia (Neighbourhood Committees). In 1981, they grouped together in a council (*majlis*). The first of these committees came into existence on an *ad hoc* basis after a cholera epidemic in Jordan, which the people of Acre feared might reach them. The committees then cleaned up their quarters, clearing them of garbage, rats, and so on. In the face of official neglect, there was such obvious need for self-action that the council continued to meet.

The present-day majlis consists of about 35–40 people. They have taken the initiative in restoring some of the houses, rebuilding walls and blocking crevices used by drug dealers. They have organized lectures on health and identity, and shown films in the alleyways. The majlis's demands include an end to evacuation of the Arabs from Acre, renovation of old homes, and provision of electricity to homes without it.

Meanwhile, *al-Ittihad* reported on the authorities' continued manoeuvres to 'de-Arabize' Acre's old city (12 September 1987). A tiny item in an official newsletter, headed 'New quarter for old city inhabitants', mentioned hitherto unknown

plans for a new quarter in a deserted area east of Acre, the
former Tantour area. The item said there would soon be a
meeting between Amidar Co., the Jewish firm responsible for
development in the city, and the ministers concerned to see how
to move people out of dangerous buildings in old Acre. *Al-
Ittihad* called on the Acre Arabs to resist attempts to move them
to Tantour, and insist on proper housing in the city itself. It
also called on the councils of the new towns of Maker and
Jadida, which had earlier been set up to absorb Acre's citizens,
to hold on to Tantour lands.

The mixed city of Ramleh (with 10,000 Arabs out of a
population of 55,000) was one of the most underdeveloped of
Arab areas: it produced no university graduates at all until
1974. Even at the end of the 1980s, it was estimated that nearly
two-thirds of the young people were semi-literate or illiterate. A
small group of concerned citizens formed Rabitat al-Jamiyyin
(University Graduates League) in 1987. They went from house
to house to inform people about the Rabitat, and received
responses ranging from interest to incomprehension. They tried
to protest against social and economic conditions, and to
promote cultural activity, by, for example, bringing the
Hakawati theatre troupe to Ramleh. But it was an uphill
struggle: the Rabitat found it hard to bring people out on
Yawm al-Salam (the Day of Peace on 21 December 1987) as
people there had so little awareness of what was going on in the
West Bank and Gaza.

One of the Rabitat founders was Dr Aref, whose father had
moved to Ramleh after losing their home in Jaffa during the
1948 war. Dr Aref's father now lives in the 'Arab ghetto', and
recalled: 'When we first moved here we were the only Arab
family, the rest were all Jews and used to insult us. The Jews
have moved to council flats. There are only Arabs living here
now.' As for Dr Aref and his family, they live in an apartment
block where the majority of the families are Jews.

> At the hospital here, I have no problems with my Jewish
> colleagues, but I do have problems with some of the Jewish
> patients. Once, for example, I went in to examine a Jewish
> patient. Her husband told me, 'Call the doctor.' 'I am the
> doctor,' I replied, but the man refused to let me touch her. I

had to call a Jewish doctor, who asked the man why he wouldn't let me examine his wife. 'Because he's an Arab.' My colleague promptly asked him and his wife to leave the hospital.

In the Jaffa of the 1980s, the Arab part of the population was estimated at between 10,000 and 17,000, accounting for only about 3 per cent of the population. Here, the League of Jaffa Arabs was established in 1979 under Ottoman charity laws. Jaffa had become part of the Tel Aviv municipality, and the Arabs were worried about plans (the Medron Yafo scheme) to redevelop parts of Jaffa, including the Arab quarters, into luxury housing and hotel complexes, thus eliminating all trace of Arabs in Jaffa. In August 1980, the League issued an 'Appeal to Jaffa citizens'. It said, 'Brothers, sisters, it is time that those officials show some understanding for our conditions, and time for them to practice justice, if only a little. Those who wish to live in peace must cease their discriminatory practices, if only a little.'

In 1985, the League began an active programme to help families improve and repair their homes in the Jaffa Arab quarters, al-Ajami and Jabaliya. It helped them to build kitchens and bathrooms, and to repair floors, windows and doors. The League offered some funds itself but, so as not to create dependency, insisted that the families also bore part of the costs. In 1987, the Jaffa Arab Cultural Centre was set up as part of the League (see the story of Adeeb in part two), in order to tackle Jaffa's wide-ranging social problems.

The League also paid attention to public buildings. For instance, it had plans to turn an abandoned water storage tower which commanded a good view of the Arab part of the city, but was strewn with garbage, into a coffee shop for locals and tourists. However, the Jaffa Arabs were not allowed to restore and renovate a closed Coptic monastery of great beauty, which they had wanted as a residence for Arab students.

Conservation takes off
During the 1980s, a movement also developed to protect and renovate Muslim religious sites and trusts. One of the active voluntary groups in this respect was the Haifa-based Muslim

Initiative Association. Its secretary Fathi Fourani, in a
pamphlet on 4 September 1987, listed the religious sites and
trusts lost to the community:

> Transactions and deals with pseudo-representatives [of the
> community] are struck to legalize the destruction of mosques
> and cemeteries. 'Taso' cemetery (81 dunums) was handed
> over in such a deal. Hassan Bek's mosque was rented to
> Gershon Peres (Minister Shimon Peres's brother) for 99
> years with the aim of erecting a tourist centre on the site.
> 'Sahsak' mosque was replaced by a plastic factory, a
> Bulgarian restaurant and a night-club. A Hilton hotel sprang
> up on the ruins of 'Abed al-Nabi' cemetery. Similarly, Tel-
> Aviv University mushroomed on the ruins of 'Sheik Mu'nis'
> cemetery.

Fourani has written several articles on the subject, published in
1984 in a book called *In Defence of the Roots* (Arabic).

The loss of many of the Muslim waqf sites (personal property
that Muslims endow for use as a service to God in charitable
purposes) was a serious blow to the '48 Palestinians (for details
of the extensive waqf property, see Michael Dumper's 1983
thesis, Lancaster University, 'The Palestinian Muslim waqf: a
study in the transformation of a religious symbol'). For
example, it was estimated that before 1948, between 12 and 18
per cent of agricultural land was waqf property. Nearly 100,000
dunums in Palestinian towns were also waqf property; up to 90
per cent of Acre used to be waqf property before 1948. The
income from waqf property was used to build schools, clinics,
orphanages, public baths, and other services, as well as to
administer the charitable system. After Israel was created, the
waqf was deemed to be 'absentee' property, partly because the
members of the Supreme Islamic Council were no longer there.
The Arabs then protested that this property was in the service
of God, and God could not be considered an 'absentee', but to
no avail. Most of the property has, in one way or another, been
transferred to Jewish ownership.

'In the meantime,' Fourani wrote with heavy cynicism,

> vigilant statisticians keep exact records of our demography –
> our fast rate of increase and our slow rate of decrease. Every

now and then there is a paranoiac cry of warning that this highly potent minority is growing out of bounds, which is invariably followed by a reassuring analysis listing facts which prove that the possibility is non-existent and that therefore, the fear is unwarranted but that nevertheless it is always safer to be suspicious and watchful and that meanwhile, until a practical solution can be found, it is imperative that the Arab minority should – to use an understatement – be kept at a safe distance, on their own side of the fence. This goes to explain the presence of ghettos in towns like Haifa, Jaffa, Lod and Ramla. This explains the strategic siege of Nazareth and many an Arab village which are engulfed by a heavy chain of settlements frustrating their economy, stunting their growth and stifling their very breath.

There were some success stories. In Jaffa, the Arabs managed to hold on to the Hassan Bek mosque. This had been deliberately neglected by the authorities until the minaret collapsed in 1983. After protests from all over the country, the Arabs were allowed to renovate the mosque in 1984, and funds were collected by the Palestinian community to do so. However, the renovation has proved no easy task. In 1985, there were dire threats of sabotage if work on the mosque continued, and two hand grenades were thrown at the mosque on 7 July 1985. In 1986, the head of the Tel Aviv–Jaffa council insisted that work should be stopped on the grounds that the minaret was 1.5 metres higher than it should have been according to planning permission, but it later resumed.

Also in Jaffa, an Islamic Association was elected by some members of the community for the first time in April 1988 to challenge the committee appointed by the Israeli authorities. It insisted that it be recognized as the true representative of Jaffa's Islamic community, and be given responsibility for the waqf. They recalled that the waqf board appointed by the Israelis had recently signed a deal to sell a local Islamic cemetery to property developers. 'We do not trust this board of trustees', they declared.

In Haifa, the Muslim Initiative Association tried in the 1980s to stop the demolition of the al-Saghir mosque, which was scheduled to make way for a post office. It commissioned

reports to show that the building's foundations were sound, and
that it should be preserved. A meeting was scheduled with the
authorities to protest the plans but, just the day before,
bulldozers were sent to the site and destroyed half the mosque.
The bulldozers were only prevented from destroying the rest by
a court order.

The Muslim Initiative Association also organized a clean-up
of the Haifa Islamic cemetery during the month of Ramadan in
spring 1988. They reported that all people from all religions in
Haifa had participated in defending the historic Arab presence
in the town. Meanwhile, it was being remarked that more and
more young people were turning up to care for and tend
Muslim cemeteries.

Fighting villages
The mixed towns were not the only area where Palestinians
were becoming organized and assertive. Committees were also
established in several villages to carry out a range of activities,
from building roads and sewers to setting up kindergartens. For
example, the village of Musmus (with a population of 3,000), in
the Northern Triangle, was one that still lacked a local council
by the 1980s. The argument used by the authorities was,
apparently, that the village was too small to warrant a council.
Al-Amal al-Tatawe (the Volunteer Work Association) was set
up by the villagers in the late 1970s. In the early days, the
volunteers say, some of them were harassed and imprisoned
by the authorities to stop the association taking shape.
Nevertheless, al-Amal al-Tatawe was registered as a non-profit
organization in 1984.

Most of Musmus's workers were wage labourers, as the
village had lost a large part of its land. The village lacked
proper sanitation facilities, decent roads, clubs, and kindergartens. Over the years, al-Amal volunteers levelled several roads,
including one to the cemetery. They bought a tractor, bulldozer
and trailer, which were used to collect the garbage, and to
empty cesspools. The machines were hired out at less than cost
price to the villagers. They found a dumping ground for their
garbage outside the village, but the authorities forbade them
from using it on the grounds that it was state land, and
threatened to imprison the driver.

Al-Amal volunteers also set up two kindergartens. Perhaps their best achievement was the public library, stocking some 2,500 books. In a typical month, they reported, 709 people, of whom 541 were students, visited the library. On the health front, al-Amal collected the money to equip a clinic. Until then, mothers had had to take their children into town for check-ups or medicines, and the village had been staffed by one doctor for three hours a day. The villagers were also concerned to preserve Musmus's cultural heritage. The well in the middle of the village was the main historic site remaining to them, so they repaired it and planted a small garden around it to renew the 'bond between the well and the new generation'.

Villages also confronted major public health challenges, such as incomplete or non-existent sewer systems. By the early 1980s, none of the Arab villages or Bedouin groupings had a central sewage system. Adjacent families often quarrelled about sewage seepage from percolator pits. There was an outbreak of typhoid in Arraba in the late 1970s. Umm al-Fahem, which then still had the status of a village, had achieved notoriety because of what came to be known as the Umm al-Fahem disease – a sickness and rash brought on by insanitary conditions and the sewage that ran through open drains down the streets. By the 1980s, with assistance from the Galilee Society for Health Research and Services, a few villages had accomplished the task, and others were well on the way, through a revolving loan fund (the health services offered by the society are elaborated in chapter 3). By 1987, Umm al-Fahem's streets had been turned into construction sites instead of sewage canals, as the installation of its first sewage system got underway.

The concept of self-reliance to offset the lack of central government assistance was most visible in the voluntary work camps which were organized abundantly in Arab towns and villages in the 1970s and 1980s. The Nazareth municipality set the trend with 1,500 volunteers (Arabs, Jews and visiting foreigners) at its first work camp in 1976. The numbers rose to 7,000 by the eleventh work camp in 1986. In the 1976 work camp, 46 projects worth $250,000 had been completed; in the one of 1986, 90 projects worth $650,000 were carried out. In the 1986 work camp in the village of Tiraan, 500 work days were spent in the third voluntary camp, and 950 tons of material were used to asphalt roads. In the 1986 work camp in Umm al-Fahem, 600 volunteers built 250 metres of walls, asphalted four kilometres of streets and three basketball courts, expanded the plumbing in two schools, and worked on the five-dunum municipal park.

Unrecognized villages, 'illegal' homes
In fighting back, the '48 Palestinians have unwittingly discovered a way that sends shivers of recognition down Israeli spines: by creating facts. As the Zionists had demonstrated only too well, facts, once established, are very difficult to dismantle. The Palestinian facts, born out of sheer necessity, consist of thousands of homes built by the '48 Palestinians without permits because permits were impossible to obtain. Some of the 'illegal' homes are in clusters, making up to sixty unrecognized villages; others are spread through 'recognized' Arab towns, villages and Bedouin encampments. What began as an unplanned response over the years to the pressing need for living space has become an organized struggle to hold on. In this struggle, Palestinians have had homes demolished, paid large fines and even served prison sentences – but the vast majority of 'illegal' homes have remained in place.

The first organized force for recognition in this area was the 'Committee of Forty', which was formed over the course of 1987 and 1988 to represent the interests of those villages and hamlets whose existence was unrecognized by the state. It was called the Committee of Forty because it initially brought together representatives from forty 'unrecognized' villages, and it kept the name even though by 1990 it represented almost sixty villages.

Of these hamlets, the smallest houses some thirty to forty people, while the largest is home to around 400. Altogether, the villages are believed to accommodate close to 10,000 people. As they are 'unrecognized', these villages have no running water, electricity, paved roads or sewers, let alone schools or clinics. Some have managed to 'tap' into such facilities from neighbouring Jewish or Arab villages. Others use tankers or donkeys to ferry water. In the majority of cases, the villages were built on agricultural land owned by the people themselves – but it is illegal in Israel to build on agricultural land.

The spark for forming the Committee of Forty came from the village of Ain Houd Abul Haija, home to a population of 160 who live in 27 houses. Ain Houd lies on the western slopes of Mount Carmel, overlooking the sea. The story of how and why Ain Houd came into being is a good illustration of the situation.

Muhammad Abul Haija, one of the leaders of the Committee of Forty, described their odyssey to *al-Ittihad* (1 July 1988):

> The present citizens of Ain Houd became refugees from their homes in the village of Ain Houd in 1948. The village was afterwards transformed into an [Israeli Jewish] artists' colony with the name Ain Houd. The original inhabitants came to this place where they had pastured their flocks, and lived in shacks on the slopes of the mountain overlooking their former village.

Muhammad Abul Haija was born in the new Ain Houd,

> Some time after we came to this place, the authorities started putting pressure on us and harassing us to leave. In 1958, the court decided that the land we lived on was state land. After that, negotiations began between the Israel Land Authority and the people of Ain Houd about the fate of this land. During these negotiations the Israel Land Authority offered my grandfather three proposals: to buy the land we were on; to mortgage it; or to exchange it for land we owned in the original Ain Houd area. My grandfather turned down their offer, affirming that the land we lived on was part of our confiscated property. The Israel Land Authority continued nevertheless to try to evict us, while leaving the door open for negotiations.
>
> In 1962, my grandfather told the official from the Israel Land Authority that he was willing to buy the land we were on; he had tired of their pressures and harassment. But at that point, the Israel Land Authority refused to sell on the grounds that state land could not be sold to Arabs. The Authority then confiscated 100 dunums of the villagers' land, put a fence around the village houses, and planted cypresses among the olive groves, in order to isolate the village, besiege it and prevent the villagers from cultivating their land. We

lost a major part of our livelihood. The authorities continued their attempts by declaring, in the early 1970s, that the land where we lived was a national park. A few years later – when Sharon was Minister of Agriculture – orders were issued that we had to sell our flocks, and we lost our last source of livelihood. We thus had to go out to work as wage labourers outside the village, and suffer the daily exhaustion of commuting.

Abul Haija continued with his village's story.

In the mid-1950s we began to move out of the shacks into stone houses, and by 1964 there were 15 stone houses here. At that time the law on building regulations which is now being used for orders to demolish homes had not yet been passed ... In 1978 a local committee was set up in Ain Houd, and we began negotiations with the Council of Hov Hakarmel to get some services. In 1980 a zoning map for the village was drawn up, but the authorities rejected it. In 1985 an Arab–Jewish committee to defend Ain Houd was set up. In July 1986 orders were issued to destroy three homes in Ain Houd. We went on strike for fifty days, during which time we contacted all government and popular institutions to stop the demolition. Because of the widespread Arab–Jewish support, we managed to stop the demolition.

However, a further seven demolition orders were later issued against Ain Houd home owners.

Ain Houd's villagers have managed to provide some basic services for themselves. The houses are equipped with solar energy systems, and they use a nearby kibbutz for health and postal services. The inhabitants have built a two-room school, and the teachers receive their salary from the government. Five of the village youth are now university students.

There are similar stories from other villages, such as Arab Qumeirat. Here, no new building has been allowed since 1948, and an average of three families are estimated to live in each of the 24 houses in the village. The villagers say they have been there since Ottoman times, and that they began to build stone houses during the British Mandate. The whole village is deemed to be 'illegally' constructed on agricultural land, and the first demolition order was issued 25 years ago. One house was in fact demolished in 1985.

The Committee of Forty has organized tours for concerned people and journalists to publicize the villages' plight. The 12 June 1988 edition of *al-Fajr* reported:

> As we made the journey to the villages, my companions and I were worried that our guide, engineer Muhammad Abu al-Haija, had lost his way. As we travelled through the western part of what is called 'Area 9' we saw only signs to Jewish settlements and none to Arab villages. Then, just before the watchtower of the Jewish settlement of Eshtar, our guide turned, travelling down a rocky, perilous path, impossible for cars to pass. The taxi driver who was carrying a Jewish journalist from our group decided to turn back, saying he did not wish to risk damaging his car. Ahead we could see corrugated iron huts, which turned out to be homes, and, as we got nearer, two boys on donkeys carrying water. We had arrived in Arab an-Na'im . . . Nimer explains that the village suffers from being situated in 'Area 9', part of the fertile Arab lands confiscated and used for military manoeuvres. The villagers are often forced to take shelter in caves and behind trees in order to escape stray bullets.

The Committee of Forty is fighting back by commissioning town planners to conduct social and economic surveys of the conditions and to draw up a unified zoning map that would integrate the villages into the country's official development plan. On 18 June 1988 the Committee of Forty held its first public conference in Shafa Amr. The following day, the demolition decrees against the homes of seven Ain Houd villagers were cancelled. Abul Haija hoped that the problem could be solved through negotiations.

Once a fact . . .
As noted earlier, it was estimated that by the end of 1986 the number of 'illegal' houses was 4,500, and that many were to be found in officially recognized Arab towns and villages. Here, restrictions on housing and space are so severe that young men and women find it difficult to marry and start families. Many

villages simply have no zoning plans at all. Even where families own the land, building is illegal unless their land is within a zoning plan. And many of those Arab towns and villages that do have zoning maps are working to ones set two decades ago, and are unable to get these amended to reflect population expansion.

Arab towns and villages are further squeezed by measures such as those forbidding building near a main road. For example, in the Arab village of Majd al-Kroum, inhabitants cannot build within 100 metres of the Acre–Safad road; however, in neighbouring Jewish Carmiel, building is allowed within 25 metres of the main road. Thus, many families have been forced to build without permits, in spite of the threat of fines, prison and demolition.

The Israeli authorities make regular attempts to demolish the 'illegal' homes. In the summer of 1988 two houses were destroyed in Ara, four in Muawiya, two in Taybeh, and five in the Negev village of Hora. In November 1988, 15 houses were demolished in Taybeh, the most recent Arab 'village' to become a town, with a population of nearly 20,000. The Taybeh demolitions were protested even in the Israeli Jewish press. *Al-Hamishmar* wondered why building code violations by Jews earned fines, while Arabs had their houses demolished. The *Jerusalem Post* commented, 'Its collective eye focused mainly on Jewish houses, the Housing Ministry does little to ease the problem in the Arab sector ... Matters can only get worse so long as it is the bulldozer's shovel and not the building crane that symbolises housing policy in the Arab sector.'

In spite of these forceful responses, the problem of 'illegal' construction in the Arab sector has the usually inventive Jewish state at a loss. The difficulties were recognized by a Commission set up in 1986 to study the problem, headed by Yaakov Markowitz, the acting director-general of the Ministry of the Interior. This duly produced the Markowitz Report, which was immediately attacked by the '48 Palestinians. The Markowitz Commission was one of many such committees set up to study the illegal housing problem in the Arab sector – although the problem exists in the Jewish sector as well. In fact, in a telling example of double standards, the report recognized that the problem existed in both Arab and Jewish sectors, but stated baldly, 'Under its powers the Commission has focused on studying the situation in the minorities sector and has therefore not addressed itself to the situation that prevails in the Jewish sector.' It explained this by saying,

> Illegal construction in the Arab sector has drawn special attention. It seems that one of the chief reasons for this is that in this sector there are quite a few cases where the construction is illegal not because it departs from the conditions set forth in the permit but because it takes place without any permit at all.

The report pin-pointed 4,532 Arab houses which lay outside development plans and against which demolition decrees·had been issued in the north, the central, Haifa and Jerusalem regions. Further down, in the southern, mostly Bedouin region, it pointed to 5,944 'illegal' constructions (161 buildings and 5,783 shacks) and 818 tents. It recommended bringing most of the buildings in the north, central, Haifa and Jerusalem regions within development plans – barring a few hundred houses to be coloured grey, that is demolished. For the southern region, it recommended lifting the 'existing freeze' on building in the Bedouin areas of Hora and Laqqiya, the approval of development plans, and then, after four years, implementation of demolition decrees.

Explaining some of the reasons forcing people to build illegally, it stated, 'Many Bedouins have written assurances from the Israel Land Authority for the purchase of land for construction purposes, but the Authority is unable to identify and locate the lots purchased for construction purposes. As a result, temporary buildings are being erected by the Bedouins without permission.'

The Markowitz Report implicitly admitted that facts had been created: 'The results are nearly irreversible, since thousands of demolition decrees which have not been carried out so far testify to the failure of the authorities to stem the wholesale violations of the law.' It stated that, unsurprisingly, Experience has shown that the law-breakers do not execute the court orders which require them to do the demolition.' Besides, The law-breakers take advantage of the existing legal proceedings to obtain recognition of the facts created on the ground.'

The report further explained,

> The instability in enforcing the law in this domain has stemmed in part from manpower shortage for the purposes of inspection and prevention of illegal construction. That was supplemented by the practical and public difficulty involved in demolishing buildings. This difficulty, which manifested itself acutely in those cases where the demolition involved riots and violence, contributed to the restraint of local authorities, and perhaps of state authorities as well, when it came to executing demolition decrees.

An illustration of these terse statements, should one be needed, is amply provided by the mini-uprising in Taybeh when 15 homes were demolished in November 1988. There were riots in which stones and bottles were thrown at the police; forty people were injured.

An eyewitness account in the January 1989 newsletter *al-Hadaf* vividly evoked the scene after the demolition squads moved in:

> I woke up at 9 a.m. to hear loud voices in the street. Hundreds of students with posters were marching along the street singing patriotic Palestinian songs. I tried to call Jerusalem, but the lines were cut off. The first destroyed house belonged to my aunt. She has eight sons. She kept weeping as they were pulling down the house. Hundreds of pupils were in the area, shouting at the soldiers, 'You are savage beasts, we are waiting for the failure of your state . . .' Then the soldiers went on to pull down the other three houses. They were huge ones. About a hundred students were on the roofs trying to prevent the soldiers from carrying out their task, but all their efforts were in vain, for police and border guards rushed into the area and forced them to scatter, using tear-gas. It felt like fire in our breasts; we fell down and we could not see anything . . . The soldiers formed a corridor, with six of them standing on each side. They began beating the girls on the head; blood was running down their faces.

The next day, Taybeh came to a complete standstill in protest, and the Regional Committee of Heads of Local Arab

Councils called a general strike on 15 November 1988. *Al-Hadaf*
noted that this coincided with the meeting of the Palestine
National Council, which declared an independent Palestinian
state. When this was pointed out to some '48 Palestinian
leaders, they retorted sharply, 'We're not the ones who have
blurred the Green Line' (by occupying the West Bank and
Gaza), and 'It is the Israeli authorities who have wiped away
the "Green Line" by transferring their repressive methods from
the occupied territories to here.'

The '48 Palestinians have objected to the Markowitz Report
as a whole. They note that not a single Arab was on the board.
They object to being called law-breakers, and blame the delays
in approving zoning plans for their situation. They also say the
authorities have begun to act on the demolitions, but not on
other aspects of the report, such as provision of adequate
development plans.

The whole question of land and property goes to the heart of
the Palestinian–Israeli conflict, and it is clearly as unresolved
now as it was in 1948. In spite of their control over most of the
resources in the part of Palestine that became Israel in 1948, the
Jewish establishment seems insecure. As we have seen in the
previous pages, it is clearly reluctant to accept an Arab
presence in Israel (to say nothing of even natural Arab growth).
No doubt the Palestinians' very existence is a reminder that the
country was, just four decades ago, Palestine, and the Jews were
themselves, not so long ago, the minority. Moreover, the Arab
presence is a challenge to Israel to live up to its claims to be a
democracy, and to treat all its citizens equally. The dilemma for
the Jewish state is that, once it becomes a democratic state,
with the plurality that that presupposes, it will cease to be a
Jewish state.

For their part, the '48 Palestinians do not have the luxury of
space and the comfort of facilities to brood on existential
questions. They have dug in to preserve what little they have
left, through voluntary committees and associations, in groups
or as individuals, working within a system that is heavily
weighted against them. One can only hope, as Muhammad
Abul Haija of Ain Houd hoped, that the problem will be settled
through negotiation and not by force.

3

Serving

Israeli Arabs are perceived as passive victims of 'higher order' conflicts, and until political relations are dramatically transformed, the individual citizen remains powerless in the face of conflict . . . [We insist] that, on the contrary, it is necessary to create independent institutions that can provide services relevant to our society and its needs.

Dar al-Tifl, educator

Alongside the struggle to hold on to their resource base, the '48 Palestinians also worked to enhance their community's social and economic development. Dozens of voluntary associations have been formed over the last 15 years to serve the community, in fields such as education, youth and health. By the end of the 1980s there were estimated to be some eighty major voluntary associations. Unable to access funds from Israeli government bodies, and given that the budgets allocated to Arab municipalities were a fraction of those given to their Jewish counterparts, these groups fund-raised actively from the community itself and from development agencies and charities abroad. By working to breed Palestinian self-reliance, they also bred self-respect and nutured a sense of identity.

The discrimination faced by the '48 Palestinians in the socioeconomic field has been well-documented. Ella Westland, a teacher who worked with the '48 Palestinians in 1969, described the changes over twenty years in the 19 January 1990 issue of *Middle East International*. She wrote that the mood among the '48 Palestinians at the start of the new decade was summed up in the key words *baqa'* (staying put) and *sumud* (steadfastness). But she warned that they might find such an uphill struggle wearisome, and long for the release of an intifada.

Among the people I met, the increasingly impressive level of education and aspiration in the post-1967 generation of Arab

school-leavers has in many instances simply pushed down
one barrier only to bring them up against the next.
Discrimination is rife, especially in employment. Farid buys a
bar from a Jew as a going concern and finds that he is being
denied a licence to continue to operate it. Nabil writes in the
Communist party magazine and finds that the school offering
him a job cannot get the necessary government approval to
take him on. Laila gets clerical work in a bank, but after 20
years realises that she has been repeatedly passed over for
promotion. It is extremely hard for any Palestinian, however
well qualified, to find work in a field like electronics. Jobs in
any area that can be defined as remotely sensitive are barred
to Palestinians on 'security' grounds.

The discrimination against the '48 Palestinians was the
subject of a recent study, commissioned by the Israeli Jewish
International Center for Peace in the Middle East and funded
by the Ford Foundation, entitled *Conditions and Status of the Arabs
in Israel*. Its results were widely publicized, and revealed such
statistics as: 40 per cent of Arab households fell below the
poverty line; 26.4 per cent of Arab families lived in highly
crowded conditions as compared to 1.1 per cent of Jewish
families; and Arab local councils lagged behind their Jewish
counterparts in all fields, especially in budget allocations.

The Palestinians also sought to analyse and document their
problems in the social sector (see chapter 2). Hence the
conferences on education (1984), health (1986) and social and
economic conditions (1987).

The 1987 conference sparked a good deal of interest, and paved
the way for the June Day of Equality. It was co-sponsored by the
active Nazareth Graduates' League (established in 1973), the
Committee for the Defence of Arab Land, and the Regional
Committee of Heads of Arab Local Councils. As Graduates'
League secretary Marwan Duweiri, a research psychologist, said
bluntly, 'People feel that social and economic conditions in the
Arab sector are at their most painful.' In preparation for the
conference, the organizing committee held forty meetings in Arab
villages and towns, which helped survey conditions in each
locality.

When the conference convened, 457 Palestinians attended (including 39 heads and members of local councils; 74 teachers and social workers; and 70 unionists, economists, doctors and lawyers. Women accounted for nearly 32 per cent of the total). Speakers assessed unemployment at between 20 and 23 per cent of the Arab labour force. They said 50 per cent of Arab workers received below the minimum wage, and the average Arab wage was 60 per cent of that of a Jewish worker. Housing was in crisis: some 24 per cent of Arab families lived three or more people to a room compared to 1 per cent of Jewish families. In Hay al-Ajami in Jaffa, 13 per cent of Arab heads of families had been in prison, compared to 6 per cent of Jewish heads of families; 31 per cent of Arabs were drug abusers compared to 15 per cent of Jews; and 34 per cent needed social welfare compared to 17 per cent of Jews. School drop-out rates were high, so that about 50 per cent of Arab students did not reach secondary level.

Education for change
By the 1980s, the Arab resurgence was in full flow. Much of the effort was concentrated in the field of education. They sensed that education was crucial to the individual's political and economic development, as well as to that of the community as a whole. This was, in any case, an area where much effort was needed. In a piece in *al-Mawakib* (2–11 December 1985), the late Palestinian educator Dr Sami Mar'i noted that, while Arab functional illiteracy had dropped from 64 per cent in 1961 to 30.5 per cent in 1979, the sector was ridden with problems. In the 1981–2 academic year, Arab schools had had to rent nearly 5,000 classrooms to accommodate their students (compared to 1,000 rented in the Jewish sector); of 11,990 Arab pupils who started 9th grade in 1974–5, only 3,827 reached 12th grade, the end of the secondary cycle.

In another article in the *Journal of Palestine Studies* (1985), Mar'i tackled the content of Palestinian education. In addition to the curricula reflecting Zionist thinking and information, the Palestinians were further fragmented because, after Israel was created, the private Muslim schools were shut down, while the

Christian ones were allowed to continue to operate. Although half the student body in the Christian schools was Muslim, Mar'i reported that these

> nonetheless continuously bring into focus the existential experience of separation between the different Christian denominations as each maintains its own network, and between Christians and others (Muslim and Druze) as belonging to the state's public education system . . . Druze schools, on the other hand, are designed to further sectarianism as they are organisationally separate and, at the same time, as they further a Druze, non-Arab, non-Palestinian identity in a direct manner through their curricula and policy. (1985, p. 64)

He concluded with a call for unity in Palestinian education.

Approaching the same problem in an interview with the *Jerusalem Post* (2 September 1986), Majid al-Haj, Head of the Follow-up Committee on Education in the Arab sector and lecturer at Tel Aviv University, complained that the curricula were too Jewish-oriented, and avoided what the establishment considered 'sensitive issues' such as Arab culture, social history and nationalism. 'Arab educators should have far more to say in the drawing up of curricula than they do at the moment', he insisted.

As with other sectors, the '48 Palestinians began by collecting the information they needed to wage their battle, and holding several conferences on Arab education. Then they went on the offensive: 1987 was declared the Year of Arab Education. An Arab Education Week was held in June 1987 and, on 1 September, the school year began with a one-day strike as the 230,000 Arab students protested about services and staffing levels; the Arab local councils also shut down in protest. This was the fifth strike in the year organized by the local councils and schools to protest against conditions. The Arab local councils – their Regional Committee had set up the Arab Education Follow-up Committee – wanted 300 classrooms built every year for five years in order to catch up, and called for the recruitment of 4,000 more Arab teachers. The Arabs also

demonstrated outside the Ministry of Education in Jerusalem
on 9 September 1987, shouting slogans such as 'We refuse to be
hewers of wood and drawers of water' (this is how the early –
and later – Zionists spoke of the Palestinians).

Reporting on the events, the *al-Hadaf* September 1987
newsletter commented drily:

> The Jewish sector was not entirely strike-free on the first day
> of the school year. Parents in the town of Beit She'an, to the
> north of the West Bank, kept their schoolchildren away from
> school to protest the shortage of air conditioners in the
> classrooms. In our community, we would be grateful for the
> luxury of classrooms in which to put air conditioners.

Finally, the government produced a five-year plan to solve
the Arab classroom crisis. This was welcomed by Majid al-Haj,
who attributed the government's move to the Arab citizens'
struggle (*al-Ittihad*, September 1987).

> The Ministry had openly acknowledged a lack of 400
> classrooms only. But the Follow-up Committee carried out a
> detailed field survey, which was presented to the ministry in
> several meetings last summer . . . showing that over 1,400
> classrooms were needed . . . The five-year plan provides for
> building a total of 740 classrooms, i.e. at a rate of 148
> classrooms a year, over and above 100 classrooms a year
> previously approved to accommodate natural increase. So
> over the five years the total number of rooms will be 1,240.

The struggle for education epitomized the tactics of the '48
Palestinians. On the one hand, they protested and demonstrated for the equal rights Israel nominally offered its citizens.
On the other hand, as we shall see below, they did not wait for
the government to deliver, but adopted a self-reliant policy of
providing and improving facilities.

Arab parents' committees sprang up throughout the country,
putting pressure on local government authorities to act. For
example, in Jaffa, Arab parents lobbied hard for a new
government school in the late 1970s. They had only one
government school and four private ones serving the community

in 1978, and the private schools had had to turn away 200 applicants. As a result, an old building was converted into an elementary school attached to the comprehensive secondary school. In 1980 it was separated from the comprehensive, and called the Ukhuwa school.

The head of Ukhuwa school described its progress in the 26 February 1987 edition of *al-Ittihad*:

We started with 187 pupils from first to sixth grade in 1980, before being separated from the secondary school . . . When the school year began, the pupils' parents organized a strike and asked the municipality to move their children from the decrepit building, and we moved here in April 1981, the same school year. This building had been used as a Jewish school, which itself had moved elsewhere. It was run-down, so we renovated and improved it, and tore down a storehouse in the centre of the school yard. We repaired the walls and paved a large area of the yard, planting nearly fifty trees. We also planted a garden. The parents' committee helped by offering building materials, and plants for the garden.

According to *al-Ittihad*'s journalist,

The visitor to Ukhuwa school in Jaffa forgets, even though briefly, the ruined state of the city. It is a really attractive school with a clean, wide yard. Murals adorn not just the walls of the yard, but also the rooms and staircase. In nooks and crannies you see small 'museums' of artefacts produced by the children.

By 1987, the school had 432 students in the elementary cycle. Part of the school budget was covered by the municipality, but most was provided by the parents and the waqf.

Similarly, in the Arab–Jewish town of Ramleh a school had housed 730 elementary pupils in several rented rooms all over the town. Two of the buildings had been damaged by burst water reservoirs and had had to be demolished. The parents organized a three-week strike during the 1986–7 school year to force the municipality to fulfil an agreement to move the students to a building that had housed a Jewish school. The parents later petitioned the Supreme Court, with help from the Follow-up Committee.

In the Amal elementary school in the Arab–Jewish town of Acre, where the pupils had to carry umbrellas in the classrooms, the principal resigned to protest the terrible conditions and the authorities' unwillingness to respond to his requests for repairs. *Al-Ittihad* reported (8 January 1988):

> At first glance, you think you're entering a training camp or a deserted building because of the cold. There is no heating in the school; the classroom roofs embrace the rains, which pour through the ceiling and form puddles under the pupils' feet. The teachers had to push all the desks into a corner of the room, where the roof did not leak. The worst thing was seeing the pupils shiver with cold, particularly as one of the school buildings is right by the sea.

Finally, as a result of the pressure by parents' committees, some repairs began to be made, and the principal returned to his post.

In Arraba, an additional floor at the school was built at the parents' expense, and they took part in construction work. Indeed, according to the Follow-up Committee, over a five-year period in the mid-1980s, 333 classrooms had been built and funded from private sources; the government had built 383 classrooms during the same period.

Parents' committees were also active in trying to modernize school facilities, for example, in purchasing computers for their children's schools. This was seen as essential for their future careers, and they were ill-equipped compared to the Jewish schools. It was estimated that each school needed some $30,000 to purchase enough computers. Through local and international donations, parents raised enough for 14 schools in 1985, and for another 17 in 1986. In Carmel school in Haifa, and in Tiraan in Eastern Galilee, the parents donated their labour to build a special classroom for computer training.

In addition to the parents' committees, teachers' committees formed spontaneously to try to increase their students' enthusiasm and skills, and to promote excellence. The results indicated that any underachievement by Arab students was more the result of lack of opportunity than lack of enthusiasm.

In 1986, a group of maths teachers organized country-wide competitions for pupils from the 4th to 10th grade (see *Tanmiya*, March 1988). The response to the first set of maths questions was overwhelming: 2,700 students wrote in. As one committee member put it, 'We had not expected such a response from the students. Although it is a time-consuming operation to prepare questions, examine answers and reply to each student, the committee managed to do so.' In June 1987, 1,427 pupils took part in a maths competition from over 100 schools. Nearly 70 were awarded certificates of excellence at a ceremony in Nazareth, and 350 others were sent theirs by post.

Showing similar proof of the pupils' thirst for knowledge, a children's magazine, *al-Hayat Lil Atfal*, was set up by Arabs in Haifa in 1985. It was soon receiving some 3,000 letters in response to its quizzes. The science teachers of the Arab Orthodox School in Haifa also began publishing a bimonthly called *Sigma* in 1984, and another bimonthly magazine called *al-Orbital* began to appear in January 1984.

Students also organized themselves into committees at both regional and local levels. For example, the Arab Students' Association in Acre was set up in 1983 in a rented waqf building, and has about 600 members. The students collected books from graduates and sold them to other students at the cut-rate price of one shekel. The money raised went to buy other books. They also organized classes to improve the educational standards of secondary school students, which were taught by university graduates on a voluntary basis. The students tried to help drug addicts and their families, by teaching them a trade and by distributing books free of charge to their children. On the cultural side, they formed a Palestinian folklore group.

Moving on to higher things
More and more Palestinians were entering university. Majid al-Haj estimated that the number of Palestinian university graduates had soared from 350 in 1960 to 10,000 in 1988, of whom 22 per cent were women. Again, they had to study within the Zionist frame of reference, without access to 'sensitive' subjects like electronics, and they still faced covert but effective discrimination even in subjects like medicine.

An early example is given by Elrazik, Amin and Davis (1978):

> Following the 1973 war, the School of Medicine at the Hebrew University of Jerusalem also introduced a new stipulation whereby any candidate who has not served in the Israeli army – in which Arabs generally do not serve – must, prior to his application to the School of Medicine, complete two years of approved 'national service'.

Meanwhile, Arab doctors who had evaded such rules by studying medicine abroad complained that they were being discriminated against as a result of a decision taken in late 1988 that those studying abroad had to pass an Israeli exam to practise in Israel. They said that only 4 per cent of Arab doctors had passed.

> None of the Arab doctors who graduated from the Soviet Union, Czechoslovakia or Hungary passed, while 85 per cent of the Jewish immigrants from these countries passed. The committee has demanded that the Health Ministry acknowledge these figures, cancel this arbitrary ruling and find a new, non-discriminatory way to train Arab doctors. (*Al-Fajr*, 23 January 1989)

There were further incidents. For example, in May 1987 the government decided that university students who had not done military service should pay more – an underhand means of charging higher fees to Arabs, who do not undertake military service. The Arabs would have had to pay $1,550 when Jews were paying $1,050. This raised an uproar among both Arabs and Jews. To their credit, three universities – Haifa, Jerusalem and Beersheba – immediately refused to implement the two-tier fee structure. According to *al-Ittihad* (May 1987), the president of Tel Aviv University said, 'The university that respects itself will refuse to abide by the efforts to turn it into a tool to implement a measure which is clearly discriminatory.' Many Jewish professors sent telegrams of protest to the government. A professor at Beersheba University was quoted as saying, 'I will lecture today about the Nuremberg Laws. I am a proud Zionist, but I feel shamed and insulted by the government's racist decision.' A month later, the government backed down, deciding to charge all students $1,350.

The authorities thwarted Palestinian efforts to set up an Arab university to evade discrimination. As Mar'i noted,

> the lack of such an institution limits the access of Palestinian Arabs in Israel to research and scientific productivity. It inhibits their own awareness and study of social issues, as well as their ability to identify, in a scientific manner, social problems to be coped with in order to prepare the grounds in the present for a desirable future. (1985)

Meeting special educational needs

The '48 Palestinians were also active in almost totally neglected special sectors such as kindergarten education and technological education. At the pre-school level, the gap between the Arab and Jewish sector was startling. The figures most often quoted show that whereas only 10 per cent of Jewish children were not enrolled in kindergartens, only around 10 per cent of Arab children were. Further, such kindergartens as did exist in the Arab sector were started on an *ad hoc* basis, by volunteers or as money-making enterprises whose staff were often untrained.

The Arab pre-school sector provided an opportunity for pioneering work by a group of enterprising Arab women, the Acre Arab Women's Association (AAWA), headed by Dr Mariam Mar'i. The association had been established in 1975, as their information material put it, 'as an independent, non-partisan organisation to meet the needs of Arab women in their process of change from a traditional society to a modern one, without losing their cultural and national identity'.

At a practical level, the AAWA faced the problem experienced by women world-wide. When they wanted to meet, many had nowhere to leave their children. They took turns looking after each other's children, while others attended the meetings. This raised their awareness of the absence of childcare facilities, given the changes in the Arab family and in women's economic roles as they moved from a home-based to a wage economy. But the AAWA wanted to do more. Some of the group were educators who were aware that the earliest years of a child's life are the most formative, and their children were not well-served (see Siham's story in chapter 5).

The AAWA established a pioneering project for early childhood education, catering for children below six: Acre's Dar al-Tifl al-Arabi (House of the Arab Child). This is a regional resource centre which offers in-service training for kindergarten teachers and counsellors, a workshop for the creation of low-cost educational materials, awareness sessions for parents, and a model kindergarten where methods and materials can be tested. The centre first made a survey of the situation and found that out of 43 kindergarten classes served by 87 teachers, 99 per cent of the teachers working with children under four had no qualifications of any kind. All the teachers expressed an interest in taking courses.

The association began with an intensive 400-hour training session for kindergarten teachers: 300 hours of instruction at the centre, and 100 hours of in-service observation. It covered music, art and drama as well as class observation and child psychology. At the end of the first year, they had trained over 100 teachers a year. Within the first three years, Dar al-Tifl had taken out a mortgage on an old house and adapted it to be used for the centre; it was furnished and provided with clerical equipment as well as equipment for the educational workshops, including a lamination machine, an enlarger machine, video tape and television systems, a slide projector, a tape recorder and a sewing machine.

In addition to retraining teachers, developing toys and educational materials, and upgrading facilities, Dar al-Tifl started three-month training sessions for parents, which were so popular that many parents asked for a further three months. A visit to Dar al-Tifl's model kindergarten shows boys and girls learning how to make Arabic 'pizzas', topped with olive oil and thyme. The educators are aware of the importance of both sexes sharing responsibility in home management.

Perhaps the most impressive aspect of the AAWA and Dar al-Tifl is that many of the women who work there are volunteers. The philosophy that guides them, as one educator put it, is that:

Israeli Arabs are perceived as passive victims of 'higher order' conflicts, and until political relations are dramatically transformed, the individual citizen remains powerless in the face of conflict. The AAWA has consistently rejected this argument, insisting that, on the contrary, it is necessary to create independent institutions that can provide services relevant to our society and its needs.

Another interesting effort in the field of special education was the establishment of the Fund for the Development of Vocational and Technological Education in the Arab Sector. This voluntary effort was mounted by Arab educators, led by Ibrahim Auda, and supported by the ubiquitous Regional Committee of Heads of Arab Local Councils. Nearly $120,000 was raised at the constituent conference on 18 November 1985. There was no doubt about the enthusiasm of the '48 Palestinians for the Fund. For example, a wedding in the village of Musherfeh near Umm al-Fahem in September 1985 was transformed into a spontaneous fund-raising event for the Technology Fund after a poet spoke about its activities.

The Fund had two complementary aims: to advance Palestinians at the level of education and training; and to develop high-tech industry. There was no question that the Arabs had lagged far behind in this field. The Fund reported that while 60 per cent of all Israeli secondary students were in technological education, Arabs accounted for only 6 per cent of the total. There were only two technical and two agricultural schools serving the Arab sector.

Even at the end of the obstacle course, Elrazik et al. (1978) gave a telling example of the employment difficulties faced by Arabs who had managed to enrol in and graduate from technology courses.

To illustrate the case: some two years ago a special committee was set up at the Technion under the Chairmanship of the former Dean of Students, Prof. Dori, to facilitate the placement of Arab Technion graduates in engineering in Israeli industrial plants and corporations. The committee laboured hard for six months without succeeding in placing a single Arab Technion graduate in engineering in any relevant job in an Israeli plant, and has consequently been dissolved.

Not surprisingly, in the mid-1980s, it was estimated that as many as 42 per cent of Arab engineers were unemployed or worked in fields other than that of their specialization.

In 1986, the Fund gave 23 high schools soft loans to upgrade their facilities in science and technology. In 1988, it helped ten schools in ten villages to open electrical and electronics sections. Elementary schools in Jisr al-Zarqa and in Kufr Kanna received $20,000 worth of equipment from West Germany, via the Fund, for their sewing sections and metal works. The Fund also sent 16 secondary-school principals to West Germany to study curricula and methods relating to technological education.

The Fund was not yet able to do much to promote high-tech industry, although there was a keen awareness that this could be a way of compensating for the loss of agricultural land, and could alleviate the serious Arab unemployment problem. According to the 18 June 1986 edition of *al-Ittihad*, many Arab financiers were ready to set up industries if there were incentives and development zones, as in the Jewish sector.

But by the 1980s, there were only two major Arab-owned factories: one iron and steel works owned by the Qadamani family, which employed 150 people, in the Galilee village of Yarka; and a marble factory owned by the Boulos family, employing some 65 people, in the town of Carmiel. The paper reported that the Boulos family had wanted to set up near their village quarry of al-Ba'neh, but could not afford to as it was not a development zone, and did not enjoy incentives in taxation, funding and facilities, which the Jewish town of Carmiel did. The Boulos family faced difficulties in Carmiel, as Arabs were discouraged from moving into Jewish towns, but eventually they managed to buy a plot of land and build a factory in the development zone. This is sometimes held up to demonstrate that the government does not discriminate against Arab industrialists. However, it remains the exception rather than the rule (see also chapter 2).

Unemployment, drugs and youth
The economic underdevelopment of the Arab sector has led to a severe unemployment problem among the '48 Palestinians. *Al-Ittihad*'s correspondent toured Nazareth and surrounding areas

(2 March 1986), and reported that the main area of activity was outside the employment offices, where the queues stretched into the streets. Fakhri, a 40-year-old worker from Mashhad, 'who looked over 50', said he had been fired from his job on New Year's Day in 1985.

> I register for work three times a week, once in Kufr Kanna and twice in Nazareth, and I pay the transport from my pocket. I have not been offered any employment yet. I live by borrowing from the shops. The rest is left to God. My mates and I want work, any kind of work. We don't want to stay in this situation of torment and idleness.

Asked how he managed to live, another unemployed worker screamed in reply, 'Who told you we are living? I am ashamed to show my face to the shopkeeper I borrow from. I am ashamed to show my face to my children' (*al-Ittihad*, 24 February 1986). One worker had become so depressed that he had tried to burn down the unemployment office.

Unemployment affected all categories of workers. *Al-Bayader al-Siyassi* commented about unemployed university graduates:

> Hanna Ghareeb from Nazareth completed his studies with distinction in aeronautical engineering at the Applied Engineering Technion in Haifa. He has not found work in his field, and so has opened a shop to sell aluminium pipes in his home town . . . Muhammad Abu Samra from Bir al-Maksour received a degree in political science from the Hebrew University, and was forced, after not finding work in his field, to work in a hotel in Jerusalem; at the same time, he is studying for his Master's degree in the hope that this will improve his employment chances . . . Abdullah Gharra from Jitt village in the Triangle has a doctorate in biology from Tel Aviv University. After searching far and wide for work, without success, he is studying medicine. (29 August 1987)

Unemployment is a contributing factor in the narcotics problem (see the story of Adeeb in part two) that has become so serious in recent years that even small Arab villages are affected. The problem has also been exacerbated by a breakdown in traditional values as a result of contact with other cultures and with the consumer-oriented city culture. The

generation gap has been widened and family conflicts have
resulted. Many Palestinians blame the loss of their land for
over-rapid social change. When they were farmers, the father
was the undisputed head of the family, controlling its main
assets. Now that the majority of Palestinian workers had
become wage labourers, commuting to their place of work, and
lacking time for family life, parental authority had diminished;
respect for the old was no longer the norm. As one Palestinian
put it, 'Natural, gradual development would have been so much
better and less destructive than the sudden changes which have
created deep conflicts in the family.'

The category most affected by these troubles is the younger
generation, which is a major area of concern for the '48
Palestinians. The problems of youth start in the educational
system. As we have seen earlier, the facilities are seriously
inadequate, and the drop-out rate is high. A report from Umm
al-Fahem found that 1,007 youngsters (516 boys and 491 girls)
were outside the formal school system, out of a total of 6,200
students between the ages of 12 and 18. There are few good job
opportunities for young Palestinians, and they are the first to
suffer in conditions of economic crisis. For those who crack
under the strain, there are only seven rehabilitation centres, so
that many young drug offenders end up in gaol.

By 1988, the '48 Palestinians had begun to respond. The al-
Hilal Association to Fight Drugs in the Arab Sector had been
set up, and a hot line was opened for drug addicts. The
Jerusalem-based association met with the Regional Committee
of Heads of Arab Local Councils to discuss a plan of action.
The then MK Tawfik Toubi successfully insisted in the Knesset
that al-Hilal should be included as one of 43 associations in the
country set up as an authority to fight against drugs.

There were also efforts at the local level. On 1 April 1988 a
Centre for Cure from Drug Use was set up in the village of
Tireh, where there were estimated to be between 500 and 600
drug users. It was run by a doctor and a sociologist, and was
targeted at cocaine users. The treatment was in units of around
five, and 12 addicts had joined up by then. The Ministry of
Labour bore 75 per cent of the costs, and the local council bore
25 per cent. In fact, the local council was very active on the
issue. It provided a building, and gave incentives to youth

including free passes to the swimming pool; and it paid 50 per cent of the costs of a trip to Egypt for ten addicts under treatment. The centre faced a problem in that 110 addicts had addiction certificates, which gave them the right to treatment and a 'salary'. They were afraid of losing these payments if they were cured, but the centre pledged to help them find jobs afterwards.

As part of their response to the crisis among youth, over the last decade the '48 Palestinians organized youth and cultural centres throughout their towns and villages. Their aim has been to involve youth, to get them off the streets, and to give them self-respect and help to reinforce their identity. A good example of an active cultural centre is al-Hadaf, established in 1984–5 in Umm al-Fahem, where there was a high rate of unemployment and many youngsters had started to use drugs and form gangs.

Al-Hadaf's activities for young people were wide-ranging. They invited Palestinian film makers such as Michel Khleifi to debates (attended by 200 people in February 1986), and musicians such as Mustafa Kurd to give concerts (attended by 350 people in 1986), as well as offering music lessons. Their computer courses were highly successful, and they provided outreach services by transferring seven of their computers to high schools in neighbouring villages. Day trips were organized, including one for 58 computer students to the Israeli-occupied Golan Heights in 1987. British volunteers came to give English courses, which also reached eight nearby villages.

The centre started activities specifically for women, including adult literacy courses, accounting, sewing, lectures and debates. It later began to work on consciousness-raising among women about their rights. For example, at the end of 1989 it organized a series of discussions on marriage and family. It was stressed that since the family was the key to society, women should be 'equal and responsible' within it. 'One speaker remarked that many more women in Umm al-Fahem were now listening to news broadcasts. A small matter in itself, but one which shows that the heightened political awareness of Palestinian society as a whole is having particular and inevitable consequences for Palestinian women' (al-Hadaf newsletter, February–March 1989). Al-Hadaf volunteers had worked hard to set up a creche where the women could leave their children, and were pleased

when this took off in 1988, with 24 children. The newsletter
reported: 'Each child pays 150 N.S. [new shekels] monthly;
they get three meals, which are put together with the advice of a
nutritionist. Meat is not included, its price being too prohibi-
tive, but we are intending to include meat once the budget is
higher.'

Al-Hadaf also began to work on a documentation centre,
beginning with a collection of aerial photographs taken of
Palestine in 1918 by the German air force, which they ordered
from Germany. Perhaps their proudest achievement was
building the first public library in Umm al-Fahem, which
housed 10,000 books and was, they claimed, the biggest in the
Arab sector. It had not been easy.

> As planned, two representatives of al-Hadaf travelled to
> Egypt to buy books for the library from the Cairo book fair.
> We originally received an import licence for $20,000 worth of
> books, but owing to the uncertainty of the political situation
> at the moment we decided that we should make it a priority
> to bring as many books from Egypt as possible while we still
> have the opportunity. Accordingly, we obtained an import
> licence for a further $10,000 worth. We bought a total of
> 11,000 books, which now have to be submitted to both
> Egyptian and Israeli censors. (Al-Hadaf newsletter, March
> 1988)

By July, the al-Hadaf newsletter could report,

> The books for the library that we purchased in January in
> Egypt finally arrived at Lydda airport three weeks ago. They
> had a long sojourn with the Egyptian religious authorities of
> al-Azhar who censored them for inappropriate presentations
> of Islam before they were allowed to be exported. Luckily the
> al-Azhar sheiks found no inappropriate presentations in our
> selection and all our purchases arrived at their new home in
> Umm al-Fahem. Then the Israeli censors wanted to take a
> look at what we bought. They also like to read. In fact, the
> Israeli censors liked our book selection so much they took 51
> of them. We noticed that the censors had quite specific
> reading interests. For instance, they seemed very interested
> in books on Palestinian history and politics. We hope they

enjoy learning more about Palestinian culture and politics
from the 51 books they 'borrowed'. We have almost finished
preparing the building we will be using for the library and
hope to have people besides Egyptian and Israeli censors
reading our books by the time the school year starts.

Among other social and health issues exercising the '48
Palestinians was the question of the aged. With the changes
affecting the extended family, which used to care for its old or
sick members, new facilities were needed. It was also recognized
that, since older people now had pensions, they were no longer
as dependent on their children as they used to be. Yet there
were few facilities for older people, and it was very hard for
Arabs to get into Jewish old people's homes. Through voluntary
efforts Nazareth built a home on Muslim waqf (endowed) land
near the Salam mosque. The contributions were solicited from
mosque goers and others, and the construction was carried out
as the money became available (see also *Tanmiya*, March 1987).

In Taybeh, a club was set up for older people, the Beit al-
Razi for the Aged Association, which can cater for 150 of the
900 old folk in the town. A small bus would bring people to the
club, where facilities on offer included counselling, medical
care, hot meals, laundry services, a handicrafts workshop,
outings, lectures, and festivities. The Ailaboun local council also
founded an Old Folks Club in 1980. Most of the members (140
men and women) were retired labourers; they had campaigned
for the club themselves, to have somewhere to socialize with
their peers and to fill the vacuum after retiring. Their activities
included lectures on pension schemes, trips to the West Bank
and to their own regions, games like cards and backgammon,
and television and radio.

Another sector of Arab society receiving attention was the
prisoners, many of whom were, in Palestinian eyes, political
prisoners. One of al-Ard's founders, Mansour Kardosh, went on
to set up the Prisoners' Friends' Association (PFA) in 1984, and
it grew to 185 members by 1988. The association tried to
improve prisoners' conditions, and to help their families
financially and socially, especially where the wives did not work
and had a large number of children. The PFA met with women
who wanted to divorce husbands with long prison sentences,

and argued that the men had been imprisoned for fighting for justice and Palestinian rights; if their wives divorced them, they would be thrown into even deeper despair.

Every three months, the PFA spent $50 on each prisoner's medicine, food and clothing. It also set up a revolving fund to help rehabilitate prisoners on their release, and assist them in starting their own business. However, internal quarrels led to the founders breaking away from the PFA in the late 1980s, and Kardosh went on to set up the Human Rights Association, and the Development Association. Acknowledging the importance of funding from overseas development agencies the Development Association sought, according to its information material, 'to put an end to the prevailing common practice whereby many small associations at this end are crippled by the requirement of donor organizations to submit detailed proposals and then wait for long periods for funding'.

Another of the al-Ard founders, Saleh Baransi, set up the Research Centre for Arab Heritage in Taybeh at the start of the 1980s. It organized several festivals of Palestinian music and dance, as well as other cultural activities. In August 1987, the centre organized the first International Conference on Palestinian Heritage. Held in Jerusalem, the conference was attended by large numbers of Palestinians from the '48 regions, the West Bank and Gaza. The renowned Palestinian scholar Dr Ishaq Moussa al-Husseini remarked, 'The last time Jerusalem saw such crowds was the day of Gamal Abdel Nasser's funeral.' Visitors from abroad also attended and gave papers, including one on the American Indian experience. The Palestinians needed no prompting to see the resemblances.

Baransi also held a conference in Nazareth in 1988 on Palestinian society, 'Forty years after the Catastrophe and twenty years after the occupation of West Bank and Gaza'. As a result, he was placed under administrative detention (imprisonment without trial) for several months.

Working on the health front
In addition to activism on youth and culture, the '48 Palestinians tackled other neglected social issues, like health. The most impressive society in this field was the Galilee Society for Health Research and Services, which was established as a

non-profit-making organization in 1981. As the Society pamphlet put it, it was founded

> as a result of the spontaneous meeting of ideas of four
> physicians residing and working in Galilee rural com-
> munities. In time it has enlarged its circle of members to
> include other indigenous health professionals concerned with
> community health issues relevant to their daily lives. Thus
> our members from the fields of biochemistry, dentistry,
> medicine, psychology, public health, engineering and social
> work are responding to their perception of unique and urgent
> rural community health problems in their immediate vicinity
> by volunteering their time and skills to assist in developing
> and promoting appropriate solutions.

Again, a major push was made to collect data. The Galilee
Society, along with the Nazareth Graduates' League and the
Regional Committee of Arab Heads of Local Councils,
sponsored the first conference on health issues in the Arab
sector in April 1986. Some 420 people took part (20 heads of
local councils, 170 doctors, 49 pharmacists, 29 nurses, and 63
educators and social workers).

Participants attacked the deterioration of health conditions in
the Arab sector. Dr Hatem Kenaaneh, who headed the Galilee
Society, noted that the infant mortality rate in the Arab sector
was twice that in the Jewish sector, and that the number of
Arabs dying of 'unknown causes' was three times as high as in
the Jewish sector. Dr Imad Makhoul had studied two Arab and
Jewish population settlements in the Tamra valley, and found
that 39 per cent of Arab children suffered from intestinal
inflammations compared to 14.6 per cent of Jewish children.
Engineer Ramez Jaraysi pointed out that the Arab sector's
share of the health service budget was only 2 per cent, although
the Arabs accounted for 17 per cent of the population. Dr Nabil
Jaraysi reported that Arabs accounted for 13.7 per cent of
Histadrut trade union members, yet the number of clinics run
by the Histadrut patients' fund that serviced their needs was
only 7.9 per cent of the total. There was one doctor for every
2,900 members in the Arab sector, compared to one doctor for

every 1,800 members in the Jewish sector (see also the June 1986 issue of *Tanmiya*).

During the 1980s, the Galilee Society, staffed by volunteers, made some headway on health conditions in the Arab sector. It was concerned with preventive as well as curative medicine, and with environmental conditions, giving special attention to four areas of extra need: the Bedouin, children, the aged and the handicapped.

For example, it worked to provide a mobile clinic for Bedouin communities in Galilee, which, according to a Society pamphlet, suffered even more than the rest of the Arab minority: 'There is little published data to support this last statement, but our personal observations together with a preliminary survey the Galilee Society is conducting leads us to believe in the absolute truth of this statement.' The Society found that in case of illness a patient had to be transported

> considerable distances on tractor, jeep or even on animal back and then be transferred to a private car or by bus to the nearest facility which might be a few minutes or an hour's ride, depending on the type of care being sought. Similarly, to get to the nearest maternal and child-health clinic to weigh a baby or a pregnant woman or to immunise a child the same type of improvised transportation has to be used, or more commonly, a walk along a rocky road has to be negotiated, followed by a hitch-hiking trip to the village where there is an MCH.

The vehicle for the mobile clinic was finally received after long delays from suppliers and from customs and licensing offices. Finally, the Galilee Society was able to report,

> As the date of Monday March 28, 1988 neared, fears were expressed that the long winter with its rain and dampness would continue. Fortunately, for all those attending the opening ceremony for the Mobile Clinic Services to Bedouin Communities, it was indeed a beautiful spring day in the Galilee . . . By 11.30 a.m. the staff members of the Galilee Society joined the others to form a caravan which then proceeded to the Bedouin community of Huseineyeh, one of the seven communities being served by the Mobile Clinic.

Although the road was dry and reasonably passable, it was obvious to all that the 4 wheel drive ambulance was what was needed all year round . . . and especially during the winter months. Abu Zaher, the mukhtar of the Huseineyeh community, greeted the members of the caravan to his home where cold drinks, fruits, nuts and traditional black coffee were served. (May 1988 report)

As for the handicapped, only two mentally handicapped facilities existed in the entire Galilee Arab rural area, serving forty youths. The Galilee Society assisted a pioneering initiative by the Sakhneen local council to set up a specially equipped kindergarten to cater for children in four villages within five kilometres of each other: Sakhneen, Arraba, Deir Hanna and Kawkab.

The Galilee Society was particularly active on the question of sewers for Arab towns and villages, by assisting the local councils with a revolving loan fund to cover the cost of the village council's master plans. Hitherto, the Arab villages had been in a catch-22 situation: the plan was needed before the councils could obtain taxing and borrowing authority for construction. As the cost of the plan was $55,000, and they did not have the funds to cover this, they were unable to proceed. Once the plans were drawn up and approved, the Society then approached international development agencies for funds for construction.

By 1987, loans to 11 villages had been disbursed and the Society had begun to receive the first repayments. There had been a number of problems with the revolving loan funds. The Interior Ministry had prohibited local councils from receiving loans from sources not under its direct authority – without, however, coming up with funds of its own to help out the local councils. In the end, according to the Society's 1986 annual report,

eight out of eleven local councils whose applications were approved did actually receive their loans. This was after involving the National Committee of Arab Mayors and after threatening to go to the Supreme Court to issue an injunction forcing the Ministry of the Interior to permit the councils to receive this loan.

Minorities within minorities
Israel refers to 'its Arabs' as a minority, which is divided
further into four categories: Arabs (Muslims and Christians),
Druze, Bedouin and Circassian. The Druze have been conscripted into the army since 1956, and the tiny Circassian
community since 1957. The Bedouin have been 'allowed' to
serve since 1948, while other Arab Muslims and Christians do
not serve. Those who do serve in the army receive a range of
benefits not available to those who do not. However, increasingly large sections of the Druze and Bedouin communities are
protesting against their separation from their Palestinian Arab
brothers, in spite of the 'benefits', and have started to organize
against this. Indeed their communities have claimed that they
too have been discriminated against in comparison with
equivalent Jewish ones.

The Bedouin are estimated to number some 60,000 in the
Negev, and 35,000 in the Galilee (about 12 per cent of the '48
Palestinians). There had been around 150,000 Bedouin in the
Negev until 1948, but during and after the Arab–Israeli war of
1948 their numbers dropped to 13,000 as thousands were forced
to flee to Gaza and the West Bank and to the towns of what was
to become Israel. Unlike other Middle Eastern Bedouin
communities, the Palestinian Bedouin were largely sedentarized
when Israel was created, and most were farmers. Along with
other '48 Palestinians, they lost much of their land to the Israeli
state. From the start, they faced policies of dispersal and forced
resettlement.

Dr Ghazi Falah, a Bedouin geographer who is one of the few
in the community to have earned a doctorate, wrote: the 'Negev
bedouin is the forgotten Palestinian. The bedouin face problems
first because they are Arab and second because they are
bedouin.' Falah said the government's policy towards the Negev
Bedouin had been implemented in two phases (1989). From the
early 1950s to the mid-1960s many tribes were forced to move
to the north and central Negev, where they lived under Israeli
military rule, forbidden to leave their areas without permit.
From the mid-1960s on, an effort was made to 'concentrate' the
Bedouin in new purpose-built townships like Tel Sheva, Rahat,
Kseifi and Araara. Here they were effectively to become
landless day labourers in Israeli townships, as they had no

access to cultivable land, and there was no industry in the townships. In 1986, *al-Fajr* estimated that in the biggest township of Rahat, with some 16,000 Bedouin, between 30 and 50 per cent were unemployed (12 September).

Close to two-thirds of the Bedouin resisted the move to the townships, and still live in 'spontaneous' settlements – twenty officially unrecognized villages and hamlets (see also the section on the Markowitz Report in chapter 2). They are refusing to move not only because of the conditions in the townships, but because moving there would entail waiving any claim to their land. A large number continue to claim the land that was theirs in 1948. Disputes over Bedouin land cover 2.4 million dunums, according to Falah. In 1979, Land Settlement Department statistics referred to 776,856 dunums, the area over which 21 Bedouin groups had filed formal land claims.

As Falah (1989) put it,

> In its desire to acquire bedouin lands, the state has spared virtually no bedouin family from some form of confrontation with the authorities. The official statistics speak for themselves: as of 1979, there were 3,220 registered cases involving land disputes between the bedouin and the State of Israel. According to a 1986 official report, there were 5,944 bedouin houses in the Negev considered to be illegal and thus subject to demolition by the authorities at any time. These statistics suggest that one in every eighteen Negev bedouin faces a problem with the authorities regarding land, and one in every ten regarding housing.

The Bedouin lag far behind other Arabs in terms of education and other services. Ironically, before 1948 educational facilities in the then Arab town of Beersheba are said by some to have been better than in the rest of the country. According *al-Bayader al-Siyassi* (30 August 1986), a boys' school was built as early as 1908 (under Ottoman rule), and a girls' school during the British Mandate. By 1948, there were 36 schools in the Negev region, although these could still not accommodate all those who wished to study. Secondary education then 'disappeared' in the Negev after 1948. The Beersheba high school was transformed into an Israeli military headquarters in 1950. Only in the 1960s was a secondary class for Arabs opened in the region again. By the 1980s, the number of schools totalled 27 – less than before 1948. And some of the schools were wooden shacks which had served as temporary accommodation for Jewish immigrants. The educational standards were so low that, for example, of 210 students in Rahat who sat for their matriculation examinations in 1985, only five passed. Many Bedouin sought education in the Arab schools of Galilee and the Triangle, a drain on the region's resources estimated by Falah at $0.5 million annually.

In 1979, an Association for the Support and Defence of Bedouin Rights in Israel was established in Beersheba. It had 300 members by 1986, and had made a start in lobbying for land rights and better services. The association set up three kindergartens, and offered special courses for students with difficulties at school, as well as grants for some university students. It bought olives from landowners for five shekels and sold them to the poor for one shekel. When the intifada broke out, the association collected cash and goods for the Gaza and West Bank Palestinians.

In the mid-1980s the association began to lobby to have the mosque in Beersheba restored to the community. This mosque had been transformed by the Israeli authorities into a national (read Jewish) museum; visitors have observed an interesting time chart on the museum walls in which history stops in the seventh century AD (when the Muslims entered Palestine) and resumes only in the twentieth century (beginning with the Zionist period).

In one attempt to reaffirm the Bedouin's attachment to their mosque, the association encouraged people to go and pray there as a form of protest. On that occasion, the police rounded up the shoes the Bedouin had left outside the mosque/museum (as is mandatory before entering a religious place to pray) and took them to the police station. The Bedouin were very amused that the police had 'arrested the shoes'. In a further effort, in December 1986, the Islamic Committee in the Negev managed to get a court order to stop the Beersheba municipality from demolishing the wall surrounding the mosque/museum.

The association frequently protested against attacks on Bedouin property. In a press conference on 12 February 1986 it reported:

At dawn on Wednesday, 4 February 1986, workers for the Israel Lands Administration uprooted an orchard of olive trees approximately 10 kilometres north of Beersheba . . . Al-Bahari Salman is sixty years old. He inherited the land from his father, possessed it and worked the land before and after the founding of the State of Israel without interruption . . . The day after the uprooting of the olive orchard, al-Bahari went to the Beersheba police so as to file a complaint against the Land Administration's workers. They weren't able to help him and sent him to the local police station at Tel Sheva. There he was told, 'Go to the Israel Land Administration office.' When he replied that he came to file a complaint about the damage caused by the Land Administration workers, he was told that they did not take complaints. It was only after the association got involved, on 6 February 1986, that the police accepted the complaint from al-Bahari.

The Bedouins are particularly concerned about the activities of the inappropriately named 'Green Patrols', a unit established within the Ministry of Agriculture, ostensibly to police and protect state land and ecology. An association statement attacked the Green Patrols for uprooting, on 27 October 1987,

> olive orchards belonging to 35 families from the al-Nasasreh tribe in al-Lakiya . . . vegetable gardens planted by the families, patches of eggplant and green pepper, within the courtyards of the houses, were destroyed by tractors on the order of the 'Green Patrol'. The olive trees were confiscated after being uprooted, and a portion of them were replanted in Petach Tikva and other cities . . . The al-Nasasreh sub-tribe, which was part of the tribe Gderat al-Sana, was evicted in 1952 from ancestral land and removed by force to Tel Arad, where its people lived until 1974. The authorities decided then, once again, to 'clean up' the Tel Arad area and remove the Bedouin tribesmen. The government suggested to them that they return to their lands – which had been confiscated illegally following the Land Ownership Law of 1953, based on the claim that the owners were 'absentees' and not living on the land at the time. The al-Nasasreh sub-tribe is in the possession of documents proving land ownership and dating

back more than eighty years, and they have filed claims to this effect with the Land Court. To date, not a single claim filed by a Bedouin has been dealt with and decided upon within the framework of the land registration procedures. (31 October 1987)

In another statement (undated) on conditions in the Negev, the association warned against house demolitions:

Demolition orders are frequently served on houses built without official permits. Yet official permits are not given to Arabs in the Negev except within the new townships which the government has designated for them. Those who refuse to move there cannot legally build permanent structures on the land where they now live. A massive joint Jewish–Bedouin rally was held in the northern Negev hamlet of Lakiya on 18 April 1987 to protest this policy of house demolitions. It is feared that more than 8,000 Bedouin family homes are designated to be demolished soon by the Green Patrols if the recommendations of the government's Markowitz Report are implemented. Speakers at this rally, believed to be one of the largest ever held in the Negev, called for a government investigative probe of Green Patrol abuses.

The association summarized its demands as: an end to the policy of land expropriation; an end to the programme of 'concentration townships'; a settlement of the land ownership problem; '*equal* provision of government aid and water allotments to both Bedouin and Jewish farmers, regardless of ethnoreligious origin'; an investigation of Green Patrol activities; and a return of the Beersheba mosque to the use of the Muslim community.

Among other Bedouin self-help groups is the Sons of Laqqiya, which was set up in 1981 and began its activities in 1982 with a small club (see the story of Amer in part two). And in May 1986 the township of Rahat won the right to elect its own municipal representatives after a court case was filed by one of its residents. The town had previously been run by a council appointed by Israeli authorities.

In 1988, an Arabic weekly newspaper called *Akhbar al-Naqab* (Negev News) began to publish on a fortnightly basis. It appeared to have no party-political bias – happily carrying advertisements for all the Arab parties during the 1988 elections, plus the Jewish Citizens' Rights Party and the Muslim fundamentalists – but it was strongly pro-Arab Bedouin rights. In one editorial against house demolitions, it wrote,

> Two weeks ago the bulldozers moved towards two targets . . . the first, in the south where the authorities destroyed thirty homes of the Abu Kosh family, and the second [where the authorities destroyed] three homes of the Zabarqah family in Taybeh in the Triangle. Even though the Triangle is far away from the Negev, the bulldozer does not recognize distance. It remembers that it uprooted both the Abu Kosh and the Zabarqah families from their original homes in Tal al-Milh. And no sooner had these families begun to heal their wounds from a tragic past, when the bulldozer came in pursuit, to prove that this policy does not distinguish between the Triangle and the Negev. (16 October 1988)

The other major 'minority within a minority' is the Druze community, which is estimated to number some 60,000 citizens, mostly in the Galilee region. The small Druze Initiative Committee was established in 1972 to protect the community and to promote its Palestinian Arab identity. It considered the Druze community as the 'most discriminated' against in the country: 'Military service is obligatory, along with its tragedies and problems, yet most of our land has been taken, and we suffer from unemployment and crowded living conditions.' The committee estimated that nearly 70 per cent of the community's land had been lost since the creation of the state. Further, 'there are no development projects, no industries, no clubs, no sewers, no proper roads, no town plans, and no modern agriculture.' It claimed that Druze village budgets were one-seventh of that of their Jewish counterparts. It also said that the community's educational attainments at the university level were lower even than Brazil's, 'where there are 12 students per 1,000 population, whereas we have an average of four to six students per 1,000'.

The committee inaugurated its headquarters, Beit al-Mubadara (House of the Initiative) in April 1987 in the village of Yarka, and hundreds of people attended from all over the region. An editorial in the committee's occasional journal said, 'We have bought a building and we are now furnishing it so that it may become a thorn in the throat of those who swallow our rights' (April 1987 issue).

The committee was most active in the question of compulsory military service for the Druze. In one of its leaflets it noted that when the 1956 law conscripting Druze was passed – which it described as a 'tragedy' – 1,074 Druze had signed a petition against it. However, 16 of the community leaders approved it, and it was passed. The committee lobbied hard to persuade young Druze not to serve. In an interview with *al-Raya* (3 June 1988), committee head Shaikh Jamal al-Maadi claimed the Druze had served 3,000 prison years because they had resisted compulsory service; sixty to seventy were in prison at any one time. He declared,

> The Israeli occupation forces [in the West Bank and Gaza] always try to damage the reputation of the Druze community by highlighting Druze soldiers, as though they alone were responsible for putting down the intifada. But these attempts can be quickly seen for what they are, because the total number of border guards from the Druze sect are 150, distributed in Lebanon and the West Bank and Gaza and within Israel. So how can they be responsible for all that? Many Jewish soldiers speak Arabic and claim they are Druze to harm our reputation.

In an interview with *al-Mawaqif* (22 March 1986), Shaikh Jamal admitted that they had not yet won over the majority of the 60,000 Druze, but added that the concept of fighting against military conscription was gaining ground. There had been an attempt by MK Tawfik Toubi to cancel the compulsory military service law, and he presented a petition to the Knesset with 7,000 signatures. The committee also formed a subcommittee of those opposed to military service.

In other efforts by the Druze community to resist discrimination, the municipality of the village of Beit Jann in Galilee began an open strike on 13 April 1987 to protest against restrictions on the use of village lands (which had been declared an environmentally protected area) and discrimination in budgets. The schools followed with a strike on 28 April. The

Beit Jann strike lasted for 110 days, and became the stuff of legend among the '48 Palestinians. Many villagers were arrested in the 'battle' to defend their land in the Zaboud area in July. That month, the Agriculture Minister issued special regulations to allow the Beit Jann people to farm their land. Although the strike was lifted, the villagers said this was not enough: they wanted a law to return the lands to their owners, and a guarantee of their rights in these lands – not ministerial decrees which could be overturned.

Meanwhile, the school curriculum taught in the Druze schools was challenged by members of the community; they preferred to use an Arab programme than the 'Druze programme' with a Druze history and culture introduced by the authorities in 1975. In 1981 the head of Moughar local council, a member of the Democratic Front for Peace and Equality, declared his village to be an Arab village (it is 60 per cent Druze), and announced that henceforth the schools would use the Arab programme rather than the 'Druze programme' devised by the authorities. He was dismissed as a result. But the programme continued to be challenged. For example, the Committee of Graduates of Schools of Daliet al-Karmel protested against it in 1986.

The discriminatory practices against the Bedouin and Druze communities, who serve in the army, gives the lie to official apologists who excuse the treatment of the '48 Palestinians because of their 'disloyalty' to the state. Such treatment would be considered short-sighted if one believed that the state's aim was to create a cohesive Israeli society. However, the discrimination against all sectors of Palestinian society is so pervasive as to be considered racist. One can only assume that the state's long-term goal is to keep these citizens apart, in the hope that they will one day be persuaded that their future does not lie in Israel.

The response of the '48 Palestinians, as we have seen in chapters 2 and 3, has been based on the premise that their future *does* lie in Israel, where their homes are. They have worked on two levels: first, to pressure the authorities to fulfil their responsibilities towards them as tax-paying citizens; and second, to develop their own economic and social self-reliance. Although they have far to go, they have been so successful that, as we shall see in chapter 4, the Jewish state has devised new ways to try to stop them.

4

Reversing?

It will mean closing the last window on us. The government doesn't give us money for our local councils; if we go to the Jewish Agency, they tell us: 'This money came from Jewish people to help Jewish people'. Arab countries are considered enemy countries and if we try to be in touch with Palestinians abroad, that means we are terrorists in terms of how the government defines things.

Member of Ibillin Public Association for Culture and Art

The fight by the '48 Palestinians against dispossession and discrimination has gathered tremendous pace over the last 15 years. As we have seen in the previous three chapters, this struggle has taken the form of activism in the political sphere through organized parties, as well as spontaneous voluntary self-help initiatives at the town or village level, whose political colour may only be a commitment to equal rights and to a clearly defined identity as Palestinian and Arab.

At the heart of the '48 Palestinians' drive to organize on social issues was a determination to survive and to preserve their distinct Palestinian Arab identity. Even though a specific organization might have started out to tackle something as prosaic as sewage systems, the struggle to put these in place would take on overtones of cultural identity. It was apparent that the Jewish state's failure to provide such basic amenities was more than simple neglect; it implied pressure on the '48 Palestinians to move, to abandon their lands and their roots. It is not surprising that the '48 Palestinians imbued their countermeasures with an opposing agenda, a determination to stay and to retain their own culture.

As Rouhana wrote in 1989, the:

> drive for organisation on the community level has had three
> major motives, emphasis upon which varies from one
> organisation to another: to respond to particular require-
> ments and demands of a sector of the population whose
> concerns are neglected or not sufficiently met by the relevant
> authorities; to participate in the general effort by the Arab
> population to achieve equality; and to support the Pales-
> tinian drive for self-determination and independence. In
> many cases an organisation began with the first two goals, or
> even the first one only, but eventually became involved in all
> three. (p. 51)

The various techniques developed by the '48 Palestinians
were similar to those used by the West Bank and Gaza
Palestinians before the intifada, who established dozens of
institutions, voluntary organizations and committees in fields as
diverse as medical care, education, agriculture and culture, to
carry out their social development independently of the Israeli
occupational structures. The difference is that the '48 Palestinians are fighting, as yet, not for independence but for
equality.

In a sense, the Palestinians have become adept at using the
Israeli Jews' own language against them and challenging them
on their own terms, creating a profound sense of unease in the
process. An example of this unease is recorded by Khalil Nakhleh
in one of his articles (a critique of sociological writing on the
Palestinians in Israel) in the *Journal of Palestine Studies* in 1977.

> After presenting some of my present arguments in a
> departmental seminar at the Hebrew University of Jerusalem,
> December 1975, some Jewish anthropological colleagues were
> critical of my thrust. The general reaction of my academic
> colleagues at the universities of Haifa and Jerusalem, where
> some of these views were presented, was that of disgust and
> disbelief. One comment went as follows: 'I am frustrated and
> disappointed by your talk: why is it that whenever I talk to
> the simple Arab fellahin [peasants] in the villages I leave
> with a great hope that we can live together, and when I listen
> to you, my counterpart, I lose that hope?'

'Simple fellahin' or sophisticated intellectuals, the '48 Palestinians have come close to mastering the system in order to use it for their own ends. Political parties, cultural clubs, voluntary work camps, parents' committees at schools, kinder-gartens, fund-raising activities for community service, lobbying the Knesset, press campaigns, field studies, strikes and demonstrations: all are legal activities enshrined in a democratic system.

Given that the '48 Palestinians' struggle is legal, the Jewish state is constantly searching for 'legal' ways to counteract it. For example, when the Communist Party became strong enough to take over the Nazareth municipality in 1975, the government produced the Koenig Report which, as was mentioned in chapter 2, recommended several counteractions to consolidate the Jewish presence in Galilee.

In the mid-1980s, new Arab political and social forces had come on the scene, and the drive for self-reliant socio-economic development had started. The government response was enshrined in the Arens Report, details of which were leaked in October 1986 by the Israeli daily *Haaretz*. The Arens Report (ordered by Likud MK Moshe Arens when he was Minister of Arab Affairs) is said to have warned that 'Israel's minorities' were expected to reach 29 per cent of the population by the year 2000. It recommended that any independent political party with links with the PLO should be forbidden; that bodies working towards autonomy for Arabs in Israel should be banned; that foreign money should only be transferred to Arab bodies with the prior permission of a regulatory body or according to new legislation that will ensure that money does not enter from any sources not approved by the state; that Arab regional bodies should be integrated into official government institutions, or be totally unacknowledged; and that pro-grammes should be instituted to encourage 'minorities' to volunteer for the Israel defence forces (quoted in *al-Hadaf* newsletter, November 1987).

Emanating from one of the recommendations of the Arens Report – the restrictions on foreign funding – came the most serious threat so far to the organizations and community groups established by the '48 Palestinians, a back-handed compliment to their success. In 1989, a Draconian amendment to the

Terrorism Ordinance of 1948 was proposed, so as to allow
Israeli authorities to confiscate property, arrest people and close
down institutions, all on the suspicion that they had received, or
might have received, funds from 'terrorist' organizations.

The bill of 22 May 1989, 'Amendment No. 3 to the
Prevention of Terrorism Ordinance – 1948', was punitive.
Defining property as 'land, movable property, currency, rights
of any kind, including property which was purchased in
consideration for, or was exchanged for a property', it said that,
if 'a police officer whose rank is commissioner or higher has
reasonable suspicion that the property has originated from a
terrorist organization, he is authorized to order in writing the
seizure of such property for the purpose of its confiscation'.
Further, a police officer carrying out confiscations would be
'authorized to use any reasonable measure needed for the
fulfilment of such orders and for the prevention of disturbance
as he carries out his function; and in this case, he is authorized
to enter premises, including houses and work places'. The court
could also order the confiscation of 'another property belonging
to the person against whom the order is given'. Corporations
could be refused registration if they were suspected of being in
any way associated with 'terrorism'; worse, existing corporations could be 'liquidated' if they had any such links. Moreover,
as had been the practice in many cases against '48 Palestinians
tried under the Emergency Regulations inherited from the
British,

> the court may accept evidence in the absence of the person
> whose interests stand to be affected or his lawyer or without
> disclosing such evidence to them . . . if the court is persuaded
> that the revelation of such evidence to such a person or his
> lawyer is likely to harm the security of the state or of the
> public.

(It is worth recalling that the second amendment to the
Prevention of Terrorism Ordinance in 1986 prohibited contact
with members or representatives of the PLO. That law has been
used against both Israeli Jews and Palestinians.)

Along with other Palestinian publications, the *al-Hadaf*
newsletter vociferously protested the law in its draft form.

An alarming indication of what is behind the law came in the Ministry of Justice explanation to the Knesset Constitution Law and Justice Committee of why they consider the amendment necessary. This complains that the security services are unable to obtain results under the existing law because they are limited by procedural regulations and forced to rely on the court's discretion! For example, evidence must be revealed and witnesses brought before the court and cross-examined. The security services of many countries would surely relish such an opportunity to do away with these 'tiresome' processes, but in democratic systems the rule of law, including a judicial system which is able to protect basic civil liberties and rights such as the right to know and answer the case against you, is considered sacred. (July–August 1989)

The International Commission of Jurists noted in July 1989 (*ICJ Review*) that the burden of proof 'to establish that the property came from a terrorist organisation is that required in civil law (i.e. on the balance of probabilities) and not that under criminal law (beyond reasonable doubt)'. As it pointed out:

When such issues have arisen on other matters in Israeli Courts, the Court has accepted evidence by the security authorities that they know that the individual or organisation in question is working for or is in contact with a banned organisation, but for security reasons is unable to disclose the source of its information. If the Courts follow that practice in these cases, the other parties to the proceedings will be powerless to disprove the allegation.

When word came out about the proposed law, the Palestinian voluntary committees went into action. Several of them met on 30 April 1989 and formed the Committee for the Defence of Voluntary Work in the Arab Sector (including al-Hadaf, the Galilee Society for Health Research and Services, the Human Rights Association, and the Voluntary Work Association of Musmus). They agreed 'to raise objections to any amendment to the law aimed at stopping contributions reaching voluntary foundations in the Arab sector from foreign associations that were legally registered in their countries'. They 'stressed the right of such foundations to receive contributions in order to carry out their registered objectives as do hundreds of Jewish voluntary foundations. The Arab sector within the green line already suffers from government discriminatory measures and does not receive government money for development.'

After the bill's first reading (of three) in the Knesset on 23 May 1989, 55 voluntary agencies and municipal bodies serving the Palestinians in Israel issued an international appeal. The 55 bodies covered a range of opinion from left to right, and included friends as well as foes from the Democratic Front for Peace and Equality, Abna' al-Balad, the Muslim League (Umm al-Fahem), the Progressive List for Peace, and the Arab Democratic Party. The threat was aimed at one and all. The appeal declared, 'Although ostensibly aimed at fighting terrorism . . . the proposed amendment would give the police and the security apparatus in Israel virtually absolute powers to close down Arab charitable organizations, to confiscate their assets and to detain activists.'

The ordinance amendment was the proposal of the Justice Minister Dan Meridor. The *Jerusalem Post* reported the following conversation in the Knesset, 'MK Muhammad Mi'ari (Progressive List for Peace), who voted against, said: "This is a law that is tailor-made to hit at Israeli Arabs." To which Meridor replied that it was not Israeli Jews who had created the situation that had necessitated such legislation' (30 June 1989). It quoted Palestinian lawyer Hussein Abu Hussein as estimating that there were eighty Arab voluntary associations, and that these received 90 per cent of their funding from abroad, and that the amendment would ruin their work. It also quoted a member of a self-help group in Ibillin, the Public Association for Culture and Art, as saying,

It will mean the closing of the last window on us. The government doesn't give us money for our local councils; if we go to the Jewish Agency, they tell us: 'This money came from Jewish people to help Jewish people'. Arab countries are considered enemy countries and if we try to be in touch with Palestinians abroad, that means we are terrorists in terms of how the government defines things.

In summer 1989, a European-based development agency involved in assisting the Palestinians also launched an appeal to friends and colleagues. Its appeal said,

> Particularly worrisome in the proposed draft is the wide and imprecise definition of what the draft calls 'an illegal organization', the wide discretion given to administrative bodies, and the shift of the burden and reduction of standards of proof. The draft also gives the police wide powers to confiscate property before the judiciary is given the chance to determine whether or not such property in fact belongs to an illegitimate body.

Many bodies expected that, when the bill became law, the Israeli military occupation authorities in the West Bank and Gaza would promptly issue a military order for the occupied territories along the same lines, to deal with the already severely harassed voluntary sector under occupation.

By late 1989, several Arab and Jewish organizations had come together to lobby against the proposed law. Over 150 people attended a meeting on 5 November in Tel Aviv, organized jointly by the Committee of Arab Voluntary Associations and the International Center for Peace in the Middle East. The head of the Regional Committee of Arab Local Councils, Ibrahim Nimr Hussein, said that the 'law could do untold damage to projects which are vital to the Palestinian communities here because of the lack of sufficient government funding'. Hussein added that when Palestinians 'ask the government for money for development they are told that money for this purpose comes from Jewish donors abroad and they must themselves go out and seek such funding – but now, as they begin to do just this, the government starts trying to put a stop to it' (al-Hadaf newsletter, issue 12, undated).

A coalition of 102 Arab and Jewish groups lobbied against the measure as parliament prepared to resume discussions of it. It made news even in the New York Times (12 November 1989). The paper quoted Dr Hatem Kanaaneh of the Galilee Society for Health and Research Services: 'The intent of the law is to impede the development of the Arab sector and maintain our total dependence on the Government and the major political parties.' The New York Times itself commented:

The Israeli proposal indicates a concern that the P.L.O.
financing will increase to include the Israeli Arabs. It also
shows the distrust many Jewish leaders feel toward Israel's
700,000 Arab citizens. The Israeli authorities acknowledge
that Government financing for social services in Israel's Arab
towns is significantly less than for similar Jewish towns.

Relentless pressure

By the end of the 1980s, the '48 Palestinians faced a new
challenge with the news from the Soviet Union that restrictions
on Jewish migration were being lifted. Previously, most Soviet
Jews allowed out of the Soviet Union headed straight for the
United States. But with the relaxation of emigration in the
Soviet Union, the United States argued that Jews could no
longer be considered a persecuted group deserving special
treatment; they would have to queue with everyone else for
entry to the United States. Therefore, most Soviet Jewish
migrants will be heading to Israel (although, once there, many
might still apply for entry to the United States). By January
1990, the *New York Times* estimated that Soviet Jews were
arriving in Israel at the rate of over a thousand per week.

The flood of migrants will place further pressure on that most
precious of resources – land – as well as on development funds
across the board. There is no doubt that the '48 Palestinians,
already suffering in these areas, will be further squeezed. Their
predicament is unlikely to be resolved in the event of a peace
settlement between the Arabs and Israel and the establishment
of a Palestinian state – which would end Likud's hopes for
settlement of Jews in the West Bank and Gaza. The Palestinian
state would have to accommodate as many returning Palestinian refugees as possible from Lebanon and other Arab
countries. In any case, '48 Palestinians do not want to move to
a Palestinian state; their towns and villages in Israel are home,
and they are determined to stay put.

A confrontation is on the cards between Palestinians and
Jews within Israel. It may well be bloody, but not because the
Palestinians would initiate the use of violence. Excluding the
decade or so after the creation of Israel, there is no tradition of
'armed struggle' among the '48 Palestinians, and the last two

decades have seen the increasingly sophisticated use of democratic forms for change. However, if the Israeli Jews close all democratic avenues, and use force against the Palestinians, the outcome will be violent.

The only way out would be if Israeli Jews faced the basic contradiction of Israel's being both a Jewish state and a democracy. At the most basic level, Israel needs to turn from a 'haven' for persecuted Jews into a normal state, where, as novelist Anton Shammas suggests, the same immigration criteria are applied to all, and on the basis of how many new people the state can absorb while still providing equal opportunities for its existing citizens. Certainly, the use of anti-Semitism as an argument for the existence of Israel would have to be abandoned. Anti-Semitism would continue to be fought by Jewish citizens of other countries to end any discrimination that might face them in those countries. Any ties to Israel would be religious, like those of Catholics to the Vatican, or sentimental, like those of Americans to the 'old country'; Israel would not be regarded as an alternative homeland – a position which exposes Jews in other countries to the accusation of dual loyalty.

Once Israel ceases to be a Jewish haven and a Jewish state, it will have moved into a post-Zionist era. Thus, the answer for Israeli Jewish and Arab equality and coexistence is a 'de-Zionized' Israel. As the majority of Israeli Jews are still very far from seeing things this way, it seems likely that the next decade holds tragedy.

However, many Palestinians now believe this could be an answer. The development of the Palestinian struggle has gone through three phases. The first phase was 'armed struggle' by Palestinians in exile, in response to dispossession at Israel's hands, which kept the pot boiling but could not resolve the conflict. The second phase was civil organization and resistance to Israeli expansion in the West Bank and Gaza, which peaked with the intifada. The third phase, yet to crystallize, belongs to the '48 Palestinians, striving in the long term for a de-Zionized Israel and the making of a state that, truly democratic, works for all of its citizens.

At the present time, the '48 Palestinians' attention is focused on ways of ending the discrimination and achieving recognition of their identity as Palestinian Arabs. We meet many

Palestinian Arab citizens of Israel in part two, to hear about the
problems they have faced, and the solutions they have devised.
They tell their own stories in words prosaic enough to describe
day-to-day affairs, and evocative enough to paint a dream of the
future.

A *Portrait of Institution Builders*

About five years ago or so, I made a firm decision not to use a single Hebrew word when speaking Arabic. Once we had a meeting with some left-wing Jews, who only spoke Hebrew, so we decided to have someone translate the Hebrew into Arabic for us, although we all spoke very good Hebrew. Then after the meeting was over, one of us said something in Hebrew, and the Jews were astounded, and they cried out: 'Goodness, you are *our* Arabs after all!'

Marwan, 1989

5

The Counsellor: Siham in Acre

I asked them is it an educational institution you
object to, or an *Arab* educational institution?

Siham

'There is no sunset as beautiful as that of 'Acca', said an
inhabitant, as he gazed at the sea and the setting sun.

Acre (Arabic: 'Acca) has a population of 45,000, of which
around 15,000 are Arabs. Of the Arabs, some 10,000 live in old
Acre, a beautiful area which is, sadly, crumbling. But despite its
depressed physical state, it has a majesty about it, as if to say,
'My past was once glorious.'

The Arab inhabitants are convinced that the municipality is
allowing the area to disintegrate so that they will be forced to
move out. The place can then be turned into a tourist attraction
and a residential area for Jews, especially as many Jews from
Tel Aviv would like to move to Acre.

The authorities have already persuaded some of the Palestinians to move to a town called Maker. They convinced very
poor families living in dilapidated houses, and young couples
who wanted to set up their own homes, that they had built
them new luxury flats. Once in Maker, the people found
themselves living in tiny flats like matchboxes. They were
resented by the local Arab population who compared them to
the Jews who settled uninvited on Arab land. Many Palestinians who moved to Maker desperately want to return to their
old homes.

'The authorities are expropriating old 'Acca little by little,'
explained an inhabitant angrily. 'For example, the Arab shore
used to be an open area where families went for walks and
picnics. It has now been taken over by Jews. They are building

restaurants and night clubs, and they have erected a fence to keep the local population out. The only way anyone can go in is by paying four shekels.'

The Israeli Jewish authorities are also trying to move the fishermen, but they are putting up strong resistance (more so, it would seem, than in Jaffa). Other pressure is therefore being used – such as turning the area into a tourist attraction with mooring for yachts and sailing boats. This has restricted the fishermen's mooring areas, giving them limited space for their nets. Moreover, restrictions have been imposed on where they can sell their fish.

Outside the walls overlooking the sea, some Palestinians live in old Arab-style houses, and some live in luxurious villas. Others live in council flats which once belonged to Jews who have moved elsewhere, and a few also live in apartment blocks.

Siham is a 42-year-old counsellor at Dar al-Tifl, and a member of the Acre Arab Women's Association. She also teaches in a secondary school, and is a lecturer at the University of Haifa. Her day starts at 8.00 a.m. and often ends at 11.00 p.m. She is tall and imposing, but with a girlish mischief and warmth. She lives in an apartment block with her two children, Ahmad, aged 20, and Alia, 15. The building consists of 32 flats: there are seven Arab families, and the rest are Jews. Siham's flat has three bedrooms, a study, a large sitting-room, kitchen and bathroom.

Her flat is very different from the house where she was brought up, and where her mother and her older unmarried sister, Lamis, still live. Their house is Arab-style, with six spacious rooms, and a large garden that has seen better days. A well-fed Alsatian keeps an eye on the house. He is tied up to one of the trees during the day, and exercises his heavy limbs by turning round in circles as far as his leash will allow. At night, he is left to roam the garden, but at no time during the day or night is he allowed indoors; according to tradition, dogs are unclean.

Siham visits her mother and sister daily; the old lady is 84, an invalid, but with a sharp mind and a mischievous sense of humour. Lamis is in her early fifties, and a practising Muslim, but not a fundamentalist. She is kind and always welcomes the constant flow of visitors throughout the day; relatives, neighbours and friends.

It was a hot humid afternoon. Siham arrived at her mother's place from Dar al-Tifl. She kissed her mother and sister, and then slumped in a chair. She was tired and hungry.

'I'll warm up the food,' said Lamis.

Siham smiled, 'I don't really have time to cook because of my hectic schedule, so I have an arrangement with Lamis: I share the expenses of the food, and she cooks a large quantity to include me and my children. I eat here every day, but my children don't always come, so I take their share home. Actually, Ahmad sometimes cooks himself a meal – a simple one of course.'

Her mother asked if her children were coming to eat.

'No,' replied Siham. 'Ahmad is still studying for his exams. Alia had her last exam today, and she is out seeing her friends before she goes to America for her summer holiday.'

Siham gazed at a large photograph hanging on the wall. It was that of an old man with a handsome face.

'It's my father,' she said. 'He was a good man, and very wise, too. You know, it was by staying in 'Acca during all the troubles that my father managed to hang on to this house. He held on to his papers and saved his home. He owned other properties jointly with a friend of his who left the country with the relevant papers. The Jews then expropriated some of the properties. They said that there were no papers to prove that my father was joint owner.

'When the country was occupied, the women mourned. They stopped going to public baths, and they stopped combing their hair. They became more segregated because they were frightened of what the Jews might do to them. Girls were withdrawn from school at an early age, and some were married off. Others stayed at home, unable to get married because their cousins had left the country and their parents would not allow them to marry outside the family.

'People were unrealistic about the situation. They thought the occupiers would only be here for a short while. Eventually they had to face up to reality. So when education became free in the 1950s, it encouraged families to allow their girls to finish school. Mind you, it was not for the sake of education as such, but it was better than having their daughters stay idle. On the other hand, boys were withdrawn from school at the ages of 13 to 14 in order to work and help their families financially. Most people suffered vast economic losses.

'My parents, like most of their generation, bewailed the loss of their land, but were not really aware of the national consequences. Their suffering was on an individual and very personal level, and their main preoccupation was not how to free the country, but how to protect the family.'

Siham's mother retorted with a chuckle: 'Today people may be more aware, but they are not more polite. In my days, we also struggled. I remember how under Turkish rule people in 'Acca were left without food or clothes. I used to walk from 'Acca to Haifa to get food. I carried it on my head, my back, my arms, and walked all the way back.

'Most of our men were in the Turkish army, and those who remained in 'Acca were too ashamed to fetch and carry the food. It was considered a woman's task. Then later, during the resistance, some of us women used to take food and tea to the fighters in the hills, and we used to spend hours trying to clean the rust off the ammunition that was sent from Egypt.'

The conversation was interrupted by the arrival of Hussain, one of Siham's brothers. He is 52, and owns a restaurant overlooking the sea. He kissed his mother, and enquired about her health. She grinned. 'They want to know about the old days.'

Siham continued with her tale: 'In 1948, my mother was frightened for us children, especially as I had a brother who was under threat of execution by the Jews. In those days, they used to arrest the young men, imprison them, and threaten them with execution to discourage them from fighting for their country. My mother wanted us all to leave the country, but my father refused. He said that the Turks had occupied us and left, the English had come and left, and now the Jews were here but they too would leave. This was his country and home, and he wasn't going to leave. He told her that he could not have her and the children on his conscience, so if she was that frightened, then she should leave with the children.

'My father stayed behind, and we went to Lebanon for a year or so. He was then allowed to have his family back, but not all of us: only his wife, unmarried daughters, and boys under the age of 16. I had two married sisters who could not return, and two brothers, one over the age of 16, and the other exactly 16. We were dispersed for the first time in our lives, and we are still dispersed.'

'In those days, there was no political awareness; what we felt was purely emotional,' said Hussain. 'I remember when we came back from Lebanon, I had to leave school to work. I worked as a carpenter in a kibbutz, building prefabricated houses for the Jews. I was there for about a year, and I was very happy. For me, it was the ideal example of socialism and I was very impressed by it. Yet there I was, building houses for the very people who had taken away our land and homes. I wasn't aware of this – we were so politically ignorant about our cause. All that concerned me was the fact that part of my family had left the country and wasn't allowed to return.'

His mother sighed: 'Yes, the Jews have divided us. They have caused us so much pain.'

Hussain continued: 'I used to sleep in the kibbutz, go home Friday afternoon, and then return to work on Sunday. My father, who was a wise man, realized that I was being influenced by life in the kibbutz, and that he was also losing his authority over me. As I was going to be in charge of the family after his death, he decided to find a way of keeping me in 'Acca. He owned a coffee shop with a partner, so he told me to take over his share as he was getting old and tired.

'At first, I didn't want to, I wanted to stay in the kibbutz, but then I gave in to his wishes. I took over his share of the coffee shop, and as there were no proper restaurants in 'Acca, I persuaded my partner to turn it into a restaurant. Later on, I bought him out. When I settled in 'Acca, I started reading the Communist paper al-Ittihad, and I listened to Nasser's speeches. I began to question what was going on around me, and that's how my awareness developed.'

Siham commented: 'My father was a religious and traditional man, but he was wise. He had sound ideas about justice. He married four times, but not all at the same time. He used to say that he did not believe that he could divide his time equally between the various wives. He had 13 children: I am the youngest. He believed that the children were his sole responsibility, so we were all brought up in the same house by him and my mother, who was his last wife. He always made sure that we were all treated equally, and that no one exploited the other.

'My father's sense of responsibility started at a very young age. When he was about 12 years old, his father died. He had to leave the *kuttab* [traditional school], and find work in order to support his stepmother, brothers and sisters. He wanted to study so badly that he used to bribe his mates who were still in the *kuttab* with sweets and money so that they would teach him what they were learning.'

Siham stopped talking and grinned: 'I talk too much,' she said. She concentrated on the food for a while, and then resumed her story:

'It was a blow for him and for all of us to end up dispersed. At first, my own awareness was also on the emotional level. Then, when Nasser came to power, the emotional awareness began to develop into a nationalist one, especially among the young people. We looked upon Nasser as the symbol of our revolution. His speeches filled us with faith in the Arab cause. In those days, the Palestinian question was not a separate issue, but part of the great Arab world, especially Egypt. And so my awareness developed as I listened to Nasser's speeches and to our own nationalists.

'My children can discuss their political interests with me. I could not do so with my parents because they, like other parents, kept telling me to keep quiet as they were afraid that I would get myself and them into trouble. The fear of the older people, combined with their inability to cope with the changes in the younger people's attitudes, created conflicts in the family. The old people were faced with a totally unknown situation, not only in terms of what was happening in the wider society, but in relation to their own children.

'In about 1961, the Jews killed some Palestinians who were trying to cross over to Jordan. There was a demonstration, and my friends and I defied the headmistress, walked out of school and participated in the demonstration. I was arrested, and I honestly did not know at that point whether I was more scared of the police, or of what my family would say when they found out. But my belief in what I had done gave me strength when I faced the police. I was in fact more frightened of my family's reaction to it all.

'I was released the same day, and when I went home I lied about where I had been. But my lie was exposed when the police came to our home in the middle of the night to question me. My parents and older brothers were angrier with me for having lied to them than for having marched in the demonstration. Shortly after that, one of my brothers was wounded by a Moroccan Jew. My parents finally realized that the situation was far more serious and threatening than they had perceived. And so they came to terms with my political involvement.

'In 1967, when we listened to Cairo radio and heard about the victories of the Egyptian army, we of course believed them and felt very excited and proud. It was then that I heard my mother speak openly about Palestinians. She said that she would open her door to all the Palestinians who returned and who had no roof over their heads. I realized then that although my parents were ruled by fear, deep inside themselves they were Palestinians.

'The disaster of 1967 changed us. We were finally confronted with the fact that the only people responsible for the Palestinian cause were the Palestinians themselves.'

The rest of the family nodded in agreement.

'Although my father was traditional, he didn't have a closed mind,' Siham went on. 'Most times, I behaved in the way he wanted me to so that I would be allowed to continue my studies. My brother had to leave school to work, and so did Lamis. My father had property, but he didn't have ready cash because he had had to close down his flour mill, which in fact had been his main source of income.'

Lamis, who is also a member of the Acre Arab Women's Association added: 'Yes, I left school at the end of the sixth grade. I was 15, older than all the other students in my class because when we went to Lebanon I didn't go to school for about a year and a half. When I left school, I worked in a Quaker centre which had a club, kindergarten and clinic. I wanted to become a nurse, but my father refused because in those days girls from traditional families did not take up the nursing profession. It was considered a lowly job.

'So I worked in the kindergarten, and then I learnt how to weigh the children and helped with first aid in the clinic. Although the reason for my leaving school was because of our financial situation, my father refused to take any of the money I earned. He felt guilty for taking me out of school. I worked at the centre for about ten years. I also learnt sewing during that time, although I hated it. But when the centre closed down, I decided to become a seamstress. I did so from home, and I had clients from towns and villages: Arabs and Jews.'

'I was very lucky to be able to continue my studies,' Siham admitted. 'At first, I went to a primary school which I hated. I was about six years old. It was terrible because they used to beat us up, and prick us with needles if we messed up our sewing. I was so terrified of the school that I couldn't learn anything. Lamis realized this, and so did my brother, and they persuaded my parents to send me to a different school. I was sent to a nun's school and stayed there until the tenth grade when the school closed down.

'My parents then wanted me to stay at home and learn how to sew. They said that I'd had enough education. I was devastated, and tried all sorts of methods to convince them to let me continue my studies. I reasoned with them, I sulked, and I cajoled until they gave in. I was sent to boarding school in Haifa. When I went home for weekends, my brother would come and pick me up and then take me back at the end of my stay. In those days girls were not allowed to travel on their own, not only because of social traditions, but because parents were frightened of the influence of the wider society and what the Jews might do to us. My daughter, who also goes to school in Haifa, commutes every day on her own.'

Siham's mother nodded, and then said with a grin, 'I used to go to school too, but I played truant. I used to play outside until it was time to go home. When my mother found out she beat me up, and so did the teacher. They made my brother take me to school every day to make sure I didn't play truant again. But then my uncle (my father was dead) made my mother take me out of school. He said that I should not learn how to read and write because I might end up writing love letters to boys,' and she giggled at the thought.

Siham laughed and hugged her. 'It was not difficult to persuade my parents to let me go to university,' she continued. 'They realized how much education meant to me, and they were also proud that I had excellent grades in my *baghrout* (matriculation). They also trusted me not to break family values and dishonour them. Although I lived my life the way my father wanted, there was one tradition I could not bring myself to accept: an arranged marriage.'

Siham was interrupted by the arrival of guests. Shortly after that, she left for a meeting in Haifa. On her way home from the meeting she dropped in at her mother's. The old lady was dozing in her wheelchair, Lamis was watching television, and the dog had his freedom for the night.

On the balcony there was a humid breeze blowing from the sea, and there was silence. After a while, Siham began talking. 'I was saying earlier that I did not accept the idea of an arranged marriage. I couldn't accept that a man I didn't know would ask for my hand not because he respected me as a person, but because I was so and so's daughter, or so and so's sister. It was a big problem for me because, on the one hand, I didn't want to break tradition and create conflicts in my family but, on the other hand, I could not succumb to something that was so much against my principles and convictions. So every time someone went to my family to ask for my hand, I would tell my parents, "Absolutely not". They tried very hard to convince me, but I wouldn't be persuaded.

'Then a friend of mine told me that a young man she knew had heard about me and was very keen to meet me. He was doing an MA, and at the same time teaching at the University of Jerusalem. I refused to see him because meeting him in secret meant breaking my family's trust in me. I was also suspicious of him because in those days we thought that any Arab who did postgraduate work, or who had a good job, must have collaborated with the Jews.

'We had such a negative view of ourselves and of our abilities. The Jews placed many obstacles in front of us to stop us from advancing in our lives and careers, so if an Arab had a good position, he was immediately suspect. Anyway, in the end my curiosity got the better of me, and I agreed to meet him at my friend's house. I saw him for five minutes only, and then I

rushed home because I felt so guilty meeting him without my
parents' knowledge. I was also frightened that they would find
out and would then stop me from continuing my studies. In
those days, if parents didn't like the way their daughters
behaved, they immediately blamed it on education.

'After thinking about him for a couple of months, and
struggling with myself, I decided to see him again. We didn't
fall in love at first sight or anything like that, but we found out
that we had a lot in common, intellectually. He wanted to
continue his studies, and he wanted me to do the same. He was
ambitious and so was I; I wasn't going to stand in his way and
insist that he support me, as another woman might have done.

'I also found out that, far from being a collaborator, he was
someone with great integrity, and an ardent Palestinian
nationalist. He had worked as a labourer for a while, and
eventually became a teacher. At university he was one of the
top students and was determined to continue his studies.

'I agreed to marry him, but I also warned him that it was
really up to my parents; if they refused, then I was not prepared
to go against their wishes. Before he approached my parents, I
told my brother about him, and my brother talked to my
parents. When they met him, they liked him, and we got
married. I totally refused to have him pay the *mahr* [dowry],
where the groom gives money to the parents to buy clothes,
gold, furniture, etc., for the bride. In those days, the sum paid
was relative to how beautiful and educated the girl was. It was
like being put on auction in the market. I found it absolutely
humiliating. He and I built our home together.

'I was in my first year at university at the time. I had started
studying Arabic, but then changed to education because the
Arabic they were teaching was geared to Jews: they taught
Arabic grammar in Hebrew, the Koran in Hebrew, and so on. I
found it meaningless. At the end of my first year, my husband
had a scholarship to do his Ph.D. in America. There I went to
college for a year. When we returned home, I finished my BA.
Then my husband had a sabbatical which we spent in the
United States, where I managed to finish my MA. Then I went
on to do a Ph.D.

'All my university education took place during my married
life. I sometimes feel it would have been nice to have been a

carefree student without having to be a mother and wife at the same time. But I suppose the way I did it had its positive aspects as well.

'My husband died three years ago, and I went through a rough period. I was so used to sharing decisions, and above all sharing the responsibility of bringing up the children, and suddenly there I was, having to make all the decisions on my own. I have not brought up my children in an authoritarian way, because I don't want to be like my parents. But sometimes, I wonder if I haven't made a mistake.

'My son can understand my views about life and about our society, but it's not so with my daughter. At times, I argue with her about the way she dresses, for example. She seems to disregard some of the values of her society and it worries me. She should respect at least some of the values. She is a Palestinian, and her society has a uniqueness which differentiates her from a Brigitte, Annie, or Rachel.

'The other worry I had after my husband's death was the change in my status from a married woman to a widow. I was worried that as a woman on my own my movements would be restricted by my family and society, and I would have to stop all my activities. But I was pleasantly surprised when I found out that I had more support than criticism, from my family and the wider society. Palestinian society is changing: you have both the traditional and the modern, and you can find this dichotomy within one family. Mind you, if I started to live my personal life in the Western way, then I would most definitely be condemned.'

The next day Siham was in her office at Dar al-Tifl by 9.00. The institution is situated on one of the main streets in the modern sector of 'Acca.

'Dar al-Tifl takes up most of my time,' explained Siham. 'It was established by the Acre Arab Women's Association in 1983, and serves as a centre for the development of kindergarten education in the whole 1948 region. The Women's Association itself was set up around 1975 with the aim of helping women develop mentally, intellectually and emotionally.

'The building we were in before was a much smaller one. When we bought this building it took us months to settle in. The municipality gave us so much trouble. When we started making alterations inside the building they took us to court, although they had no right to do so. But, of course, they lost the case because we had not broken any laws. To renovate the exterior of the building we needed planning permission, so we submitted our plans, but they kept them for months and we couldn't start anything. So back to the court we went.

'In any other country the municipality would have been proud to have such an institution and, instead of obstructing us, they would have helped us. But not in this country. They also accused us of taking money from the PLO, which is not true at all. Then they told us that it was not proper to have an educational institution on the main street alongside banks and shops. I asked them, "Is it an educational institution that you object to, or more accurately an *Arab* educational institution?"

'They don't object to the Jewish old people's home next to us. In fact, the municipality helped set it up. They said that it would have been better had our building been turned into a restaurant. I replied, "Yes, of course. For years you have been used to us working for you, serving you, feeding you. But you cannot accept the fact that we are doing something that feeds our brains for a change." Anyway, in the end we won our court case.

'When I first started, I tried to apply some of the Western ideas I had acquired abroad. We gave lectures and held discussions, but it was not successful because you cannot impose alien ideas on people; you cannot force them to accept values which do not suit their way of life. We decided instead to set up kindergartens to help working mothers so that they wouldn't be forced to leave their children in the care of different people every day.

'We also realized that to develop our Palestinian identity in a positive way we had to start with the very young. After all, they are the corner-stone of our society. To achieve this, we needed well-trained kindergarten teachers, which our society lacked. So we began to think in terms of setting up an institution to train kindergarten teachers.

'At first, we found the task daunting. It needed a great deal of effort and struggle, and it needed a substantial sum of money. But we were lucky because we met people from an independent, non-governmental organization who were visiting the country.

They told us that they wanted to finance projects which were non-governmental and which helped Palestinians in the '48 region.

'We wrote our proposal, but we also imposed two conditions on the organization. One was to guarantee us finance for five years. The other was that, once we started working, they should allow us time for trial and error, because we had to take so many different factors into account: parents, the wider society, the municipality, and the authorities. It would not have been realistic to give a detailed account of all our plans.

'They accepted our conditions, and gave us the finances to begin our projects. We carried out a survey to find out the standards and quality of the teachers, and whether they were willing to be properly trained or not. Then we set up workshops, because teachers complained that they did not have enough money to prepare their kindergarten classes in an efficient way: they lacked books, toys, equipment, and so on.

'We were successful from the first year, and when the Ministry of Education examined our programmes, they said that they could learn from us. Our institution has succeeded because it meets the real needs of Palestinian society, and because we are determined to fulfil the needs of our people. Today, some Palestinians in the '48 region realize that they can obtain finances from institutions abroad, so they write up proposals just to be able to get the money, but in fact they are still in search of ideas. And when they do get the money, they don't know how to use it because they have not properly researched the needs of the society.

'One of our main aims has been to develop the personal and national identity of the teachers. Many of the girls come from rural areas. When they finish secondary school, they find themselves in a dilemma about their future. They don't know what to do with themselves, how and where to place themselves. They feel inferior and lost, and they look shrunken. So we have counsellors who give them lectures and encourage them to talk about themselves: about their childhood, their problems, and aspirations.

'These courses encourage the teachers to get to know themselves. They have to know their strengths and weaknesses, and they have to learn to respect themselves and their profession so that they can respect the children, and interact with them in a positive way. At the end of the course, the teachers are very different people in behaviour, in the way they talk, look and walk. We want a better society, and to do this we have to make sure that children are well taught and taken care of. We can only do this through well-trained and qualified teachers.

'We also teach them about Land Day, and we have games about our land and olive trees, and what they mean to the Palestinian peasants. We teach them how Palestinian families celebrate the different festivals: Ramadan, the Eid, Christmas and Easter – but not from a religious point of view, just to show how they are part of our culture and history, which differ from the Jewish festivals and culture. They must learn that as Palestinians we too have a culture which is not inferior to the Jewish one, and which must be recognized and respected.

'We have six members of staff, and ten teachers/counsellors who are not staff members, but come in specifically to give courses to kindergarten teachers.'

At the institution there was a course in progress. There were 27 students who were being taught how to deal with children aged one day to three years. Some of the points that the teacher emphasized were: welcoming the children with warmth; respecting his or her individuality; visiting their homes to acquaint themselves with their background; teaching the parents the importance of cleanliness. She then left the room briefly and came back with a doll the size of a two-month-old baby, and a feeding bottle. The idea was to demonstrate how to bottle feed a baby properly. First she asked one of the unmarried students to demonstrate how she would do it. Some of the other students giggled as their classmate struggled clumsily with the doll. The next student to try was a married woman with two children of her own. She not only held the doll properly, but also talked to it as she went through the motions of feeding it. She pointed out that it was important to have both bodily and verbal contact with the baby to relax it, and to reassure it of its existence as an individual.

Their next lesson dealt with values and identity. The teacher began by telling them that some of the values in Arab societies tended to be repressive.

'For example, it is shameful to talk about one's body, or about certain emotions. Consequently it creates tension in a person which is then transmitted to the child,' she explained.

She then took the students out into the hallway where she showed them exercises to help them relax their bodies and faces. Some of them were shy and hardly moved their bodies. She was relentless with them until they finally began to relax. The exercises went on for half an hour, after which they returned to the classroom. She then talked to them about the importance of making the children aware of their Palestinian identity:

'A very young child will not understand abstract concepts about identity, therefore it is important to do it through festivals, songs, costumes, pictures and nature.'

'But if we talk openly about our Palestinian identity, we will get into trouble,' said one of the students.

'You will not be talking to the children about the authorities, nor will you be talking directly about political repression and injustice. You will be doing it indirectly through songs, pictures, and so on. If the children are not taught about their identity, they will be lost.'

And the lesson continued.

Later in the day, after a meeting with some of the teachers, Siham introduced one of them, who was Jewish.

'This is Hava. She trains our teachers to make games, models, pictures and puppets for the children.'

Hava pointed out some of the drawings on the walls: 'The drawings are by a Jewish lady who got the material from Egypt. She made a few adjustments such as changing the Egyptian costumes to Palestinian ones.'

The drawings were of a family dressed in Palestinian clothes, celebrating Ramadan: shopping for food, praying, breaking the fast, etc.

'The drawings are not realistic enough for the children,' continued Hava, 'so now we will take photographs of real people dressed up in Palestinian clothes. We will have families celebrating Ramadan, Christmas, the Eid, and Easter. Most of the children's books in this country are written for Jewish children. When we translate them into Arabic, we change a few things so that the stories are suitable for Palestinian children. Siham is trying to get children's books from the Arab world.'

After Hava left, Siham said: 'Unfortunately, Palestinians here still don't have the skills of people like Hava. We had a Palestinian teacher before Hava, but she was not competent at all. But we will get there one day.'

The day-care centre and nursery school, which were also started by the Acre Arab Women's Association, are within walking distance from Dar al-Tifl.

There were 96 children, whose ages ranged from six weeks to four and a half years. Some were howling, others were laughing, and some were singing a song called 'Nations of the World'.

The director, who is also a member of the Association, explained: 'In 'Acca most parents prefer to send their children to Arab nursery schools. Here we teach them about the importance of the extended family; we tell them about the land and the olive trees; we teach them all about the different festivals; and we make them wear Palestinian clothes when we celebrate the festivals. There are about 25 Arab children in Jewish nursery schools. There are a few parents who still think that their children will be better taken care of in Jewish schools, but in fact they end up unable to speak either Arabic or Hebrew properly. They have problems with their speech, their under-standing, and of course their identity. It's very sad.'

After a busy day divided between Dar al-Tifl and the university, Siham finally went home to spend a few hours with her daughter who was leaving for the United States early in the morning.

The doorbell rang. It was a Jewish woman, a stranger. Siham talked to her in Hebrew. When she came back she said:

'It's strange, some of the Jews must be really desperate for work. The woman asked me if I would hire her as a cleaning lady. It's never happened before.'

A year later, Siham was busier than ever.

'We struggle and struggle, and the authorities want to enact new laws to try to hinder us,' she said angrily as she greeted her mother and sister.

'The Jews want to pass a law through the Knesset to close down Palestinian cultural centres and institutions which they think may be getting financial support from the PLO. Even if a centre or institution is financed by an independent, non-governmental organization, the authorities will have the right to close it down by claiming that the money sent by the organization was originally obtained from the PLO. So if a policeman in the street does not like the way I look, he will be able to walk into Dar al-Tifl and close it down, claiming that it is financed by the PLO. He will have the power to do it without proof or evidence of any kind.' She sighed wearily. 'We are not going to accept this. We are campaigning against this crazy law.'

'The Israelis refuse to recognize our needs,' said Lamis. 'We are discriminated against on all levels. For example, the Women's Association is trying to set up a home for the elderly which will cater for the needs of all the Arabs here, regardless of their class or religion. In the past, our Arab society was in no great need for such a home because we still had the extended family. But now the Arab community is changing. Young people of both sexes go out to work and have no time to take care of the elderly. Also, nowadays married couples live in small flats where there is not enough room to have their parents live with them. The three homes that exist for the Arabs have been established specifically for the Christians. The public homes which are government owned claim that they cater for both Jews and Arabs. But for example in 'Acca there are only two Arabs in the public homes and it was not easy for them to get accepted. Moreover, for the Jews themselves there is a waiting list of up to four years, and they of course take precedence over the Arabs. We are asking the municipality to help us set up a home. They are not responding, but we will not give up.'

'Every step, every breath a Palestinian takes is a struggle. But we will not give up until the Israelis recognize our identity and our needs,' Siham said vehemently.

Ahmad and Alia, Siham's children, arrived. They were warmly welcomed by their aunt and grandmother.

Siham continued: 'Today's struggle is so different from what it used to be during my parents' time, and my time, when I was my children's age. Unlike my own parents, I have encouraged my children's awareness. Their struggle is a different one: on one level it is a humanitarian struggle against injustice and discrimination, and on another level it is a national one where they want their Palestinian identity to be recognized and respected by the authorities. My son was once asked, "What are you?" He replied, "I'm a Palestinian living in Israel." '

'It's true our struggle is different from the older generation,' said Ahmad. 'But I don't blame the older generation for our situation. I don't look back to the past. For me, what is more important is what is going to happen and what should happen.'

Alia added: 'I'm a Palestinian living in Israel, but I can't say I'm all that proud to be living in Israel. There's a lot of injustice here. The Jews claim that it is a democratic state, but it is not at all. The Jews have more rights than the Arabs, and the authorities treat them very differently to us. For example, in a demonstration, the police are always ready to beat up the Arabs for the slightest thing. We don't feel protected in the least. I am politically aware, and I do go on demonstrations, but I don't feel I know what is really happening. I just learn about things from different people. I would like to get to know the situation through personal experience as a Palestinian. I think this will happen when I go to university.'

'The university is a different world,' said Ahmad. 'About 85 per cent of the students at the University of Haifa, where I am studying, are Jews. One is faced with different political views, different movements. We hold discussions among Palestinians, as well as between us and the Jewish students. We usually end up shouting at each other. One thing though: the teachers don't discriminate between Jews and Arabs in the courses. Even if some wanted to I think that, out of respect for their profession, they leave such temptations at home.'

'There are Jewish students at my school. I interact with them and our relationship is good. But my friends are mainly Arabs,' added Alia.

'We all interact with Jews in one way or another,' said her mother. 'Apart from struggling with the authorities, I also interact with left-wing Jews, but mainly on a political level. I don't interact socially because there are always barriers between us. When the Jews stop thinking that their Arab neighbours are going to destroy them, then the situation will improve. This fear puts a great barrier between us and the Jews. Yet, in some ways, we have the same ambitions, and we have been through similar experiences: dispersal, the wish to have our homeland, and so on. Our enmity blinds us to all the factors that can bring us together. We always look at the negative aspects, the ones that separate us. But history proves that this sort of relationship can change. Look at the Jews and Germans today, or the French and Algerians: they interact quite happily together. Despite the pain, the suffering, and the price we are paying, I have great hope for the future. I find that we Palestinians here are much more optimistic about the future than some Palestinians living in the Arab countries. My sister and brother who live in Bourj al-Barajneh refugee camp in Beirut, Lebanon, were able to visit us through Jordan after the 1967 war. Although there was no difference in our faith for our cause, I was surprised at their pessimistic outlook. They seemed broken down; they had no hope at all for the future. Perhaps we are more positive here because we still live in our homeland, we are not refugees. I couldn't understand at first why they were so broken down. After all, they live among Arabs in an Arab world, while I live among my enemies who have caused all our suffering. The 1967 war made us finally confront the fact that the only people responsible for the Palestinian cause were the Palestinians themselves, but we still envied the ones in the Arab world. We thought they had greater freedom there, while here we were locked up and had no way of getting to know the Arab world. But when they told us how they were treated there, I realized that it's much more painful to have a brother stab you than a stranger. We Palestinians are Arabs, yet neither the Arabs recognize us or trust us, nor do the Jews.'

'I pity the Palestinians who live in the Arab world,' said Ahmad. 'The ones who live well there are very few. They are mainly the ones who have made some money. But others live in dreadful conditions. I know that from my aunt and uncle. It's difficult for me to imagine how they survive. Their way of life is so different from mine. I don't know how I would cope if I were to live in the same way. However, they accept it.'

Hussain, Siham's brother, arrived with Anan, one of their nieces. They sat down and listened to Siham.

'I really believe that the next five to ten years will see a Palestinian state in the West Bank and Gaza alongside Israel,' she said. 'I don't believe that the destruction of the Israeli state is a solution. But I believe that a Palestinian state for the Palestinians all over the world would give us a sense of security, integrity and pride. I can envisage Palestinians living abroad holding two passports: a Palestinian one, and that of whichever country they are living in. This would also apply to the Palestinians in the '48 region. I too want to have dual citizenship, because this is my homeland, and I can't see myself leaving my country to live in the West Bank. I was born here, I've been brought up here, and I shall remain here.'

Hussain joined in: 'Before the intifada, I had no doubts about my identity, but I felt stifled, especially living in a mixed town. The Jews are the majority, they influence us: they impose their laws so we are unable to live our own way of life as Palestinian Arabs. We are forced to compromise, and we adopt some of their values and way of life. But the intifada has brought hope for the Palestinians. We will eventually obtain our rights and we will have a state of our own. Our identity will finally be recognized. I wouldn't leave 'Acca, but a Palestinian state in the West Bank and Gaza would give me security and reinforce my identity.'

'I think the intifada is a wonderful thing,' said Alia, 'but if there's a Palestinian state I would not go and live there because this is my homeland. I'm not going to leave it just to satisfy people who would prefer me to say that I'm living in Palestine rather than in Israel. Besides, living in the West Bank would be difficult because their way of life and way of thinking differs from ours. They are much more traditional than we are, and I would not find it easy to adapt to their way of life.'

Ahmad added: 'The intifada had to happen sooner or later. A large number of people have been living under occupation for over twenty years. They have been imprisoned, deported, exploited economically; they live without rights of any kind. It's difficult to imagine how they are able to survive.'

Anan, Siham's niece, also joined in. She is nearly Siham's age. Her mother died when she was just a child. At the age of 13 she had to leave school to take care of her father and brothers. She is married to an employee of the municipality. She herself has never worked, nor does she intend to. She has always been religious, but is never averse to enjoying a good wedding, and participating in the dancing and singing. Of late, she has adopted the dress of the Islamic fundamentalists and has decided to stop all the frivolity. She said it was partly due to the influence of religious lectures she has been attending at the mosque, and partly due to a dream she had had one night, although she refused to say what it was. She said:

'The Islamic movement cannot solve the Palestinian question, but what it can do is influence people to follow Islam properly, which will make us stronger. To be honest, I can't see how the Palestinians in the '48 region can help the Palestinians in the West Bank and Gaza. May God be with them. We can give them donations, but we can't fight. The people in the West Bank are in a better position to fight the Israelis; for us, it's not possible. We depend on the Jews economically, and if we try to do anything our men will lose their jobs. Most families can't afford it. Economic survival is more important than anything else. Anyway, I don't know much about politics!'

Her relatives smiled wryly.

'Here too, we have to fight for our rights, but in a different way,' said Ahmad. 'The reality is that Israel does exist. To get rid of it and replace it with a Palestinan state sounds great, but it's not practical, it doesn't make sense. On the one hand, the problem is simple: we Palestinians have been robbed of our rights, and we should have our rights back. On the other hand, the solution to the problem is complicated and will take time. So far, the best solution is a Palestinian state in the West Bank and Gaza, but there is no guarantee that there will be no violence between them and the Jews. I am all for a Palestinian state in the West Bank and Gaza, but, as far as I am concerned, I am a Palestinian from 'Acca. The West Bank and Gaza mean nothing to me in relation to 'Acca. I wouldn't leave my home town to live in the new Palestinian state.'

'I can really see peace one day, especially as the peace movement in Israel is growing in strength,' remarked Siham. 'People are beginning to realize that in the end it is in their interest to have peace.'

6

The Teacher: Adnan in Yarka

Their sole purpose is to alienate us from the rest of
the Palestinians . . . instead of directing their anger
and hatred against the authorities, they want them to
direct it against us.

Adnan

Yarka is a Druze village in Galilee with a population of around
8,000. There are thirty family groups whose members vary from
400 to 30 in number. It is built on a hill; in the summer it is not
as humid as Acre, which is a 25 minutes' drive away, and in the
winter there is a sharp sting to the air.

The village has one intermediate and secondary school, and
two primary schools. There are also a number of small factories:
textile, metal works and tiles. They are not government-owned
but have been set up by wealthy businessmen from the village.
There is one main street leading to a square where most of the
shops, and the local council, are located. Once a week a market
is held in the square where the men and women do the bulk of
their shopping for clothes, household utensils and food. Most of
the stall owners come from different villages and towns in the
'48 region, as well as from the West Bank and Gaza. A large
building, the religious centre, dominates the summit of the hill
in the village.

Yarka once owned 54,000 dunums of land, both within and
outside the boundaries of the village. Since 1948, 44,000
dunums have been expropriated by the authorities, and six
Jewish settlements have been built on some of that land. Before
the State of Israel was created, 90 per cent of the villagers were
farmers; today the figure is only 10 per cent. The rest are
labourers, factory workers, businessmen, traders, teachers,
engineers, shop owners; some are unemployed.

Physically, Yarka is like any other Arab village, with broken-
down roads and Arab-style houses alongside modern ones. But
there are two distinguishing features: the beauty of the

inhabitants, and the presence of soldiers. Throughout the country, soldiers can be seen walking on the roads, waiting for buses, hitch-hiking, or driving army vehicles. Whatever their mode of transport, the common denominator is their Jewishness. The startling thing about the soldiers in Yarka is that they are Arabs.

Adnan is forty years old. He is married and has four children aged between 11 and four. He and his family live in a modern house which has five rooms, a kitchen and bathroom. He is a teacher in one of the two primary schools in the village, as well as a religious leader, and a member of the Druze Initiative Committee.

'I went to secondary school in Kufr Yassif which is not far from here, and when I graduated I went to the Institute of Teachers,' he explained, as he watched his wife, Salhia, pour the coffee. They were in the sitting-room, and next to him sat his 65-year-old mother, who lives in an old Arab-style house nearby. 'I became a religious leader in 1975,' he added.

He was silent for a while and then declared vehemently: 'Let there be no mistake. I am a Palestinian Arab of the Druze sect. I am proud of my Palestinian identity and my nationalism. My father was an illiterate man. He was a peasant – just as his father was before him, and his grandfather. My father's main concern was his land and his family. He did not give me a political education.

'My awareness began to develop as a result of what I saw happening around me. As a child under military rule, I remember how the soldiers used to force entry into people's homes and search for arms. I remember vividly how they used to beat up some of the villagers and arrest others. Some of the inhabitants used to plead for mercy, but they were never given it. My parents, like the rest of the villagers, used to be frightened and they would lock up the house, take me and my sisters and brothers, and hide in the fields until it was safe to return. Even as a child, I felt this was not a normal way to live.

'We always used to have a holiday on Eid al-Fitr, but in 1957 the authorities banned the holiday and said that the Druze had to go to school. Well, I and other children refused to abide by the new law, and we persuaded many of our friends to do the same. The reason for banning the holiday was to create divisions within the Palestinian community, and to isolate us from the rest of the Arab community.

'In 1956, when Ben Gurion decided to have us serve in the army, 1,100 Druze signed a petition against it, but it had no effect. Sixteen of our dignitaries agreed, and that was what counted for the authorities. I was called up for military service after I finished secondary school. I tried every possible way to get out of it, but I couldn't. They wouldn't allow me to work, and they hounded me until in the end I was forced to do it.'

Salhia, a handsome woman of 36, added: 'I have a brother who is supposed to begin his military service but he is trying to get out of it, especially as he doesn't want to end up fighting against his brothers in the West Bank.'

Adnan continued: 'Although I lost three years of my life in the army, military service also reinforced and intensified my Palestinian identity and nationalism. I can in all honesty say that not once during my service have I shot a single bullet at any Arab across the borders; and not once have I raised my fist or gun against any of my Palestinian brothers. After I finished military service, they put me in the reserve, but I objected and they imprisoned me for a month. After a great deal of argument, threats and struggle, they withdrew me from the reserve.'

'My awareness about my identity and cause didn't really develop until 1967,' said Salhia. 'I remember at the time my parents were frightened, and they started packing up all our belongings because they thought we were going to be deported. Then, after the war, people from the West Bank came to our region, and we learnt more about the Palestinian cause. Now I'm fully aware and I follow the news and take a great interest in the intifada.'

A man arrived and stood outside the room. Adnan joined him, and Salhia went into the kitchen to fetch some soft drinks.

'In 1948, we were frightened too,' said Salhia's mother-in-law, who is also her aunt. 'Just as in 1967 people thought they were going to be forcibly moved out, in 1948 we too packed up our possessions. But then our religious leaders put up a white flag to indicate to the Jews that we weren't going to fight them, and we stayed on. I remember when some people went through our village on their way to Syria and Lebanon we told them not to leave the country, but they wouldn't listen.'

Salhia returned with the refreshments. As she handed them out, she said: 'In a way life in the past was simpler and more peaceful; even as women our lives were more peaceful. I left school when I finished the 7th grade. In those days girls didn't go to school beyond the 8th grade. Now they go to university, which is a good thing. But they also have to go out to work even after they are married, and they end up neglecting their husbands and children. I have never worked except at home. In my parents' house I helped with the household chores, on the land, and I took care of my sisters and brothers. My parents had 11 children.'

Adnan, who had come back into the room, commented, 'I have ten sisters and four brothers. Although it's difficult to bring up so many children, I think it is our national duty to have as many children as we can in order to increase the Arab population.'

His mother nodded her head and then said: 'I've always worked hard. Before I got married, I not only worked hard in the house but also on the land. We were five girls and one boy. Around the age of 19, my brother was imprisoned for five years by the British because he was part of the resistance movement. Then, at the age of 25, he was shot by the British while he was working in the field. When my sisters and I found him, we put him on a camel and took him home. After that we didn't let him do any farming. All he did was accompany us girls to the fields and back home to make sure that no harm came to us. Since he was the only boy, and the perpetuator of the family name, we didn't want anything to happen to him, and so we pampered him. When I got married, I also worked hard, harder than before because I had so many children to take care of. I got married at 18 and my husband was 55. He was a friend of my father's, and as he was also well off, my father decided he was a good catch, especially as there was a lot of poverty in those days because there was very little employment. He was actually two years older than my father, but he was a good man, so I didn't object to marrying him. But then in those days girls didn't dare object. It was inconceivable to refuse the suitor your parents chose for you. Today, it's different, even weddings are different.'

'Yes,' said Salhia. 'In the old days, and in my days, we didn't have music and dancing. But today they do. Although our religious leaders don't allow it, the young people don't listen to them. Everything has changed.'

'In the past the work was tougher. We were all expected to help on the land,' commented Adnan. 'I remember when I was nine years old, I used to load the sacks of olives on the donkey, and take them home. I did this several times a day, and I also helped in the olive press. It was very different from today, with cars, tractors, and all sorts of machines.'

'Some of our land was near 'Acca,' his mother explained. 'We used to walk all the way there, do a hard day's work, and walk back at sunset. I still have 40 dunums near 'Acca, but it's not all mine, some of it belongs to my sons. Nowadays I go by car, it is much more comfortable, and it preserves my energy for farming. I plant watermelon, tomatoes, beans, okra, and all sorts of other things. I sell some of my produce in the market here, and some I sell to my neighbours. Another job I do is cook at weddings. I'm very famous for my cooking, and so whenever there is a wedding I am invariably asked to cook. I enjoy it.'

'Although the methods of farming are easier today, there was a community life in the old days,' said Adnan. 'People helped each other; villagers were concerned about each other's well-being. Today, we still maintain some traditional practices, such as the way we solve disputes between families. If there are conflicts between members of one family and another, a *jaha* (deputation) is formed to arbitrate between the two families. The jaha consists of the elders of families other than the ones involved in the dispute.

'The other day a man ran over two boys with his car. The accident took place in the village. Despite the fact that the driver had to appear before a court, the offender's family still sent a jaha to the families of the two boys. For the villagers, the traditional negotiations and *sulh* (reconciliation) remain more important, regardless of the decision of the court. In this case as the driver and his family took all the blame and said that they would concede to anything the other two families asked for, he was immediately pardoned by the victims' families. They did not ask for the 'utwa (truce money), and diya (blood money); and they even allowed him to go to the funeral.

'If someone kills another person deliberately, then the process is more complicated. First the jaha decides on the amount of truce money that the offender's family has to pay the victim's family. Then the next stage is the payment of the blood money. Once this is negotiated, the offender carries a white flag of peace and each member of the jaha is asked to tie a knot in the flag, each knot symbolizing the final reconciliation.

'Although I am a religious leader, I have never been a member of a jaha because I'm not an elder, not yet anyway.

'While we still adhere to some traditions, at the same time some of our social relationships have changed. The village has become a hotel. People go to other towns to work and come back at the end of the day, tired and bad tempered, and all they want to do is eat and sleep. Then, on their days off, they prefer to go and roam in the towns rather than visit friends and relatives here. People don't really care for each other any more.'

'Life was better under the English,' his mother interrupted. 'At least they didn't rob us of our land. Even the Turks didn't take our land away; all they were interested in was to have our men serve in the army. But some men were able to avoid that. My husband managed to escape conscription under the Turks by paying ten liras in gold.'

'You can't say life was better under the Turks and the English,' retorted her son. 'They treated us badly.'

'Yes,' replied his mother, 'but they did not take away our land. The Jews are more unjust. They have robbed us of our land, and they have robbed others of their homes.'

'Yes, that's true,' agreed Adnan.

'I had thirty olive trees, and they destroyed them,' continued his mother. 'They also put some sort of chemical down so that I wouldn't plant any more trees. Do you call this justice? At least the English and Turks didn't do that. I worked so hard on those olive trees. And look at what they've done around our village. They've put an ammunitions depot near us, so that if we rise against them, they can blow us and other villages up.'

'People say that the Druze are privileged, but it is not so at all,' explained Adnan. 'In everyday life, we are discriminated against like all our Palestinian brothers, and in the army we are also treated like Arabs. They don't trust us, they don't give us important responsibilities and, when we are promoted, it is just in name without the benefits. When we finish military service, we are not given the same privileges and benefits that the Jews receive. The other day, the Druze who had finished their military service held a demonstration in front of Shamir's HQ to demand the same benefits that the Jews are given.

'The authorities lie about the number of Druze serving in the army. The Druze population is between 60,000 and 100,000. They say there are between 30,000 and 40,000 Druze in the army. In reality the number is far less. One of the tactics or tricks the authorities use is to pretend that some of the Arabic-speaking Jewish soldiers are Druze. They not only distort the statistics, but they try to create a rift between the Druze and the rest of the Palestinians.

'The Druze Initiative Committee was set up in 1972, and it has branches in each of the Druze villages. Its predominant aim is to end compulsory military service for the Druze, but it also has other activities. Members of the committee are escalating the struggle. We are talking to more and more young men to encourage them to refuse military service, and we are giving them more lectures to develop their awareness. For example, we point out to them that compulsory service for us is not for the sake of defending our homeland, ourselves or our honour, but that we are being used by the Israeli authorities for their own ends. Their sole purpose is to alienate us from the rest of the Palestinians. Instead of having the Palestinians direct their anger and hatred against the authorities, they want them to direct it against us.

'An increasing number of men are refusing to do military service. One of the most popular ways to escape compulsory service is to plead insanity. Very often the police come to the village to look for those who are trying to escape military service. There are around 120 men in prison. Some are in because they have refused to serve in the West Bank and Gaza, others because they have refused to do their military service altogether.

'Lately, we have introduced a new social activity in the village, which is to hold celebrations for every man who has successfully resisted compulsory service.

'The committee has been so successful that we have bought premises where we can carry out all our activities. There is a director, a secretariat, and 11 members. Some of our other activities include campaigning against the expropriation of land and against interference in our religious affairs. The authorities have told us that they will be the ones to decide at what age our young men can enter the religious profession. What earthly right do they have to interfere in our religious affairs. It's incredible!

'We have lectures for women, and lectures on sports, and on health, especially on the dangers of drug addiction which has increased. There were even two women involved: one was a courier for her father, and the other for her husband. Recently, a decision has been taken that anyone who takes drugs will be religiously and socially ostracized. That is, he will not be allowed to enter our religious centre; he will not be able to attend religious festivals; he will not participate in any of the social activities in the village; and no one will be allowed to visit him, or attend his wedding or funeral. We also have lectures on the intifada, and we collect donations for the people of the West Bank and Gaza. I have recently been banned by the authorities from going there because I have openly supported the intifada. I can't set foot in the West Bank or Gaza for a whole year.'

'I think the intifada was inevitable,' said his mother. 'But it's not an easy situation to sustain. I think if what they are doing is going to bring positive results then they should continue. If they are not going to achieve their goal, then they should stop.'

'I think what the Jews are doing to the people in the West Bank and Gaza is cruel and unjust,' said Salhia. 'It's true the people are throwing stones, but the Jews are occupying their land, and they shoot at them. Stones are nothing in the face of bullets. The Jews should get out of the West Bank and Gaza, and then there will be no more violence.'

Adnan left to attend a meeting, and his mother said she had work to do at home. Salhia's youngest child, a four-year-old girl, began screaming for attention. ·The three older boys hurriedly left the house in case they were asked to entertain their sister; they preferred to play with their friends.

It was the following summer: 1989. Adnan had just returned from a meeting held by the Druze Initiative Committee.

'The meeting was held in Julis, another Druze village. It was specially held there because some of the young men from the village who are in a military prison for refusing to do their military service have been tortured with knives, sticks and pipes by Jewish soldiers. Two of the prisoners were so badly injured that they had to be taken to hospital. We are going to publish a statement in the newspapers about it, and we are planning to hold a demonstration in front of the prison; we are going to ask the Jews who have refused to serve in the West Bank and Gaza to join us. Our policy now is to try to co-ordinate our activities with the left-wing Jews in order to fight inequality and racism.

'Although the main topic of discussion at the meeting was the fate of the prisoners, we also talked about other matters. For example, we discussed our participation in the Committee of Heads of Arab Local Councils. We were going to have ten Druze represent us in the committee, but the Minister of Arab Affairs refused, claiming that there was no need for the Druze to be represented because they had the same rights as the Jews. It's absolute nonsense, of course. The reason they don't want us to participate is to reinforce sectarianism; they want to separate us from the rest of the Arab population.

'We also talked about how we have managed to get round a law which forbids the Druze Initiative Committee to produce a monthly pamphlet. What we do now is produce a pamphlet with a different name each month.

'I wrote in one of the pamphlets an article condemning American imperialism and Zionism, and encouraging all Palestinians in the '48 region to support the intifada. I also said that one day there will undoubtedly be an independent Palestinian state in the West Bank and Gaza led by the PLO, with East Jerusalem as its capital.'

Adnan grinned: 'The authorities don't like what I do or what I represent. The other day, I was summoned to the Ministry of Education for questioning. They wanted to know all about the activities of the committee, and why we were donating blood to the people of the West Bank and Gaza. They also accused me of subversive behaviour because I proclaim that the Druze are Palestinians and should not be subject to conscription. I told them that – since they claim that this is a democratic state – all I was doing was exercising my right to freedom of expression.

'The authorities have just banned me again from going to the West Bank and Gaza. They've also tried to suspend me from my job. But I had a letter from the principal of the school, and a petition signed by many of the villagers, saying that I was a good and conscientious teacher who was indispensable to both the school and the students.

'The committee has increased its activities since last year. For example, we are visiting young conscripts who are too frightened to refuse military service, and we tell them not to fight or beat up a single Palestinian in the West Bank and Gaza.

'We are using various methods to try to combat the increasing drug problem. Apart from giving lectures about it, we are encouraging the young villagers to participate in sports activities instead of hanging around in the streets. The other day we had a football match between two teams from the village. The motto was: *Yes to sports; no to drugs.*

'We are also giving more lectures about the intifada, and we even had a women's committee from the West Bank visit us recently in order to promote understanding between us and the people of the West Bank. A women's committee from here will be returning the visit very soon.

'At this very moment, some of the children are rehearsing a play in our HQ.'

The Druze Initiative Committee's HQ is a short walk from Adnan's house. It consists of three large rooms with very little furniture, but the walls are well covered with posters about the intifada, the struggle against racism, the fight for equality, and the rejection of compulsory military service. On one of the posters, for example, were the following demands:

> *Compulsory military service for our people must end.*
> *Security of education and employment for our people.*

Withdrawal of the army from the occupied territories.
Peace and equality for all.

The two women in charge of the children are members of the committee: one is a worker in the textile factory, and the other a teacher.

'At present we have twenty children,' explained Emtiaz, the teacher, who was supervising a noisy group of children rehearsing their play with obvious enjoyment. 'Their ages range between five and 12. We meet once a week during school term, and more during the holidays. The play we are rehearsing at the moment will be performed in a week. It's not going to be just for the parents, but for all the villagers.

'It's about a fox who invades the land of the rabbits and tries to steal it away from them. All the rabbits get together and try to find a way to get rid of him. One rabbit says that they can't defeat the fox as he is far stronger than they are and so they should just run away. But the other rabbits refuse. One of them then suggests that they should give the fox two rabbits to appease him, but the others say that it's not a good idea. Then they all decide that the best solution is to trap the fox. When they finally succeed in trapping him, some of the rabbits say "Let's kill him." Others say, "let's torture him." But the final decision is to let him go, and they warn him that if they ever see him on their land again, they will kill him.

'Through such stories we teach the children to become aware of the Palestinian cause. We also teach them poems about our land and olive trees; we teach them national songs; and we talk to them about the intifada.'

Adnan had visitors – three students, who were studying in Eastern Europe and spending their summer holidays with their families in Yarka. They were discussing a law that had recently come into effect.

'Students who have obtained their medical degrees from countries other than the United States, Canada, Britain and South Africa are now given exams in Israel if they want to practice here,' explained Mahmoud, who is studying medicine in Romania. 'What is unjust about it is that the Arabs don't get a chance to prepare for the exams, while the Jews are given that chance. They try to obstruct us at every step.'

The three of them are members of the Druze Initiative Committee, and they have all refused to do military service on grounds of mental health.

'One of the reasons that I reject the whole idea of military service is that the Israeli army is not what it claims to be: a defence army. Since 1948 it has been an occupying army,' said Mahmoud. 'Also, we are Palestinians, and what the authorities are trying to do is to divide us from the rest of the Palestinians.'

'We have to do our military service after we finish secondary school,' explained Ahmad, who is studying journalism in Prague. 'Some men refuse outright to do it and they are then sent to prison. Others enter the religious profession because religious leaders are not conscripted. Then there are others, like us, who refuse on grounds of mental health. It took three years of our lives to get out of it. We were examined by army doctors, and by army committees. I even had to spend one week in a mental institution. In those three years we weren't allowed to continue our studies or work.'

'They are harder on the Druze who refuse military service than they are on the Jews,' said Mahmoud. 'In the Knesset they said that one-quarter of the young Jews don't do their military service. Some don't do it for religious reasons; others refuse because they don't approve of the presence of the Israelis in the West Bank and Gaza. Then there are some who are exempted because they come from very poor families and they need to work to support them. There are many Druze who are also very poor, but they are not exempted.'

'The young Druze who serve in the army are ignorant people; they have no awareness about the Palestinian cause,' commented Kassem, who is studying medicine in Russia. 'It's not enough that we refuse military service, we must also develop the political awareness of the young people so that they all end up by refusing to do their military service. When we are here in the summer we try to encourage the younger generation to refuse military service. We explain to them that we are Palestinians and that the policy of the Israelis is to divide us from the rest of the Arab population. We also talk to them about the injustices and inequalities we suffer as Palestinians.'

'The problem since 1948 has been that of fear,' explained Ahmad. 'Many people are poor and ignorant, and they don't dare confront or oppose the authorities. The Israelis exploit this. For example, they tell the young men that if they don't serve in the army not only will they never be able to work, but their fathers and brothers will also be dismissed from their jobs. Consequently, poor families with six or seven children are too frightened to resist military service. The young men in such families prefer to serve in the army rather than lose their jobs.'

'They also get paid in the army which the poor families consider a bonus,' added Mahmoud.

'It's not only through military service that they try to separate us from the rest of the Palestinians, they also use other methods,' said Kassem angrily. 'In 1957 they passed a law saying that the Druze were a different people to the Arabs, and therefore they had to be registered as Druze and not as Arabs. A Druze who had the word Arab on his identity card was not allowed to work. This law still applies today. I always put Arab when I register, but when they actually write out our identity cards, they automatically put Druze.

'Another way of separating us is through the educational system,' he continued. 'The teachers in our schools are now required to teach a so-called Druze history and heritage. They are trying to brainwash our youngsters into believing that they are not Arabs but Druze. They tell them that the Arabs have always been a defeated people, but that the Druze are different. Unfortunately some of the youngsters believe this and so end up serving in the army.'

Ahmad nodded and said, 'Yes, because the number of young men who are refusing military service is increasing, the authorities are intensifying the pressure on us, not just to make us comply with their demands, but also to separate us from the other Arabs. How can they separate us from the rest of the Arabs? We are Arabs. We speak the same language, we wear the same clothes, we eat the same food. We are not just part of the Palestinian Arabs here, but we are part of the Arabs in the Arab world.

'When we come back after we graduate, we are going to find it very difficult to get jobs because we haven't done our military service. They try to make life miserable for the Arabs hoping that they will all end up by leaving the country. But we will never leave, we will never give in to their pressures.'

'I'm willing to starve and die if necessary to obtain justice,' added Mahmoud vehemently.

And they all nodded their heads in agreement.

Kassem commented: 'The future is ours. The negative and oppressive policies of the Israelis won't get them very far, especially after the latest development in the PLO. The Jews keep screaming that we want to throw them in the sea, but that's not true at all. We are prepared to live with them in peace provided they give us equality and justice, and accept the creation of an independent Palestinian state in the West Bank and Gaza.'

'When there is an independent Palestinian state, perhaps there will be no more conscription,' remarked Adnan.

'I will never serve in the army,' said Adnan's 11-year-old son who had listened quietly throughout.

'Good lad,' replied Ahmad with a smile.

'Let's hope by the time your turn comes, there will be no compulsory military service,' said his father. 'In the meantime the Druze Initiative Committee will continue to encourage the young men to refuse to serve in the army.'

Salhia walked in and said that lunch was ready. She had made *kibbeh nayeh* (raw minced lamb with cracked wheat and spices), in the famous Druze way.

'That's one of the dishes we really miss when we're away,' commented Ahmad. And they all stopped talking.

7

The Playwright-actor: Marwan in Majd al-Kroum

My father never had any problems with his identity.
He wasn't brought up in two cultures like my generation. We have to fight and be really strong so as not
to be drowned by Israeli culture.

Marwan

In Galilee, Arab villages are reminiscent of villages in Syria or
Lebanon. But then a word in Hebrew by one of the Arab
inhabitants, or a road sign in Hebrew, dispels the illusion that
this is an Arab country.

The hills surround Majd al-Kroum, an Arab village in
Galilee with a population of about 8,000. It was once a farming
village, but most of the land has been expropriated by the
authorities. There is a high rate of unemployment, and most of
those who work have jobs as labourers on construction sites, or
in service industries such as restaurants, petrol stations, etc.

'It's like a big hotel. People go to work in the town during the
day, and then come back, eat and sleep,' a villager said.

The architecture is mainly modern, although there are a few
semi-traditional buildings. Some houses reflect their owners'
poverty, others reflect moderate prosperity. One house in
particular, owned by a wealthy businessman, is referred to by
the children as 'the palace'. It is a large villa rather than a
palace, but size is relative and, in the eyes of the children, it is a
palace.

There is one main street running through the village. This is
the centre of activity; the local council, the public library, and
shops are also all located here. Young men's favourite pastime
is to stand about in the street, chatting with one another or
staring aimlessly at the hills. Women and girls are not allowed
to indulge in this pastime. They use the street to walk from one

particular destination to another, furtively eyeing the youth. Little boys play football or other games in the main street, while little girls stand by, watching enviously. There are still a few old men wearing traditional clothes, who ride down the street astride their donkeys, returning from the little plot of land they have been lucky enough to keep.

Abu Imad and Umm Imad's (Abu means father of, Umm mother of, the eldest son) house lies at the entrance of Majd al-Kroum. The house is semi-traditional, with a porch facing a garden, the main road and the hills. The garden is planted with tomatoes, aubergines, okra, figs, grapes. At the back of the house there is a shed; outside it stands a cow.

Across the road from the house are four dunums, owned by Abu Imad, and a grazing donkey.

Umm Imad is 63 years old. Her strength of character is reflected in her rough, lined face. Her eyes dart shrewdly here and there, missing nothing. She once had ten children, but is now left with five.

She sat on the porch with Khadijeh, her eldest daughter, preparing lunch; it was cooler than indoors. Umm Imad was chopping up *molokhia* (a green leaf, cooked with meat or chicken to create a dish beloved of many Arabs; molokhia translates loosely as 'fit for a king'). Her daughter was pounding garlic, the resounding sound stifling the noise of passing cars.

Khadijeh is unmarried. Her face is set with bitterness, for she has not fulfilled the two requirements expected of her which would have turned her into a full woman: marriage and children. Time is no longer on her side, and in the eyes of the community she is a failure. And as she pounded the garlic, every blow seemed to be directed at the fate that robbed her of womanhood.

A car stopped outside the house. It was Abu Imad and his 30-year-old son Marwan, returning from Nazareth where they had been seeing their solicitor about their property.

Abu Imad is a short, wiry 78 year old. He always wears the traditional Palestinian peasant clothes. He lost the use of one eye many years ago, and his mind rambles at times, partly due to old age, but perhaps also because the present is so incomprehensible that it seems easier to cling to the past.

He sat down with a heavy sigh and declared: 'If people love one another and are happy then it is enough to live on dried lentils. But if we're unhappy and full of worries and we have plenty of rice and meat to eat, it is useless because we cannot digest it. In the old days, we did not have plenty of food to eat; there was no electricity in the streets – they used to light them with lanterns. Our homes were not as comfortable as they are today, and we worked hard. We farmed from dawn until sunset. We had no tractors, no modern equipment. We farmed with our hands, and ploughed with oxen. At times, my brothers, our women and I, could not do all the farming on our own, so we hired landless peasants. Some were paid eight piastres a day, others preferred to be paid in crops. It was hard work, but we were happy. Our land was ours, and our goats were ours.'

He gazed at the passing cars, and then at his land.

'Even under the English, life was better,' he continued. 'There was more freedom. I could come and go as I pleased, and my livelihood was not threatened. In 1946, the English passed a law which said that every four peasants had to form a co-operative and buy a tractor. I did so with my three brothers. The tractor decreased our work load, but two years later the Jews occupied the country and took our tractor away. So, once again, we had to farm with our hands and plough with oxen and horses.

'The tractors were not the only thing the Jews took away. In 1953, they seized land that belonged to Palestinians who had left the country. The Jews expropriated the land, removed the rightful owner's name from the registry, and registered it in the name of the state. They are still doing this today. When they expropriate the land that belongs to absent landowners, we say it is God's will. But when they seize land that is legally owned by people who have not left the country, people who are still farming it and whose livelihood depends on it, then what do you say to that? What law is that?' shouted Abu Imad angrily.

And still angry, he continued: 'I have 30 dunums, on which I have grown watermelons and wheat. It is land that is rightfully and legally mine. It is registered in my name. About two years ago, the authorities banned me from farming it. They said that they needed it for development, meaning they would give it to a settlement. Well, I took no heed and continued to farm it. It is my land. Three days ago, I went to check my crops and I found that they had driven a tractor over my watermelons and wheat. They ruined all my crops. My son and I went to the police station, but they said there was nothing they could do about it. We went to the solicitor and he said that I had broken the law because I had continued to farm the land after they had forbidden me from doing so. He said I should let him know the value of the crops and he would try to make them pay me compensation. What is this that says they can ban me from farming my own land? They actually want to expropriate my land by ruining my crops and making life hell for me; they think that I will give in to them and let them take away my land. It's their policy.'

Fatma, his youngest daughter who is 25 years old and unmarried, joined the family.

Abu Imad resumed his tale: 'They take our land, they destroy our houses, and they forbid us to build. This is my house, and I want to build a second floor so that when Marwan gets married he can live in it. But the authorities have refused to give me planning permission, and they won't tell me why. I can't see any good reason for refusing me permission. Everything is forbidden. Today we have comforts we did not have in the past. We have electricity in our homes, running water and machines. Even now, we can rent a tractor for twenty shekels an hour for farming. But what's the use of all this when life is so bitter under the Israelis? If we trespass on Jewish land, we are fined or imprisoned, but they can trespass on mine, ruin my crops, and steal my land. They are free to do what they like, while I'm robbed of my rights and livelihood.'

He gazed with his good eye at Marwan. 'My son cannot even begin to imagine what life was like in the old days.'

Marwan is a member of the Hakawati theatre group based in East Jerusalem. Like his father, he is short in stature; his attitude to people and to life alternates between impatience and nonchalance. He gazed silently at his father.

It was Fatma who responded impatiently to her father's woes: 'The older generation's life is still centred around the land. To us younger people, farming doesn't mean anything. Our struggle is on a different level.'

'Today's youngsters spurn such work,' the old man said disdainfully. 'We gave Marwan the education I never had. I sent him to good schools, and then to university, and now he lives in East Jerusalem, and he refuses to live here. I have asked him to settle here so that he can help us but he doesn't want to. He tells me he doesn't like our way of life.'

'I come for a couple of days to help gather the olives,' protested Marwan.

His father snorted: 'In the past, men, women and children worked on the land side by side; we worked as a team. Our existence depended on the success of our crops. The merchants would buy the crops while they were still in the ground. After harvesting, we sold what was left over to the villagers. We did it from home. If we needed extra money to buy trousers for one of the boys, we would also sell a barrel or two of olive oil. Today, we have to pick the crops first, and then sell it to people who come by in their lorries. We still sell vegetables and fruit to the villagers, but we don't sell olive oil any more: nobody wants it. They prefer to buy the artificial oil produced by the Jews. Nowadays, people who make their own bread are accused of being backward. The women prefer to buy ready-made Western bread. This is not so with my family. My eldest daughter makes the bread, and I take it to the baker's oven. We have a cow, so we produce our own milk, and we have chickens, which give us fresh eggs. We still eat olive oil, and we eat our own vegetables and fruit. I refuse to buy or eat canned food, or any of the modern junk they produce today. The only things we buy from the shops are rice, sugar, salt, and fresh meat.'

The old man gave a sigh: 'We also had goats once, about seventy or eighty of them. But we don't any more, of course. There are no more shepherds to look after goats. People don't realize that goats bring in more money than working as labourers. But young men today prefer to work as labourers. They want quick ready cash to buy cars so they can take girls out in the evenings. In my time, if a man so much as looked at a girl, her brothers and father would go to him in the middle of the night and beat him up.'

Everyone burst out laughing.

'Go ahead and laugh,' said the old man. 'In the past, if a girl refused the suitor her family had chosen for her, they'd bring a pickaxe and cut through her neck. Today, a girl marries the man she wants. I approve of this change because I think it is wrong to force people to marry one another if they don't want to. But I don't approve of other changes, such as boys and girls going out together. Each era produces its own generation. Young people today have their own ideas and attitudes. They struggle for different things, and in different ways. Look at the intifada . . .'

Marwan interrupted impatiently: 'We all know about the intifada. Did you fight in your days?'

'Of course I did,' Abu Imad responded defensively. 'I was in the 1936 uprising. I was in the prime of my youth, and ready to fight and die for my country. The leaders came to Majd al-Kroum and told the young men to take up arms and fight. They brought us arms from Syria and Lebanon, but they were not very good, they were rusty. And when we ran out of ammunition, they would tell us to send an order to Syria. "But we can't wait that long, we need ammunition now to defend ourselves against the tanks," we used to protest. It was the peasants who bore the brunt of the fighting. All the so-called leaders did was spend their time in the towns; they wore the fez and sat in the coffee houses. There were also many city dwellers who were collaborators. They too wore the fez and sat in the coffee houses. Then our leaders banned the members of the resistance from wearing the fez. To celebrate the new rule, they brought a donkey, put a fez on his head and marched him through the streets. Oh yes, it was us peasants who did all the fighting. We fought as best we could.'

'Today, they throw stones, but at least they hit their targets. In your day you had rifles but you hit nothing; you hit the air,' Marwan said, somewhat unkindly.

His father took off his headgear and wiped the sweat off his head. He looked at his son and said quietly, 'Today people are more educated. They are more politically aware.'

Nothing was said for a while. They were all engrossed in their own thoughts, unperturbed by the noise of traffic, the braying of the donkey, and the clucking chickens scurrying around the garden.

Umm Imad nodded her head and broke the silence: 'Yes, today's generation is far more aware and educated than my generation. We were not educated. I spent my life working on the land, and I still do. Fatma doesn't help me with the harvesting.'

'It's not my kind of work. But I do help during the olive season,' said Fatma grinning.

'During the olive season she stays at home to keep an eye on the olives we bring in,' said her mother. 'These days, youngsters from the village tend to steal. They even steal our olives before they have been picked. Our olive trees are not all on one plot of land, they are scattered. For example, we have ten olive trees on one plot, and further away on another plot of land we have more olive trees. We don't have enough people to help us cover all the plots at the same time. While we are working on one lot of trees, youngsters go to the other plot, steal the olives and sell them. Youngsters today have no morals, they have no shame. In the old days the young listened to their elders and obeyed them, but today they walk all over their parents. Even girls misbehave; they don't listen to their elders either. Can you imagine there are Arab girls who live on their own abroad; they live in flats all by themselves. What kind of behaviour is that? In my days, we were ruled by our fathers, brothers, husbands and mothers-in-law. We never disobeyed. If I wanted to visit my married sister and my brother forbade me, I wouldn't dare put my toe outside the house, I would tremble with fear. And if I was allowed to visit my sister, I didn't go on my own, I had to be accompanied by a brother or my mother. I wasn't even allowed to choose my husband. In those days, a cousin had priority over outsiders, otherwise it created conflicts and feuds between the relatives. My father was dead when Abu Imad, who is also my cousin, came to ask for my hand, and it was my brother who decided for me. I was 18 years old when I got married, and I wasn't asked whether I wanted him or not.'

She looked at Abu Imad and said with some bitterness, 'I'm in your house, I'm your wife and the mother of your children. But if I had been free to choose my partner, I wouldn't have married someone 15 years older than me. I had other suitors who were of my own generation, and who were educated.'

Abu Imad remained silent, looking hurt.

His wife continued: 'Today, if someone comes to ask for my daughter's hand, she would have to see him and talk to him first, and then it is up to her to accept him or to turn him down. It is not my decision or her father's. If she accepts him, and then the marriage doesn't work out, at least it was her decision. The freedom to choose one's partner is the only good change in the social values practised by the younger generation.'

'Do you mean that everything else we do is bad?' protested Fatma.

'Yes, all your other values are wrong,' replied her mother vehemently.

Like her eldest brother Imad, Fatma has congenitally defective eyes. She is a determined woman, with a will to match her mother's.

'The conflicts between me and my parents are continuous,' she said. 'The day will never come when any of us will give in. I will never be able to convince my mother to accept my way of thinking, and I'll never accept hers. There is no comparison between my mother and me. For example, she would like me to cover my hair, and to wear a long dress with long sleeves, but I refuse and I wear what I like. She doesn't like it, of course.'

'O, how I wish you'd get married,' her mother said with exasperation.

Fatma grinned: 'She disapproves if I talk to men. She thinks that if I talk to a man it means we are in love, or that we are going to do something shameful. I don't think in this way. I talk to men just the way I talk to women: on an equal basis. I'm not going to stop talking to men just because she doesn't want me to. We have very different views. On the other hand, there are certain things that my parents stopped objecting to which other parents don't allow their daughters to do: like going to 'Acca, or al-Nasra (Nazareth), unaccompanied. One of the reasons they allow me to travel alone is because they need me to go from time to time to check documents concerning my father's land. Young women are also not allowed to be out on their own in the evenings. When I applied for my secretarial course, they objected because it was in the evening. They said it would bring shame on the family, but at the same time they wanted me to study. So when I was accepted, they had to agree. I used to come back at nine in the evening, and for the first week or two my mother used to wait up for me. But then she got used to my being out late and stopped worrying. There's a . . .'

Fatma was interrupted by a little boy who came to buy onions from Umm Imad. He offered her a tattered one shekel note.

'I'm not taking this,' she yelled at him. 'Go and buy your onions from the shop.' And she refused to give him the onions.

'But my mother sent me,' the boy protested.

'I don't care. Go somewhere else.'

The boy left, and Umm Imad muttered inaudibly.

Fatma began again: 'There's a big gap between my parents' generation and mine, even in terms of political awareness, and the way we struggle for our rights. Our struggle is more planned; we use organized channels; and we know how to make use of the law to fight for our cause. When I was a little girl in school, I was never taught about Palestinian history or heritage, but I used to hear my parents and other adults speak about how the Jews had taken our land, and how they had expelled thousands of Palestinians. My father was deported to Jordan, with many others from Majd al-Kroum and other villages, but he managed to sneak back through Lebanon.'

'Yes, I did,' said Abu Imad. 'After all it is my homeland, and my wife was still here. There were some who were too frightened to come back, and there were others who got caught by the Jews and thrown back across the border.'

Marwan, who was gazing thoughtfully into the distance, spoke. 'Although my father's outlook towards his losses and the whole nakba (catastrophe), is more emotional than political, as an individual he has never had any problems with his identity. He has always been a Palestinian; he never questioned it. He wasn't brought up in two cultures like my generation. We have to fight and be really strong so as not to become schizophrenic, or be drowned by Israeli culture.

'I remember when I was in primary school, we used to celebrate independence day. We used to go to the hills, pick flowers and decorate the school. As children, we enjoyed it, we didn't know what it was all about; it was just a holiday with festivities. No one taught us that this was not really a day to celebrate. We carried Israeli flags, and no one told us that this was not our flag. Some accepted the flag as theirs because they lived in the State of Israel. Others were too frightened to tell us that this was not our flag. Independence day was also celebrated in secondary schools. Then, in 1975, people began to object to the celebrations. There was a whole new generation of teachers who had gone to university and who were far more aware than the previous generation, and so they said, "Wait a minute, this is not our independence, this is not an occasion that we Palestinians should be celebrating."

'Before 1967, we thought of ourselves as Israeli Arabs. We learnt their language and worked for them. We were aware that we were being discriminated against, but we kept quiet for fear of being deported. People were muddled, they did not know whether their loyalties were to the Israeli state or to themselves as Palestinian people. But in 1967 we realized that we were Palestinians who had no intention of leaving our homeland, which had become the State of Israel. We realized that we had our own national identity, but without equal rights, and so our goal was to struggle for our rights. Then in 1976, Land Day, our identity was reinforced because we realized that we could demonstrate for our rights. We could say no to what the Israelis wanted to impose on us.'

'My cause is part of my existence,' said Fatma. 'There are Palestinians of my generation who don't care about their cause, they are just interested in having a good time. I'm not like that, I want justice and I want my rights.

'I used to work in a solicitor's office, but I had to change my job because of my eyes. I found work in a Jewish cosmetics factory. We are six Arabs and four Jews working there, which means that the Arabs outnumber the Jews. When the owner turns on the radio, it is always to listen to Jewish songs. So one day, I brought my own little radio to listen to Arabic music. I sat in my corner and turned it on very low, but he didn't like it and made me take it home. You see, he doesn't take into account that the Arab employees want to hear Arabic music from time to time. I don't want to hear Jewish songs or plays all the time. They impose their culture on us, whether we like it or not. If we don't like it, they tell us to go home. There is no compromise. If we are unhappy about something or other at work, they don't care at all. They tell us, "If you don't like it, leave." What can we do? We are forced to work with them.

'I personally don't let them walk all over me. If I am discriminated against, I speak up. For example, the owner told the Jewish girls that they could each buy a pair of shoes and the factory would pay for it, but he did not make the same offer to the Arab girls, although some of us had been working there far longer than some of the Jewish girls. When I heard about it, I told the other Arab girls, "let's go and ask for new shoes too. We should have the same rights as the Jewish girls." But my colleagues refused. They felt inhibited and frightened because they had not been taught to stand up for their rights. I decided to go to the owner on my own. After all, I had nothing to lose. All I had to put up with was rejection, but at least I would have made the effort to ask for my rights. The girls asked me to speak for them too, but I told them that they should have the courage to speak for themselves. When I went to the owner, and asked him for the money to pay for a pair of shoes, he said there was no law which obliged him to pay me. After arguing a while, he finally agreed. The other Arab girls did not ask for their money, and so they didn't get any. We must demand our rights; they will never give them to us of their own free will. It's good that the intifada has happened. Perhaps if all the Palestinians struggled in the same way, then we might reach a solution. We must not be frightened to struggle for our rights. If the older generation had been more organized and had had the same awareness as today's generation, then perhaps we wouldn't be in the situation we are in now.'

'People today are more aware,' commented Abu Imad with some exasperation.

'It was at university that my awareness matured,' explained Marwan. 'At first, I did not want to go to university here. I wanted to go to Italy or America to study film or theatre. But my parents objected, especially as those who went to universities abroad studied law or medicine, certainly not film or theatre. So my parents refused, and I had to give in to them because, at least for the first year, I would have needed their financial support, and they were not going to give it to me. So I ended up at the University of Jerusalem where I got a BA in sociology. I remember that on the day I was leaving the village to go to university my mother sat me down next to her and gave me some advice: "Keep away from politics, and keep away from girls." But fortunately, or unfortunately, I became involved with girls and politics. I was involved in the student movement;

I attended political meetings; I walked in demonstrations. We all regarded ourselves as the liberators of our people.

'In my third year, I got to know some students who were part of the Hakawati theatre group, so I joined them, but I also went on with my studies. After the BA, I did an MA in criminology, and continued my acting career at the same time. When I finished the degree, there was a vacancy in the Bureau of Social Affairs, so I applied and was accepted. My job started at 8.00 a.m.; I hadn't been awake that early since my school-days. So I set my alarm for 7.00 a.m., and dutifully woke up, washed, shaved and went to work like a conquering hero. There they gave me a cup of coffee, and then the director called me and said: "I gather you work with the Hakawati?" I replied, "Yes, and I gather you once saw a play of ours. Did you like it?" He said: "I like what the Hakawati produces. But you can't work here and with the Hakawati. I give you one week to decide." Well, I worked in the office for one hour, and then left, never to return. They owe me an hour's pay. The decision was easy because working in the office was not a question of making a career for myself, it was just to try to earn more money. The career I really wanted and still want is in the theatre. Mind you, at times when I am feeling depressed, I say to myself: what am I doing in the theatre; why not work in the field that I specialized in at university? But then I think about it for a while, and I decide, no, I couldn't stand working in an office from 8.00 a.m. to 2.00 p.m., surrounded by hundreds of files.

'Of course, my parents are not happy with what I'm doing. They did not want me to be a labourer, but they certainly did not want me to end up in the theatre. They would have liked me to get a degree in medicine or teaching, and then return to work in Majd al-Kroum. As I did not obtain a degree in either of these subjects, they would have liked me to come back after university and work on the land alongside my father. I don't mind helping them from time to time, but I certainly wouldn't take up farming as a lifetime job. Anyway, you can't make a lot of money from farming, especially with the primitive methods my parents use. The crops are limited because they have no irrigation, they depend on the rain. I can't live like this. I don't want to follow in their footsteps. I want to live my own life and do what I enjoy most. My parents want me to live up to their expectations, and I want to live up to mine. So what does one do? I come from a traditional village where I am expected to respect the family, elders and traditions. So while I pursue the career I want, I make an extra effort to compromise in other things. Every two or three weeks I come to the village, help them on the land for a couple of days, and carry out other duties; then I return to my world.

'Majd al-Kroum has actually changed a great deal. In the past, there was more of a community life. People not only worked the land together, but they also helped one another in other ways. Today, those who work do so in the towns. All they are interested in is earning a salary, and their ties to the community revolve mainly around the rituals of birth, marriage and death. And of course there are all those young people who are unemployed, and who roam the streets in the village or in the towns. In many ways they feel lost; they are fully aware that they are Palestinians but they fall prey to Israeli culture. I remember how I struggled against this influence, and I have managed to overcome it.

'The youngsters in the streets cannot overcome Jewish culture on their own. So I and several others from Majd al-Kroum decided to start a cultural club to develop awareness about Palestinian heritage and culture, and to give the youth a purpose in life. The only other alternatives in the village are a sports club and a Histadrut club, where girls are taught sewing. Sport doesn't fulfil our cultural needs. They may beat the Jews in some game or other, but then what?

'The youngsters must have a means to express themselves as Palestinians, and the way to do it is through cultural activities: Palestinian music, dancing, plays, lectures. We have rented two rooms and we've managed to obtain finances from an independent, non-governmental organization. We will set up workshops for theatre and Palestinian music and dancing, and organize a permanent group which will be taught theatre production, acting and script writing, until it becomes independent and can perform around the country. We will also invite literary figures and others to give lectures once a week. Apart from a salaried manager to supervise the club, everybody else will work on a voluntary basis. As I live in Jerusalem, and am busy with the Hakawati theatre, I can't possibly be involved full time with the club here. So it is important to have a manager who is not only efficient, but also interested in the activities of the club. At the moment there are no activities because we are going to have the two rooms painted as they badly need it.'

Marwan looked at his watch and said that he had to go and see one of his cousins.

The little boy who had wanted to buy onions returned with his mother. 'Why didn't you want to sell him the onions?' she asked Umm Imad.

'I don't take old tattered notes,' retorted Umm Imad.

'Well, I've brought you clean money,' said the woman.

Umm Imad got up with a grunt and went to fetch the onions.

Marwan had dutifully spent his two days in the village, after which he drove off to return to his world. He did not however go back to Jerusalem but to Sakhneen, another village in Galilee where he was to meet other members of the Hakawati theatre group to perform in a play called *Taghreeb al-Abeed* (Alienation of the Slaves). Apart from several performances in Jerusalem, they had also performed in various villages and towns across the country. They had taken two days off before ending their tour in Sakhneen. There they hired a hall which well-to-do villagers used for weddings, and where other large functions took place. As the group put the scenery up, villagers of all ages walked in; some of them watched and asked questions; others helped.

'We like it when the people take an interest and help us out. We like them to identify with it. Most of our plays symbolize our predicament as Palestinians,' explained Marwan. 'The Hakawati theatre group was formed in 1977. The plays are based on the social and political experiences of members of the group as well as outsiders. They express Palestinian cultural nationalism, disguised in symbolism to escape the wrath of the censors with whom we have had problems in the past. The process of producing a play requires the creative and technical involvement of all those taking part. Some of the actors are not long-term members, but are only hired for a specific play.'

As people of all ages arrived for the performance, the hall echoed with their chattering as they waited expectantly for the actors and actresses. The play was about Palestinian workers in varying jobs who came together during one of their breaks to assess their social, political and economic situation. The play was both funny and tragic, and the audience's participation was spontaneous: they laughed, they cheered the good characters, and they jeered at the bad ones. And when the performance was over, members of the audience congratulated the actors and actresses, having thoroughly enjoyed the evening.

The group packed up and made its way to Jerusalem. It was very late at night. Ghassan, one of the actors who had been hired for the play, was worried because he came from the West Bank and it was too late to find transport to take him home. The authorities did not allow people from the West Bank and Gaza to stay overnight in Jerusalem, or in any part of the '48 region. However, as he could not walk all the way home, he had no choice but to spend the night at Marwan's place.

Marwan was at the theatre at about midday. The building was a converted cinema situated in a cul-de-sac.

'It's good to be back,' he said. 'But I can also say that living in Jerusalem is not so vastly different from Majd al-Kroum; it's not like living in New York or Paris: Jerusalem is like a big village. The main difference for me is that in Jerusalem I live on my own: I come and go as I please, and I talk to whom I please. I'm not tied down to duties and obligations, I'm not obliged to socialize with relatives and neighbours.

'I have a meeting now to discuss a play I've written.'

And he rushed off, impatient to get back to the life his parents could not accept.

Within a year, Umm Imad had lost a considerable amount of weight because of heart problems. She was sitting on the porch having come back from a relative's wedding. Her eldest daughter, who had also been to the wedding, changed her clothes and began kneading bread. A man arrived and asked Umm Imad if she had okra to sell. She brought him some, weighed it and gave it to him. She sat down and said: 'I can't work as hard any more because of my health.'

Shortly afterwards, Fatma returned from the wedding. She looked severely at her mother, and then said: 'Why did you leave so early? And why were you so silent?'

'I wasn't enjoying myself,' replied her mother.

'Nothing ever pleases you,' Fatma said angrily.

'Your own wedding would,' retorted Umm Imad, and then a smile lit up her face. 'The other day Marwan told me that when he decides to get married, he will marry someone from the village and not an outsider. It made me very happy because I always thought that, with his way of life, he would end up marrying an outsider.'

Relatives arrived; it was an old couple in their eighties.

Umm Imad asked Fatma: 'Where is your father?'

'He's still at the wedding,' replied her daughter. And then she went on to explain: 'My father has been having a bad time because the court hasn't yet sorted out the fate of his 30 dunums. So he decided that as long as his case was still in court, he would plant wheat on his land, which he did. He used to go from time to time to make sure it was all right. When he went to harvest it, he found that the authorities had done it before it was actually ready. It was all ruined. He was very upset; in fact he was furious.'

One of the old relatives who had arrived earlier, quoted a saying:

Is it possible for the stone to produce leaves?
Is it possible for the sea to dry up?
Is it possible for the fish to survive out of the sea?

Then she added: 'Who would have thought that such a disaster would strike us? Who would have thought that one day we would lose our land? But then everything depends on fate, and no one knows what fate has in store for us.'

'We once owned 36 dunums,' her husband said, 'and now we own nothing. It is not that we were happy under the Turks or the British. The Turks were cruel; they made us starve. The British were cruel too; they used to make us walk for miles, carrying heavy bags of sand. They also made us pay such high taxes that some of the peasants had to sell their land because they couldn't afford it. But whatever the Turks and the British did, at least they did not steal our land and homes. It's the Jews who took our land, and forced people to leave the country. Our people are dispersed. We have relatives in Lebanon, Syria, the Gulf and even Norway.'

'Today, life is bitter,' said his wife. 'There is no happiness and no kindness. People are intolerant, selfish and aggressive. Even our own young people have learnt to be selfish.'

Then they turned to Umm Imad and began talking about some of their relatives. When they left, Umm Imad and her eldest daughter went indoors. Fatma stayed on the porch. She gave a deep sigh and said, 'The old people cannot let go of the past.'

She gazed at the hills and added, 'Although I live with my family, and am surrounded by relatives, life can be lonely at times. I can't share my dreams and thoughts with the old because they live in a different world, and while I can communicate with those of my own generation, many of them are only interested in making money, or in marriage. Marwan is perhaps the one I'm closest to. He has just come back from Holland and Germany where they were touring with his play. He came to see us two days ago.'

Marwan was in Jerusalem trying to organize another tour, this time to England.

'The play that I finished writing last year has been performed here and we have just been showing it in Germany and Holland. It's called *The Birds*. It has three characters: a hunter, whom I play; his old servant; and a young man. The hunter is the oppressor; he kills not only birds, but anybody who opposes him. The old servant acquiesces to all the hunter's demands: he is passive and has the victim mentality. The young man represents the new rebellious generation. The play has been a great success. We have had some good reviews.'

'The Birds' is a transparent – and not transparent – political fable ... The Hakawati does seem to excel at doing something which Jewish theatre in Israel has gone sadly slack at: capturing its audience's heart. The emotional commitment of the actors in their recent production of the original Palestinian play 'The Birds' is profound. We see them reaching deeply into themselves to forge a link between their personal experience and the events of the drama. (*The Nation*, 1988)

'The Birds', an emotional allegory bristling with rebellion and relevance, is as populist and compelling as the intifada. (*Al-Fajr*, 1988)

'Unfortunately not everything has been a success,' said Marwan. 'Having been busy with the play for the past year, I did not have much time to devote to the cultural club in the village. When I came back from abroad, I discovered that the manager we hired had not carried out his duties, and the club was monopolized by members of one of the political parties who wanted to impose their own brand of cultural activities. For example, they took over a music group we had formed and wanted to give it a name which identified it with their party. I had also persuaded my father to let us build an open stage on some of his land, but even that became political. Members of the party wanted to use it for their own purposes. I pointed out to them that the whole idea was to have an independent cultural club open to everyone, and not affiliated to any party or group of people. Well, I'm planning to go back to the village soon to sort it all out. I'm also planning to hand the running of the club to a committee of young people from the village, and I will remain the supervisor.

'It's important to have cultural clubs and centres to encourage the development of our identity and awareness. If they become affiliated to a political party they lose the cultural perspective. We must struggle against the influence of Israeli culture, otherwise we will lose our heritage and identity. As I said before, I had to struggle against it, and I have succeeded in overcoming it. In fact, about five years or so ago I made a firm decision not to use a single Hebrew word when speaking Arabic. Once the Hakawati had a meeting with some left-wing Jews, who only spoke Hebrew, so we decided to have someone translate the Hebrew into Arabic for us, although we all spoke very good Hebrew. Then after the meeting was over, one of us said something in Hebrew, and the Jews were astounded, and they cried out: "Goodness, you are *our* Arabs after all!"

'Our struggle is very different from what it was in 1948. Things have changed tremendously since those days. I find that some Palestinians abroad live in a dream world. They think that life here has not changed since 1948. I have an uncle, one of my mother's brothers, who lives in Lebanon. I met his son in Europe, and he told me that his father still thinks that Majd al-Kroum is the same as it was in 1948. His son likes to hear about the past, but he also looks to the future. He knows he may never be able to return to Majd al-Kroum, so for him the other option is a Palestinian state in the West Bank and Gaza.

'To some of the Palestinians abroad, a peasant's life is considered romantic. It's fantasy. A peasant's life is hard and harsh and we don't want to go back to such a life, or to traditions that no longer serve our cause. We don't want to go back to the victim mentality. It also makes me angry when Palestinians abroad, especially some of the educated ones, think they know more than the people who live here. They have dreams of liberating Palestine which are not realistic. They don't know the reality, nor do they want to accept it.'

His impatience with the old and the unrealistic was portrayed by the young man in *The Birds*.

8

The Social Worker:
Adeeb in Jaffa

Yaffa has become the mother of the stranger. It
welcomes him and feeds him, while it neglects its
own sons and leaves them to starve.

Riyad (Adeeb's father)

Jaffa (Arabic: Yaffa) is about 65 kilometres north-west of
Jerusalem, and has both an Arab and Jewish population.
Unlike Acre, it is a sprawling town. The faded old buildings
have none of the dignity and beauty that can still be found in
old Acre. In Jaffa, the weariness of a downtrodden existence
dominates all that was once beautiful. The hot humid summers
bring impatience; and in the chilly winters there is a huddled
grimness.

According to one set of statistics, Jaffa's Arab population is
10,000; according to another, it is 18,000. The Arabs live
mainly in two areas: al-Ajami, and al-Jabaliyeh. About 67 per
cent are between the ages of twenty and thirty. Nearly 780
families live in overcrowded and poor conditions.

The town is part of the Tel Aviv municipality, and Arab
inhabitants believe the municipality wants to transform the
Arab areas into Jewish ones, just as it wants to turn the ports
into a tourist attraction, depriving the Arab fishermen of their
livelihood. They say that the policy of neglect by the authorities
is designed to make it impossible for people to live in the
houses, so they will eventually be forced to move out.

Adeeb is a short, stocky and balding 37 year old. He is
married and has three children: a girl aged ten and a half; a boy
aged seven; and an 18-month-old girl. He is a social worker, a
member of the League of Jaffa Arabs, and a member of the
Cultural Centre which is part of the League; he also organizes

156

tours to Egypt. His hours as a social worker are from 7.30 a.m. to 3.30 p.m., after which he goes home for lunch and a rest. At about 5.00 p.m. he goes to the Cultural Centre and remains there till 8.00 p.m. or later, depending on the activities of the day. He is kind and considerate with everyone he deals with.

He lives in the al-Ajami area with his family and his parents. They live in an old Arab-style house which was once a large villa owned by a Palestinian who left in 1948. The house has since been divided into three separate quarters, with a common entrance. Each quarter is divided by a wall. Adeeb has half the house: three rooms, a kitchen and bathroom. His parents have a quarter, and an unrelated family have the other quarter. There is an enclosed front garden which Adeeb and his parents share.

Adeeb was sitting outside, hoping it would not be as stifling as indoors. He explained their housing situation:

'We own our shares of the house jointly with a government company which has taken over the properties of absentee owners. We have lived in al-Ajami since 1970. Before that we lived in a different area, but the authorities expropriated our house and moved us out, along with all the other Arabs, into the Ajami and Jabaliyeh areas, which have effectively become Arab ghettos.'

Adeeb's father, Riyad, is a sprightly man of 72. He had finished his work for the day at his grocery shop, which is situated at the entrance of the garden. He sat next to his son and listened intently. When Adeeb finished talking, Riyad said: 'When I first got married, I built myself a house which had three rooms. The land belonged to another Palestinan family, and I used to pay them rent for the use of the land. When the Jews came to power, they took the land and destroyed my home, and the homes of many other Arabs.'

'Up until 1987 the policy of the municipality was to demolish the houses in the Arab areas, claiming that the buildings were derelict and too dangerous to live in,' said Adeeb. 'Many houses have already been demolished, and they would like to demolish the rest to make way for villas and expensive apartment blocks for the Jews. Of course, all of these plans do not take into account the Arab population. Their ultimate aim is to expel the

Arab population from Yaffa. In fact, the head of the municipality said outright that he did not see any reason why the Arabs should continue to live in Yaffa. As far as he was concerned, they could go and live in Lydd, Ramleh, or the Triangle. The League wrote a strong critical article about it in the newspapers, and he was forced to withdraw his remarks.

'The League then took the municipality and town planners to court to stop them from destroying the rest of the Arab houses. In late 1987, the court ruled in favour of the League. The authorities have come to realize that they cannot move the Arabs out of Yaffa. We have lived here all our lives, and so did our parents and grandparents. They now realize that we are not prepared to give in to them; we are going to continue struggling for our rights. The League has done a great deal in the restoration of Arab houses, giving the municipality no excuse to kick the Arabs out.'

Adeeb was interrupted by the appearance of his mother, Samia, who placed a tray of soft drinks on the table. She is an attractive woman of 61, whose whole life revolves around her family.

'The League', continued Adeeb, 'is encouraging the Arabs not to be intimidated by the authorities into moving out. We must encourage them to fight for their rights.'

'Before 1948, the Arabs and Jews had occasional skirmishes, but on the whole we lived peacefully together,' said Riyad. 'Then the British rubbed salt on the wound and inflamed the conflict. Look at the mess we're in now. Yaffa has become the mother of the stranger. It welcomes him and feeds him, while it neglects its own sons and leaves them to starve.' He lit a cigarette and gazed sadly at the ground.

Samia joined in: 'I remember how I had to leave Yaffa in 1948. We had two sons at the time, and a four-month-old girl. People began to evacuate the town, so I sent my eldest son away to his father's mother, and the other one went to my mother. I refused to leave my husband behind and so stayed with my daughter. But then when all our neighbours left, my husband told me: "You can't possibly stay here any more. I'm a man, and I can take care of myself, but you have a baby and you must leave." So I was forced to leave, and I went to stay with his parents in Birzeit, where they originally came from.

'They closed all the roads, and my husband and I were unable to see each other except on Christmas day. Eventually, he managed to send me the necessary documents which would allow me to return. But his father, who was also my mother's brother, refused to let me go because he had heard of the atrocities that the Jews were committing against the Arabs. As it so happened, the director of the Red Cross was a friend of my brother, and he persuaded my uncle to let me return by promising that he himself would guarantee my safety. And so I left with my two sons; my daughter had died while I was in Birzeit. There were five buses full of families returning to Yaffa. On the way, we stopped and picked flowers, and decorated the buses to celebrate our return home.

'When I settled back in Yaffa, I had Jewish neighbours from Morocco, Iraq, and Poland. I was friendly with them. It was the children who used to fight. The Jewish boys used to tell my sons: "Go to Jordan. This is not your country, it's ours." One of my sons, Michel, was very bright and strong, and he used to reply: "No, we Arabs have always lived here. This is our land. You go back where you came from." Another time, Michel and a Moroccan Jewish boy were playing outside the house when the Moroccan boy yelled at Michel: "You dirty Arab." Michel flung himself at him and began beating him up. The Jewish boy's mother rushed out to stop him and then called me and began to insult me. I said nothing, and stood in utter silence. It made her angrier, and she yelled out: "You don't even answer me." So I replied quietly: "Neighbour, why don't you come upstairs and we'll have a cup of coffee together. They are children but we are adults; we are sisters and we shouldn't fight together." And then I kissed her. So she came up to my flat, and we had coffee together. I remember when she was moving out, she said to me: "You are the best neighbour I've had. Forgive me for all the bad things that have happened." '

Riyad commented, 'When I worked as a cargo inspector at the port till 1972, I was on good terms with all my Jewish colleagues.'

'Yes, they used to visit us, come to our children's christening, have supper with us,' his wife said mournfully. 'I tried to teach all of my five children not to discriminate between Arabs and

Jews. I used to tell them that we were all brothers and sisters and should live together peacefully. We never imagined that the situation would develop into what it is today.'

Nora, Adeeb's wife, joined the family. 'She's finally gone to sleep,' said Nora, as she sat down with a heavy sigh. She had been indoors clearing up and putting her 18-month-old daughter to bed for her afternoon nap. Her eldest daughter Abla, who had been helping her, sat next to her.

Adeeb took up the conversation: 'The people who remained in Yaffa were mainly poor and uneducated. The few educated ones who did not leave were too frightened to talk and to stand up for their rights as Palestinians. We were brought up to fear the authorities and not to criticize them. We were not encouraged or even allowed to become politically involved.'

His father replied somewhat defensively, 'The older generation did struggle too, you know. They went on strikes and demonstrations. I myself did not participate in any of this, but I was a member of the Mapam party until the 1950s.'

A silence followed, interrupted now and then by the noise of children playing in the street.

Nora is a very energetic and gregarious thirty year old. She teaches Arabic at the Freres. It was she who broke the silence: 'When I was at school, they didn't teach us about our cause or history. And at home, too, they didn't talk about our cause. Everybody was too frightened. I personally lived a happy life, totally unaware of what was happening around me. Then when I finished school and began my teacher-training course, I began to notice the misery, the injustices and discrimination. I began to take more interest in newspapers, listen to people discussing politics, and read books about our history; and so my awareness developed. Adeeb also played a big role in developing my awareness. Abla is much more aware than I ever was at her age.'

Abla was amazed that when her mother was ten she was ignorant of the Palestinian cause. 'I'm very much aware of my identity, not only through my parents, but through contact with people at the League and the Cultural Centre where I go and participate in activities. I also listen to the news and read *al-Ittihad*. Also, at school, one of the teachers talks to us about our Palestinian identity and history. I am proud of my identity.'

'The children I teach are between 10 and 14 years old,' said Nora. '95 per cent of the students in the school are Arabs, and 5 per cent are Jews. The Arab students are much more aware of their identity and cause than my generation were at their age. But then the teachers today are also very different from the ones we had when I went to school. Most of the teachers where I teach are Jews, but that doesn't stop the Arab teachers from encouraging awareness among the children. For example, I teach them about some of our Palestinian writers. I refuse to celebrate independence day, and I refuse to work on Land Day. When the Jews commemorate those who died in the wars, the Arab students have to stand up with their Jewish class-mates. So I tell my Arab students to think of the people who have died in the intifada. A ten-year-old boy once asked: "How come we have to stand up for the Jews, and they don't stand up for us on Land Day." In my days no one would have dared ask such a question.'

'It was different when I went to school,' said Adeeb. 'The primary school I went to in Yaffa was run by priests. We were taught in French, and Arabic was a second language. At around the age of 12 I began to become aware of my Arab identity, and I felt I was missing out on my own language. So I persuaded my parents to send me to school in al-Nasra (Nazareth) for two years. Al-Nasra was considered the centre of Palestinian Arab nationalism. After that, I returned to Yaffa, where I finished my secondary school. I then did a teacher-training course and taught for a year at a girls' convent.

'I was also active in the scouts, and as a result I came into contact with many families who opened my eyes to the enormous political, social and educational problems that the Palestinians in Yaffa were facing. I wanted to do something about it. I wanted to help my people, so I decided to study social work at the university.

'At the time, I was the only Arab student majoring in social work; all the rest were Jews. I had contacts with some of the left-wing Jewish students, but we never developed a friendship. I did not feel that I was really fully accepted. I became involved in student activities, and I got to know Arab students from the Triangle and al-Jaleel (Galilee), who were much more politi-cally aware than the Arabs in Yaffa. It was really at university that my political awareness took on a greater dimension and strength.

'After university, I taught for a while at the Terrasanta in Yaffa, and I also became head of the boy scouts. Then an incident happened which reinforced the political and social commitment I had to my people. In the 1977 elections, I was asked by the head of the scouts, the headmaster and other dignitaries of Yaffa to organize the scouts to welcome Yigal Allon. He was Minister of Foreign Affairs at the time, and he was going to tour Yaffa on behalf of the Labour Party. I refused, saying that he had been in office for four years, and had never set foot in Yaffa to find out how we Palestinians were faring. I told them I could not see the point of welcoming him just because he wanted to campaign for his party and win Arab votes. The scouts were then asked by the dignitaries to welcome him anyway, regardless of my stand. But I managed to persuade them not to. I pointed out that by meeting him, they would be condoning the policies of the state towards the Palestinians. We ended up by staging a demonstration against Allon, which led to my dismissal from both the school and the scouts.

'I was not really upset, because I began working at the Social Affairs Bureau. For me it was much better because it meant I could get involved on a wider scale with the welfare of my people. The school I'd been teaching in was very sectarian. My work consists of talking to families with problems: drug addicts, abuse within the family, truants, deviants. I try to find ways of solving their problems through fostering, youth clubs, or psychotherapy centres for drug addicts, and so on.'

Loud angry voices interrupted the conversation. Adeeb shook his head: 'They're our neighbours across the road. They're a good example of a very big problem we have here: drug addiction. The father died of alcoholism, and the mother works part time. She has fifteen children: eight boys and seven girls. Of the eight boys, six are drug addicts, as well as one of her daughter's husbands. Three of her sons are imprisoned. One of their brothers informed on them and then ran away. Poor housing conditions, unemployment, despair, have pushed teenagers and older people into drugs as a means of escape. It is estimated that nearly one-third of the Arab population in Yaffa is taking drugs: mainly cocaine and heroin. In order to finance their addiction, they commit crimes. The municipality deals with addicts over 18. Once a doctor proves that they are addicts, they are given a synthetic drug as a substitute. It doesn't actually help them because they just end up addicted to it.'

He looked thoughtfully at his watch and said: 'Come on, let's go and visit our neighbours.'

When Adeeb rang the bell, the voices behind the door were silenced. He rang the bell again, and there was the sound of people scurrying. Then a woman's voice:

'Who is it?'

'It's Adeeb.'

She opened the door and welcomed him.

'Is Aref in?' he asked.

'Yes.'

The house was oppressively dark. Aref appeared. He was in his early twenties, thin and pale. He had two gold chains round his neck. He apologized for the darkness in the house:

'We haven't opened all our shutters because some of my brothers are still asleep.'

Adeeb asked him about his health, and whether his three other brothers were still in prison.

'Yes they are,' he replied.

'I hope you haven't started taking drugs too.'

Aref shook his head vehemently. 'No, never. My older brothers have managed to persuade the younger ones to take drugs, but I have refused to give in to them because I see what the drugs are doing to them. They're not entirely to blame. My father was an alcoholic and he used to beat us up regularly. He didn't care about our education. I left school when I reached the 6th grade. I worked as a shoemaker, but then I had to leave the job because my health has not been too good.

'So many people take drugs out of despair. The Jews treat the Palestinians so unjustly. No one cares about us, no one cares about anybody. But I have some hope now because of the intifada in the West Bank and Gaza. It finally makes me feel proud to be a Palestinian. I support them all the way. Although my brothers are aware of their own Palestinian identity, mainly because of the way they're treated by the Jews, they are too immersed in their addiction to take any real interest in what is happening in the West Bank and Gaza. Perhaps one day they will wake up.'

There was an uneasy silence. A young man in his pyjamas shuffled outside the door. Aref remained quiet, and Adeeb said it was time to leave.

Ramy, the other neighbour we visited, lived a few houses down the road. He is 45 years old, married and has four children.

'You still haven't managed to find a job?' Adeeb asked him.

Ramy shook his head, and then explained: 'I used to work as a supervisor in a shoe factory where I supervised the work and put the finishing touches to the shoes. But then I lost my job because I became a drug addict. I started taking drugs to help me cope with our miserable social and political situation. You see, in the past, despite what the Jews had done to us, we learnt how to live with them. We worked with them, and we even socialized with them. But we also had a complex: we were ashamed to be Palestinians, and we never talked about it. Then when Nasser came to power, he gave us strength and we were proud to be Arabs. After the 1967 war, the Jews began to humiliate us: they insulted us, beat us up, made fun of us, of the Egyptian army, and of the Arabs as a whole. It was traumatic and it pained me so deeply that I began to spend most of my time in coffee places and that was where I began to take drugs to drown my sorrows.

'I took opium for three years, and did not know that I had become an addict until I was imprisoned. When I was released, I took heroin for five years, and in the meantime, I had lost my job. So in order to finance my addiction, I became a drug pusher. When I realized the suffering I was causing my family, I decided to do something about my addiction. I went to a centre, a Jewish one because there are no Arab centres, where they gave me a synthetic drug as a substitute. It has not really helped, because I am now addicted to that and will probably remain so for the rest of my life. I haven't worked for 11 years. I live on social security.

'Before 1967, there were very few people who took drugs. After 1967, the pushers came out into the open, and the authorities did nothing about it because we were Arabs and they did not care what happened to us. Now the number of addicts has increased. Unlike in the past, when they started to take drugs in their twenties, today they begin as young as 13. Their reasons for taking drugs are: a future without work, discrimination, inequality, and miserable family and home conditions. All these youngsters are fully aware that they are Palestinian because it is the consequences of this that has pushed them into addiction. Unlike my generation, they are not ashamed of being Palestinian. But some of them are so involved in drugs that they think of nothing else. Their minds are eaten up by drugs so they don't think in terms of freedom, or struggling for their rights.

'The intifada, however, has triggered off some feelings of pride, and hope. When we demonstrated in support of the West Bank and Gaza on 21 December 1987, the Jews were frightened because they had never seen us Palestinians in Yaffa demonstrate for our cause.'

Back at home Adeeb said: 'It's all so depressing. But then, ironically, sometimes the misery of one family results in gains for another. One of the cases I worked on was a family which consisted of mother, father, and five children. The father was a drug addict. He had forced his 13-year-old son to find work so that he could earn money to finance his addiction. The boy was electrocuted at work and was killed instantly. The father, who at that time owned his house, sold one of the rooms. All the money from the sale of the room was spent on drugs.

'He persuaded his wife that they should sell the whole house and leave Yaffa, as it was the only way he could escape from the world of drugs. He told her that they would go to Beer al-Sabei' (Beersheba), where he originally came from, and there he would buy a piece of land and build a new home. He had married his wife when she was 15 years old, and so had trained her not to oppose him. The house was sold for the equivalent of $20,000, and the new owners were supposed to move into it two months later.

'Part of the money went on paying his debts to the bank; the rest he spent on drugs, and consequently they never started ɛ new life in Beer al-Sabei'. The relationship between him and his wife deteriorated to a point where he used to beat her up badly. One day she woke up to the realization, not only that he was becoming increasingly violent, but also that she was going to become destitute in two months. She finally gathered up enough courage to come to see me.

'The office cannot directly interfere in a housing crisis. There is a government housing agency which deals with such crises. Legally, however, this family was not entitled to have financial assistance from the agency. Once they had sold their house, they had lost the right to buy another house through the agency. The other alternative would have been to borrow money from the bank, but they were not in a position to do so. These were all the obstacles that I could not resolve. However, after a lot of discussion and argument, I managed to persuade my superiors at the office to give them financial assistance to rent a house. They agreed to do so for a year.

'Having sorted out the immediate housing crisis, I then concentrated on the relationship between the members of the family. Two of the sons were sent to a boarding school in al-Jaleel, and the others went to school in Yaffa. I had long sessions with the parents, and tried to persuade the father to go to a drug centre. He promised to do so, but of course never did. After the year was over, we tried with the help of the League to get them a loan or housing benefit from the Ministry of Housing, but they absolutely refused. They said that this family had lost all its rights to housing assistance, including the assistance they were getting to rent a house.

'The only solution left for them was to squat in the house of an absentee owner which had been boarded up and declared unsafe by the authorities. They lived there for a while, until they were evicted by the police, but they soon found another house to squat in. Shortly after they moved in, the woman was forced to call in the police because of her husband's violence. He was then ordered by the court not to live with her any more, or go anywhere near her. The police wanted to evict her, but when they saw the state she was in, they took pity on her and let her be. The League helped her restore some of the badly damaged areas of the house, and she began to make a new life for herself. Unfortunately, it was not for long.

'The woman came from a traditional family in Gaza. When her brother heard that she was living on her own, although she had some of her children with her, he immediately went to see her and told her that she was disgracing the family by living alone. I tried to persuade him to let her get on with her life, but he wouldn't listen to me. He gave her two alternatives: either to have her husband back, and accept her fate, or to return to Gaza and live with her family.

'I couldn't of course make the decision for her, but I discussed with her the pros and cons of each alternative. In the end, she returned to Gaza because of all the pressures around her. But happiness eluded her there too. Her family, especially her brother, treated her badly and made her work like a servant in the house. After a while, she could no longer bear it and returned to Yaffa. Her husband, who had been imprisoned for a while for drug dealing, is now destitute and moving from one town to another.

'The positive side of this case is that it has encouraged other families with housing problems to squat in the houses of absentee owners which have been boarded up and declared unsafe. In reality, they are not dangerous to live in. The aim of the authorities is to destroy them and build apartment blocks for Jews. There are about thirty families who have managed to solve their housing problems by squatting. The law says that if a family has squatted for over a month, then the authorities cannot forcibly move them out unless they take them to court. Well, a court case can take months and months, so a compromise has been reached and the families are allowed to stay on, provided they pay a monthly rent.

'Sometimes I feel despair because of all the obstacles from the authorities, and the policies they have towards the Palestinians. Do you know that what they give us for social services in the Ajami area does not cover 5 per cent of our needs? At times I ask myself whether I will ever be able to overcome all the obstacles; will I ever be able to change anything? Such questions make me feel like giving up, but then I say to myself: if we give up, how will anything ever improve?

'In a way, I find the voluntary work I do at the League and Cultural Centre more rewarding. It is not enough to try to solve the problems of my people within the boundaries of my profession. I must also participate in non-governmental institutions and activities to develop people's cultural, political and social awareness.'

Adeeb jumped up as he looked at his watch. 'I must go to the Centre,' he said.

The Centre is a five-minute walk from his house. At the front gate stairs lead on to a large balcony. There is a large hallway, part of which is used as a library, and a large room used for conferences and meetings; there are two kindergarten classrooms, and a couple of offices.

'The Yaffa Arab Cultural Centre was set up in 1987,' explained Adeeb. 'It has nine members, and is part of the League of Yaffa Arabs. One of the problems we encountered when we first started was that people were afraid to participate in case the authorities punished them. But we have managed to overcome this problem, and the Centre is now attracting many youngsters.

'I spend every afternoon at the Centre. One of our main aims is to develop educational, political, social and cultural awareness, especially among the young people. We have lectures on Palestinian culture, history and heritage. We have extra lessons for primary school children, and we have a library. We have also managed to persuade the Christians and Muslim clubs to co-ordinate their resources and help us with our kindergarten. We took advice from Dar al-Tifl in 'Acca, and we have managed to employ well-trained teachers. We have 15 children in each class, and they come from 7.30 in the morning till 2.00 in the afternoon. We tend to give priority to children whose mothers are working. They pay I£65 for ten months, but in fact we teach them for eleven months, and we pay the teachers for twelve months.

'We have a youth committee whose members help us on a voluntary basis in restoring the old buildings. They also go to rural areas to visit Arab villages, and they participate in the summer camps, where they help to improve our roads, paint walls, and so on. By having summer camps, we show the authorities that we can take care of ourselves and we don't need to rely on them. We also want to open an Arab centre for drug addicts because the Jewish institutions refuse to take Arab teenagers. They say that their traditions and way of life differ from those of the Jews. But it's not going to be easy to open a centre. Not only will it require a great deal of money, but also trained and dedicated people.'

Adeeb's help was required to sort out some administrative problems.

It was dark outside. The humid air engulfed the town, and there was not a ripple on the sea; the cars hooted impatiently, and the people walked lethargically.

Back at the house, the children were watching television, and Nora was preparing supper.

'Adeeb is always so busy,' she said. 'I wanted to visit some friends, but I didn't want to ask my parents-in-law to baby-sit. They are perfectly willing to do it and sometimes I do ask them, but I don't like to impose my children on them. I would prefer it if Adeeb could baby-sit, but it only happens about once a month, if at all. His work takes precedence over his household duties because he feels that at home there's me, and his parents, to fulfil the necessary demands and obligations.'

Adeeb's parents walked in, and shortly after that Adeeb arrived.

'You work too hard,' Nora told Adeeb.

'I must do my job properly, otherwise there's no point in doing it at all. The summer camps are due to start and we must make sure they're well organized. The work at the Centre and the League involves a constant struggle against the authorities. They accuse us of subversive behaviour. They tell us we are brainwashing the youngsters with anti-Israeli propaganda, and they accuse us of taking money from the PLO, which is not true. They are frightened of institutions such as ours because we are non-governmental and non-sectarian, and we reach a wide variety of people. Unlike the religious clubs, we are not afraid to criticize and fight the authorities.'

'Today's generation is different from ours,' said Adeeb's mother.

'Yes,' agreed her husband, and continued, 'but the difference is not just in the way they fight for their rights, but also in the way they behave in everyday life. We used to respect our elders, but today, if I admonish a five year old, he will look at me and say, "It's none of your business." Today, instead of helping an old man across the road, the youngsters laugh at him, and insult and humiliate him. All this is the result of modernization and adopting alien values.'

'Of course, some of our values have changed because of our interaction with the Jews,' said Adeeb. 'Within the Jewish community itself there are many different and conflicting values, because the Jews have come from all over the world. Some of the changes in our values are negative, others are positive. There are some traditions which we still practice, which I find outdated. In the old days, it was the parents who chose the bride or bridegroom for their children. I do not accept this, because if two people are going to get married, they must get to know each other. If there is no great romance between them, there should at least be an understanding and sympathy. My father disagrees. I met my wife when I was teaching at the Terrasanta and she was a student there. We fell in love, and we got married after she finished school. My father objected strongly because he wanted me to marry one of my cousins. I refused and said that I was not going to marry anyone except the girl of my choice, and so he had to accept my decision. He didn't want me to break a tradition that people have been practising for generations.'

'On the other hand, there are some practices which haven't changed at all,' commented Nora. 'For example, I don't find any changes in the relationship between husband and wife. When Adeeb wants me to do something, I have to do it immediately, regardless of whether I can or not. I can't oppose him. He expects me to fulfil his demands in exactly the same way that the older generation of men expect their wives to comply with their demands.'

'Actually, one of the biggest differences between the generations is the struggle for our cause,' said Adeeb. 'My father is still frightened for us when we criticize the authorities. I tell him this is supposedly a democratic country, so I'm free to fight for my rights and speak up for my people. Of course, in reality, this is not a democratic state at all. I'm not afraid to say that I am a Palestinian, but my parents still hesitate, they are still afraid. I don't blame them, I can understand what makes them so frightened, but I don't agree with them. I don't accept their attitudes, and I don't accept the way they want to implant this fear into us. Today, we're not the same, and I'm sure that my children will be more aware and better informed than my generation.'

'Today, the younger generation is influenced by outsiders,' muttered Riyad. 'Take the intifada for example: it is the PLO which gives them orders, and if they don't follow these orders, they are killed. The intifada is not something that was started by the people themselves.'

'It is the people who started the intifada,' said Abla with passion. 'The Jews treat the Arabs badly; why shouldn't the Arabs fight back, even if it is violent? I read in one of the newspapers that a Jewish lady said she enjoyed seeing Arabs being beaten up. It made me so furious that, had she been in front of me, I would have beaten her up.'

'If we despair and give up they will break us, and we shall be lost,' said Adeeb. 'But if we continue to struggle and get rid of our fears, if we think of our cause before our self-interest, then we can stop the authorities from beating us up, from expelling us, from demolishing our homes, and from discriminating against us.'

There was a sudden deafening noise of music from their neighbours across the road, followed by shrieks of laughter. Adeeb sighed: 'This will go on till the early hours of the morning. They sleep during the day, and then wake up late afternoon, early evening, and stay up all night. I have complained to them so many times about the noise. At times they listen to me and calm down; but most times it's like talking to the walls. They're unaware of what they're doing because they're always under the influence of drugs. Their mother and sisters cannot do anything either because they're frightened of them.'

Almost a year later, there had been a number of changes.

'You know that family across the road?' said Adeeb as he sat down for lunch. 'Well, six of the boys are now in prison, including Aref. Although he was not actually taking drugs, he began dealing in them. The temptation to make money was too great. Somebody must have informed on them, because one evening as they were sorting out the amount of cocaine they had, the police raided their house. They will be in prison for a long time. I'm very sad about Aref because he has wasted his life.

'I actually wrote a play about the problems of drug addiction. It has been shown recently at the Centre. It's called *Who's to blame?* The characters in the play are: a mother, father, two sons, a daughter and her husband. One of the sons, Ehab, is about to take his degree in law; and the other son, Diab, is a school drop-out and a drug addict. Both Ehab and his brother-in-law know about Diab's addiction. The mother refuses to either accept or acknowledge that her youngest son has a problem. Her husband and Ehab get upset by her ostrich-like behaviour and blame her for spoiling Diab. Every time his father or older brother reprimand him, the mother defends him and says that Diab is a good boy and is incapable of ever doing anything wrong. She is finally faced with the reality of her son's behaviour when he is ordered to appear in court for dealing in drugs. His brother tells him that they will all stand by him if he promises to mend his ways, and that he and their brother-in-law, who is also a lawyer, will defend him. Diab says that he is lost forever and cannot cope any more. They all try to persuade him to begin a new life and promise to give him all the support he needs. But Diab does not believe them, and says that had every member of the family really stood by him from the very beginning, he would not have ended up a drug addict or pusher.

'The people who attended the play were parents, and specialists such as social workers, psychologists, educators. After the performance, we discussed ways to overcome the drug problem. Some of the parents whose children are drug addicts asked whether the young people are taking drugs because of the political situation; or because of the way they are brought up at home and at school; or because of the housing problem; or because there are no recreational facilities, so they spend their time hanging around in street corners. The discussion was interesting, and the parents were very keen to talk about the problems.'

Adeeb's mother rushed in to say goodbye as she was going to the West Bank for a couple of days to visit relatives.

'We haven't been to the West Bank for a long time,' said Nora. 'We haven't even been to Jerusalem for some time. We're afraid to go because our car has an Israeli licence plate, and Palestinians there wouldn't be able to tell that we're Palestinians too. We might end up being stoned. When my mother-in-law goes to the West Bank, she goes in a taxi which has the West Bank licence plate. But that of course means they are stopped by the army and searched.'

Adeeb had gone to see his mother off. When he came back he said: 'I'm going to Cairo in ten days' time. I'm organizing three tours this year. Nora will come with me on the last one.

'The tours I organize are to help the Palestinians to have a break from the oppressive conditions under which they live. The trips also give me the opportunity to develop their political awareness. We go by bus to Egypt, so it gives me plenty of opportunity to talk to them. For example, I tell them all about the Centre and the League; and if some important social or political event happened in Yaffa, we discuss it. Then, when we go past Jewish settlements built in areas which were once Arab villages, I tell them all about the history of the villages, and how they were taken over. Of course I don't lecture them throughout the whole trip. We also sing, and tell jokes. When we arrive in Egypt, I talk to them about the wars of 1948, 1956, 1967 and 1973. I tell them about the history of Egypt, about the 1952 revolution and about Nasser. The trip and the places we go through give me the chance to discuss all these subjects. Organizing tours is one of my hobbies. When I first started, the trips were only in Israel and the West Bank. Then when we were allowed to go to Egypt, I organized tours for people to go there. They enjoy going to Egypt.'

Adeeb's youngest child sat on his lap and showed him a scratch on her finger. He kissed it and told her that it would soon get better.

'I'm sending this little one to the kindergarten they have at the Muslim club. My relatives are horrified. I told them that I abhor sectarianism and discrimination, and since I preach about equality, I must practise it too. I pointed out to them that if they want social and political equality, then they too must practise it.'

'Sectarianism is a bad thing,' said Nora. 'I used to be active in the Orthodox club, and I used to participate in the church activities. But then I gave it up because it conflicted with my nationalism. The people I worked with were sectarian; they were not interested in developing political awareness. Some Palestinians don't realize that our identity will not be recognized if they themselves don't acknowledge it. I have an Arab friend who wanted to send her child to a Jewish kindergarten. She claimed that she would be better looked after there. She had heard that the children were badly treated in Arab kindergartens, which is of course absolute nonsense. I said to her: "Do you want your child to come home and talk to you in Hebrew, sing Jewish songs, and celebrate Jewish feasts? How could you live with that?" So I took her to the kindergarten at the Centre to show her how the children were treated. I'm glad to say she changed her mind, and she won't be sending her child to a Jewish kindergarten.'

'We've had to increase the number of children in the kindergarten at the Centre because there aren't enough kindergartens for Arabs,' said Adeeb. 'We now have 22 children in each class instead of 15. After all, the Centre was created especially to improve the conditions of the Arabs in Yaffa. If we don't do it ourselves, who else will do it?

'One of my responsibilities this year is to co-ordinate the activities of the Arab kindergartens in Yaffa. I make sure that they are running smoothly, and that there is no discrimination or negative interference from the authorities. We are now insisting that all the Arab teachers in Arab kindergartens must take courses in Dar al-Tifl in 'Acca, or be trained here by an Arab teacher. That way they learn about our Palestinian heritage, about Arab feasts, Palestinian identity, and the types of games, songs and stories which meet the needs of Arab children. We have already sent some of our teachers to Dar al-Tifl, and occasionally a teacher from there comes over to give courses at the Centre. Unfortunately, the improvements we want for the other services are at the moment on paper only. To actually implement them is a different matter altogether.

'We have also reorganized our administration at the Centre. It now consists of five members who all share the responsibility of running the Centre. This year I am spending more time on the restoration and development programme in the Ajami area. Apart from restoring the houses so that the authorities don't have an excuse to destroy them and kick us out, we are also preparing a project to improve various services in the Arab community, such as our health services, services for old people, helping poor families who have a large number of children, and improving our kindergartens.

'The development programme is being funded by American Jews in Los Angeles, by the municipality of Tel Aviv, and by the Ministry of Housing. The funds are also for the Jewish community. But what we are trying to stress to these people is that the Arabs in Yaffa have been grossly neglected at all levels, and it's time something was done about our situation. Members of the municipality don't like the League or the Centre, not only because we criticize them, but also because we give them solutions which are appropriate to the Arab community. After all, we know what our problems and needs are: we encounter them in our daily lives. The municipality resents us because it wants to impose its own solutions.

'After winning our case in the high court in 1987 to stop the authorities from driving us out of Yaffa, they are now trying to appease us by giving us half a sweet here and half a sweet there, so to speak. For example, they are allowing us to restore some of the houses, but at the same time they are still trying to destroy others. They don't fool us; we are not stupid. We will go on confronting them until they meet all our needs and give us our rights.'

It was time for Adeeb to go to the Centre. He said that on his way he was going to visit a family whose house needed repairs. He explained the situation of the family:

'The family consists of father, mother, and four children. The father is unemployed; the eldest son, who lives with his wife's family, is a drug addict and has been in and out of prison. The eldest daughter, who is also married, is the only member of the family whose life is in some sort of order. The two remaining children, both teenagers, live with their parents. The son is mentally unbalanced. The wife had a son from a previous marriage who committed suicide because he killed his best friend in a car accident. As a result, she had a nervous breakdown and was in and out of mental homes; she also tried to commit suicide.

'They live in an Arab-style house, where most of the rooms have been sealed off by the authorities. The father, however, has forced open one of the rooms. They now have two bedrooms, an entrance hall/sitting-room, bathroom and kitchen. The entrance hall and bathroom ceilings leak, and one of the outside walls needs repairing.

'The authorities want the family to move out so they have been harassing them by telling them that the house is not theirs, that it is dangerous to live in it, that the ceiling is going to collapse over their heads. The League wants to repair the house, but our policy is that families have to pay one-third of the costs. This family is in no position to pay anything, so I have advised them to apply to the Makassed al-Khaireya (a charity organization), for a grant. They want me to help them fill in the forms because they're incapable of doing it themselves.'

The family welcomed Adeeb warmly.

Ibrahim, the father, is in his fifties. He has a rough face, with the pained expression of a man who seems to have lost any reason for his existence.

He showed the forms to Adeeb: 'I don't want to move out. But then I am unable to fight for my rights, certainly not on my own. I'm tired of life. My spirit is broken. When I was 18, I spent 12 years in a Jordanian prison. They accused me of spying; the only crime I had committed was smuggling. They tortured me. Look at my legs, they're full of scars from cigarette burns. When I was released, a friend of mine smuggled me into Jaljulia, which was where I originally came from. I was then detained by the Israelis, who took away my passport. Eventually I managed to obtain identity papers, and then I moved to Yaffa where I got married. I first worked as a garbage collector; then I became a fisherman. But I had to give up my job after losing one of my fingers. I can't find another job, and so I'm living on welfare.'

Maha, Ibrahim's wife, gave a deep sigh. She is in her forties, thin, pale, and bitter; she moves slowly carrying the weight of life.

'Yes, we are tired of life,' she said. 'I don't mind moving out immediately if they offer us another home. I neither have the interest nor the stamina to fight. I don't even care if the

Palestinians in Yaffa are displaced, just as I don't care about the intifada. It's true that I am a Palestinian, but I have my own personal problems. I don't care about the West Bank and Gaza. What use is the intifada to me? It doesn't concern me.'

Her 16-year-old son reiterated her feelings: 'Who cares about the West Bank and Gaza? Let them do what they like. I'm not interested either.'

Ibrahim looked at them, and suddenly a spark appeared in his eyes, perhaps because he realized that life was not as hopeless as he imagined it to be. 'Well, I am proud of the intifada,' he said, 'and I feel pain and sympathy when I see how cruelly my Palestinian brothers are being treated.'

Adeeb helped them fill in the forms, and then made his way to the Centre.

The library had disappeared. Adeeb smiled and said: 'We are going to have a new library. It will be on two floors and well insulated from noise. People will be able to read and work in peace. We are also getting 4,000 books from Egypt.'

There were a number of people sitting in the hall, talking and shouting in Hebrew. Adeeb explained:

'This is a Jewish theatre workshop, which also includes Arabs. In some of our programmes to develop awareness we decided to include progressive left-wing Jews who understand our cause and who sympathize with it. We want the Jews who believe in equality, justice, and an independent Palestinian state to be included in our struggle. They meet once a week for three hours. They work on different subjects which portray our political and social struggle. They do it all spontaneously. They act out some of the conflicts and contradictions which exist between the Jews and Arabs. Sometimes you hear them screaming, or you hear them imitating animals. At other times you hear them arguing and fighting; or they are serene and their voices are accompanied by music. They experiment with various methods to find solutions for the conflicts. Unfortunately, they do it all in Hebrew because the Jews in the workshop don't know Arabic, while the Arabs can speak Hebrew. When they have finished experimenting they will produce a play which will also be in Hebrew. We want it to reach the Jewish community, to reach the Jewish people who don't know anything about our cause, and who are prejudiced against the Palestinians. We can't reach them if the play is in Arabic. Also, the Jews will be more inclined to listen to other Jews than to Arabs.

'We have also increased the number of cultural, political and social lectures. We had someone from the Naqab (Negev) talk about the Bedouins and their problems; we feel so cut off from them. Then we had a lecture about Islam and Christianity, and we also had an Arab poet talk about Palestinian poetry. We had various exhibitions: one was about the intifada; another was about the architecture of Yaffa from 1900 to the present day; and we had an exhibition of the cartoons of Naji al-Ali. We are also going to have a music group which will only play Arabic instruments. We have been doing quite a lot since last year.'

There was a scream from someone in the workshop, followed by utter silence.

'I have a meeting later on,' Adeeb said. 'In the meantime I'll go home. I've had a tiring day. Nora and I work hard at our jobs, but what we earn is not enough. I get the equivalent of $700 a month, and she gets the equivalent of $430 a month. The Jews have advantages and bonuses. For example, those who have done their military service get child benefit, which of course does not apply to the Palestinians. The Jews get bigger loans for mortgages, and they get a better old-age pension.'

He sighed wearily: 'One day we will attain our rights. I'm very happy with the new PLO developments. The intifada has brought results, and will continue to bring results. If there's an independent Palestinian state in the West Bank and Gaza, which I'm sure there will be, it will alleviate the conflicts and pressures here. I shall be part of that state, but I will remain in Yaffa because it is my home and it is where I was born. If there is a just solution, then I don't think we will be in need of borders, armies or wars. We shall have open frontiers, and we will be able to come and go as we please.'

Adeeb went home. Darkness descended; and there was no noise from the neighbours across the road.

9

The Caretaker:
Amer in Laqqiya

> The intifada has affected us in more than one way. It
> has developed the awareness of the Palestinians who
> were politically ignorant; it has intensified our
> struggle to demand our rights; and it has even
> affected tribal procedures for resolving conflicts.
>
> Amer

The afternoon heat brings a stillness to the village. People find
refuge in their homes from the scorching sun; and even the
cows, donkeys, goats and dogs are silenced by the pressure of
the heat. Only the little three year old finds the stamina to
stand on top of the hill. He scratches his bare bottom as he
gazes thoughtfully into the distance. Behind him is a corrugated
iron hut; in front of him lies the rest of his village – a Bedouin
village of about 7,000, situated 14 kilometres north of
Beersheba. The houses are loosely clustered together according
to family groups; the roads are dust roads; and what remains of
the olive trees softens the harshness of the area. Beyond is the
rest of his homeland, and further away is the world. The boy
takes a deep breath and walks slowly towards the hut. A few
people live in huts like his, but some are luckier and live in
wooden homes; and there are a few buildings made of stone.

The village is under constant threat of being demolished by
the authorities, who claim that the inhabitants have no legal
right to be there. Occasionally, the authorities do destroy
people's olive trees, and houses too.

Amer is 44 years old, of slight build, and with an ironic sense of
humour which brightens up an otherwise sad and weary face.
He works as a caretaker at the University of Beersheba. He

lives with his wife and four children in a house built of wood
with stone floors. The front room is a sitting-room with a
television, pictures on the wall, and a 'God bless your home'
sign. The next room is where Amer and his wife Fatma sleep.
The third room is where Fatma does her sewing, and where
Abeer, their five-year-old daughter, sleeps. The kitchen entrance
is from the back garden. It is a dark windowless room, and in
the summer there is scarcely need to turn on the stove: the heat
of the room alone is almost enough to cook a meal. Alongside
the kitchen there is an extension to the house where there is
another bedroom in which their other three children sleep: their
eldest son Nidal who is 15; their daughter Orouba who is 13;
and Esam who is 12. Next to their room is a bathroom which
contains a shower and a washing machine. The garden is small
but lush: there are rich vines, two or three olive trees, and
flowers which Fatma has planted. In one corner is an outside
lavatory enclosed by wooden planks, and in another corner is a
tap where the dishes and vegetables are washed.

Amer finished his lunch by munching a red chilli pepper. He
got up and went over to sit on a mattress on the porch, where
he lit a cigarette and gazed over at the same hill on which the
little boy had stood. He was no longer there, but a horse
galloped up the hill and disappeared over the horizon.

'I wonder if its owner let it loose, or if it just ran off.' Amer's
remark was addressed to no one in particular.

The horse's freedom was short-lived, for it soon returned with
its master on its back.

'So much for its freedom,' said Amer with a sigh, and lit
another cigarette.

'Stop smoking so much,' Fatma said as she sat next to him.

She is in her thirties, a beautiful woman, tall and slim. A
white veil loosely covers her long dark hair, and she moves
majestically in her traditional Palestinian Bedouin dress.

He shrugged his shoulders, ignoring her remark, and said: 'It
is now 1988, and we still have no decent roads and no decent
buildings. We are not allowed to build permanent homes. We
have a primary school, a new intermediate school, a clinic, and
even a football team, but we are still waiting for permission to
build permanent homes. We are still having endless meetings

and discussions to see whether they will sell us this land to build on. Can you imagine, selling us our own land back? They want to force us to live in urban areas so they can take our land away. But even in urban areas, they won't let us have our own industries. What they want is to turn us into cheap labour for the Israeli economy.'

He was interrupted by the arrival of Salma, his 48-year-old mother-in-law, who is also his paternal uncle's wife. She is a handsome woman, and like her daughter, she wears the traditional embroidered Palestinian Bedouin dress.

She sat down and began sorting out some wool. She was going to start weaving a satchel for one of her ten children – of whom Fatma was the eldest.

'Look at how we are living,' she said. 'I'm not saying that the old days did not have hardships, but we were Bedouins with our own way of life, our freedom.' She stopped talking and concentrated on the wool.

'Our family is part of a very large tribe called the Sane',' Amer explained. 'Before 1948, some of us lived in Laqqiya, and some lived in a place called al-Sharia, which is about 20 kilometres east of Gaza. We also had land near Beer al-Sabei' (Beersheba), which once used to be an Arab town; there were no Jews there at all, unlike some other places in Palestine. When the Jews came to power in 1948, they drove all the Arabs out of Beer al-Sabei', and they also drove us out of al-Sharia. Some went to a refugee camp in Gaza; others joined their relatives in Laqqiya.

'In 1952, after we were issued with Israeli identity cards, they forced us out of Laqqiya, and sent us to the West Bank, near the village of Dahriya. We were there for about two months, then, as a result of negotiations between the Israeli authorities, the United Nations, the Red Cross and Jordan, the Jews agreed to let us return to Laqqiya. But once we were inside the borders, they went back on their agreement. Instead of allowing us to settle in Laqqiya, they put us in Tel al-'Arad, 45 kilometres east of Beer al-Sabei'.

'We were in the middle of nowhere. We lived in barren surroundings. There was no water, no electricity, no health services, no schools, and no transport. We had no radios or newspapers. We were totally isolated, and didn't know what was happening in the country. We lived in tents; we were scorched by the sun in the summer, and our limbs froze in the winter. We dug holes in the hills and lived in them to protect ourselves from the cold and heat; and we dug holes in the ground to collect the rain-water to quench our thirst. We lived in abject misery. In comparison, the people who lived in refugee camps were better off. They at least had UNRWA (the United Nations Refugee and Works Agency), which provided them with food, clothing, and education. We had nothing. But despite our hardships, we survived. We refused to run away to Jordan which we could easily have done.'

Amer stopped, and waved his hand to indicate that he wished to keep quiet for a while. The stillness around was now interrupted by the occasional shriek of a child, the temptation to go out and play having outweighed the discomfort of the sun. Amer gazed at the village, and at the land denied to them.

He went on: 'Despite our miserable conditions, the parents did not want their children to grow up illiterate, so they got a member of the community to teach them the Koran, Arabic, and arithmetic. Then, in 1962, we had our first primary school. It consisted of one room, and the children were taught in shifts. Finally the authorities also allowed us to farm some land, but we had to pay them rent for it.

'As a youngster, my awareness developed through listening to people. My father never gave me a political education: he never spoke about Palestinian identity, never advised me what to read. But I did hear him and the other elders speak about their disaster and dispersal. This aroused my curiosity, and I used to ask questions. Why has this person left his land? Why are people forced to live in refugee camps? I also remember how we were treated as third-class citizens under military rule. We weren't allowed to move freely in our own homeland. If we went from one place to another without permission, we were punished. We were isolated from the Jewish population, and treated with violence and brutality.

'When I grew up I became a teacher. I taught for five years until they imprisoned me. They accused me of supporting Fateh, and they locked me up for three years.'

Fatma sighed. 'They were a miserable three years. I hope we never have to go through that again.'

Amer continued: 'Of course, as a result I lost my job and have not been allowed to teach again. While I was in prison, the secret service came to offer me a job other than teaching. In return for finding me work, they wanted me to become a collaborator. They tried to persuade me by saying that I was educated, and came from a well-known tribe, so I couldn't possibly end up working as a labourer, and that they would find me a job that befitted my status. For me, it was all nonsense of course. I told them that 90 per cent of my people are now labourers, so why shouldn't I be like them? After all, I'm no better than they are. After my release, I did join the labour force. I worked on construction sites, and I even farmed for the Jews. I had no alternative; I needed the money to support my family. Anyway, I finally ended up in my present job where I take care of the grounds at the University of Beer al-Sabei'.

'While I was still in prison, the authorities wanted to move all the Arabs of the Naqab [Negev] into an urban ghetto and impose their own brand of change on them. But when I came out I found that part of my tribe had moved back to Laqqiya. It was a wonderful surprise. Although they have expropriated our land, we do not accept it. Our land is dear to us, and it is ours, not theirs. We will never give it up.

'Our village is represented by Bene Shamon, which is a Jewish council, and which also represents about nine kibbutzim in the area. The man representing our village is a Jew. We have been asking them to let us have an Arab representative, but so far the council has refused. They deal with our village on a tribal basis. The village consists of three main clans, each of which is divided into family groups. The council meets with the heads of clans, which to us is meaningless because the sheikhs are too frightened to oppose the council. The sheikhs are supposed to represent us, they are supposed to defend our cause, but they don't because they are collaborators. We don't recognize them. Neither they nor the council represent our interests.

'When we first moved here there was no water or electricity. Three years ago, after endless arguments with the authorities, we managed to obtain drinking water. But sometimes in the summer they cut off our water supply, not for an hour or two,

but for days. They don't do that to the Jewish settlements. Of
course, they did not provide us with electricity, so we sorted it
out ourselves. Each group of families bought a generator for its
own area. We can only have electricity in the evenings, but it's
better than nothing.

'The only services rendered by the council relate to the
primary and intermediate schools, and even in that we have no
say. They want to exercise control over the schools in order to
win the youngsters over to their own way of thinking, in order
to make them toe the government line. The contradictions of
the system can be seen in the way the authorities recognize the
schools, yet at the same time they refuse to recognize the very
existence of our village. Thus they have refused to provide us
with basic services such as a decent sewage system, road
construction, garbage collection, and so on. It is the inhabitants
themselves who collect their own garbage and take it to a dump
at the edge of the village.

'The authorities realize that we are very determined to
remain in our village and on our land. While they are forever
threatening to destroy all our homes, they also use other
pressures. For example we had our own clinic set up by a non-
governmental organization. It had an Arab doctor and nurse.
We were then forced to join *Sanduq al Marda*, the health system
belonging to the Histadrut. The clinic no longer has an Arab
doctor; it now has an old Romanian Jew who does not speak a
word of Arabic. The clinic is only open from 8.00 a.m. till noon,
so anyone who has the misfortune to fall ill after these hours has
to go to the West Bank and pay for private treatment. They also
threatened to destroy the memorial that we erected for the
victims of the Sabra and Shatila massacres. But pressures from
the media stopped the government from carrying out its threat.'

Amer looked at his watch. It was the time of day when the
sun was more merciful.

'It's time I went to the club. Working there is my most
important activity. That's another place the authorities want to
destroy,' he said, getting up.

'Shalom,' cried out a little boy's voice from somewhere.

'Go and tell your mother *shalom*,' answered Amer. 'It's my
brother's son,' he said smiling wryly. 'You're a stranger, and

any stranger is immediately greeted with the Hebrew word *shalom*. They think it is best to be on the safe side.'

The club was started by the Sons of Laqqiya Society which was founded in 1982. It has 14 members. The club caters for villagers of all ages. There is a playground for children which consists of climbing frames, swings made of car tyres, and a small concrete football ground. Above the football ground is a well-kept garden which leads to a porch and to the interior of the club. On the centre wall of the porch is a sign on which is written in both Arabic and English: 'Welcome to Laqqiya Club'; below it there is another sign on which is written: 'Sons of Laqqiya Club'. The club itself consists of a lecture room which seats thirty, Amer's office which also contains a small library, a room which was once used for a kindergarten, and a kitchen.

There were a few small children in the playground, and some teenagers kicking the football around, waiting for others to arrive to start a game.

'We have a proper football team,' Amer explained. 'When we first wanted to form a football team, the council interfered and wanted to choose the players on the basis of the clan system. Not only would that have been meaningless, but it would have created animosity among the people. We refused, and we formed a team according to the ability of the players. Then the council wanted to call our team Bene Shamon, but again we refused. We ended up calling it Sons of Laqqiya.'

Amer opened his office, and then looked into the lecture room where an English lesson was in progress.

'The person who is teaching them is a university graduate. He is a volunteer. All the people who work here are volunteers. We also give social and cultural lectures with political undertones. We encourage the youngsters to struggle for their rights and their cause. It is important to develop their awareness about their identity and heritage. Unfortunately the kindergarten closed down because the teachers were untrained and could not relate adequately with the children or parents. However, with the help of a non-governmental organization, the teachers have had a training course which has just finished.'

Amer was interrupted by a boy of about nine. He was thin, with dishevelled hair and tatty clothes. 'They won't let me play football with them,' he complained.

'You can play with the younger boys later. I've heard you've been fighting again. I told you there is to be no fighting here.'

The boy began an incoherent explanation for his behaviour; his eyes flickered around as he spoke. Amer walked to the hose and began watering the flowers; and the boy walked off mumbling. 'He is not normal,' Amer said. 'He is very badly treated at home. They beat him up mercilessly. I'm planning to have a word with his parents.'

With the late afternoon breeze, people came out of their shelters. The noise of the children and the animals echoed through the village; women wearing traditional Bedouin dresses, or the Islamic dress of the fundamentalists, walked purposefully to visit relatives or friends; a few young girls stood around, talking and giggling.

'Apart from the English lesson, there's not much else happening in the club today. We are going to start preparing for the summer camp soon. We hold it here. We sing Palestinian songs, we give them lectures, and we dance the *dabka* (folkloric dance). If there are repairs to be made in the village, the youngsters help out,' said Amer as he put the hose away.

The little three year old appeared on top of the hill, pulling a string at the end of which was a tin. This time he did not gaze into the distance, but down at the boys playing football, and at the children on the swings. He turned round and trailed the tin; he preferred his own game, for it made a noise, and it scattered the dust.

Amer returned home. His youngest daughter, Abeer, was having a fight with her older sister, Orouba.

'What's all this about?' asked Amer.

'She won't give me one of her sweets,' shouted Abeer.

'I've already given her some,' protested Orouba.

'Well, give her more,' Amer said, hoping to get some peace.

Abeer has short hair, and a pretty face with glittering mischievous eyes. She is tough too; she dominates all the members of her family. She would rule the village given half a chance.

Salma, Abeer's grandmother, was still sitting on the porch, sorting out the wool for the satchel. Fatma went into the kitchen to make coffee; and Abeer finally settled down next to her father, having obtained another sweet from Orouba. She sat deep in thought with a determined expression.

'I can still remember the smell of our land,' said Salma with a sigh. 'The Bedouin women not only did the weaving in those days, but they helped the men with the harvest, they fetched the water from the wells, they carried the firewood on their backs, and they milked the goats.'

'Today we are only housewives,' said Fatma, as she poured the coffee. 'My generation doesn't even know how to weave. If we had land, we would have farmed it, but we have no land. There are only about ten girls in the village who work. Some are teachers, others work in factories. I wish I had at least continued my education, but I left school at the end of the 4th grade. In my day, they didn't allow girls to finish school.'

'I want my girls not only to finish school, but also to go to university. Education is the only hope we have,' said her husband.

'Although we worked hard, we were all free, and we sang with joy,' Salma recalled. 'We had songs for farming, and songs for weaving. Our way of life has changed so much. Even weddings have changed. In the old days, they used to put the bride on the camel and take her to her groom, and they would sing beautiful traditional songs. Everything has changed.'

'People no longer know how to sing our traditional songs, the ones my mother and grandmother used to sing,' Amer said, gently stroking Abeer's hand. 'Nowadays, at weddings they have cassettes with modern songs, or they hire a singer who also sings modern songs. The songs don't come from the people themselves. In the old days, it was the guests who sang; they made the entertainment. The men had their own songs, and the women theirs. All this is lost. So many of our traditions are lost. We are trying to remedy this by teaching our traditional songs and folklore to the youngsters in the club.

'We were once well known for our integrity, loyalty and honesty. We all helped each other in the community, and respected the elders. All this is now disappearing. We have adopted some of the Jewish values and their way of life, not because their way is necessarily better or more civilized than ours; we just copy it blindly. Take a very simple example such as coffee: the coffee stores used to sell traditional Arabic coffee with spices, but they don't do it any more. We are now forced to buy the tasteless coffee that the Jews drink.'

Abeer was asked by her mother to fetch the dish of fruit from indoors. She gave a weary sigh, got up reluctantly, and shortly returned with the plate which she placed in front of her father.

'We were once happy, but they have robbed us of our freedom,' said Salma. 'When you are robbed of hope, there is no happiness. You can even hear small children today talk of the burden of their lives. They seem to carry the worries of the world on their shoulders.'

Salma's husband appeared. He sat on the porch without saying a word. He is a respected elder of the community; he has a *diwan* (guest-room or annexe) where villagers discuss important issues, where conflicts are resolved, and where strangers passing through the village are welcomed to spend the night.

His presence seemed to stop the conversation; there was an uneasy silence, which was broken by Abeer who jumped up with a yell as she saw her eldest brother walk towards the house. She ran towards him, and promptly started a fight with him.

When Fatma's parents left, she said: 'My father has a second wife. When he remarried, we were all very angry with him. My mother wanted to leave him but, although it would have served him right, we persuaded her to stay because of the children. He now regrets what he has done. He says that he has been very happy with my mother and it was foolish of him to have taken a second wife. Well, what's done is done.' And she shook her head disapprovingly.

It was getting dark. There were no lights as yet in the village, but not so far from Laqqiya there were lights glittering. They came from a kibbutz which was built on land that had ónce belonged to the villagers.

Less than a year later, Amer had aged considerably. He had had no grey hair the year before, but now he was partially grey. His face had become deeply lined, and he seemed to have grown thinner. But his humour remained unchanged. He smiled sardonically:

'I have some amazing news. Our struggle and determination have finally paid off. About a couple of months ago, the authorities agreed to recognize our existence, but of course with certain conditions. Villagers who own land which is marked on the skeletal map will be allowed one dunum to build a house on. Those who cannot show ownership of land will have to buy the dunum for $2,000. For the first time for forty years we will have a real home, a permanent one. A home is indivisible from the homeland.

'However, in spite of the agreement, the authorities have not stopped destroying houses. In December, a man had his house destroyed because he built it without a licence. They fined him I£5,000, and forced him to work without a salary as an orderly in a hospital. Consequently, he lost his real job, which was in a factory.

'All our houses are built without a licence. The authorities make a random choice as to whose house they are going to destroy. It's their way of trying to divide the villagers. The person whose house has been destroyed wonders why he in particular has been chosen and not his neighbour, whose house has also been built without a licence. And so the seeds of suspicion begin to grow: the homeless villager begins to suspect his neighbour of being an informer. But we have become wise to their ploys, and we are fully aware that the only people to blame are the Israeli authorities.

'The other change which has taken place is that a new head of council has been appointed. The head of the council changes every four years. The kibbutzim take it in turns to have a representative as head of the council. The new one is said to be more moderate than his predecessor. He has suggested that we should elect a local committee to represent our village. But so far nothing has happened. The villagers do not quite under-stand what is expected of them; they do not know how and on what basis to elect the committee.

'Although the existence of our village has finally been recognized, the struggle is not over yet. We will need loans from the Ministry of Housing to help us build houses; and we're also looking for Arab architects in al-Jaleel [Galilee] who will design our houses for us. We want Arabs to do it because they will know what we need. We also need money to build a secondary school so that we don't have to send our children to the north to get a decent secondary education. We will need money to build roads, to improve our water and electricity system, and we will want money to build some sort of industry in our village.

'The only thing that they have built us so far is a new clinic, and that's only because the Jewish doctor and nurses – we only have one Arab nurse – complained that they could not work in the old clinic because it was too small. However, I have found a use for it. With the help of a few other villagers, I am now turning the old clinic into a public library. We are trying to get money from various institutions and publishers so that we can buy books and maintain the library. We put an advertisement in the *Al-Ittihad* newspaper on 30 June. It cost us I£100, which for us is a lot of money. We wrote:

> The Educational Association of the Sons of Laqqiya are opening a public library, which is an important service for the villagers. Because of our meagre finances, we are obliged to ask charity associations, public organizations, publishing houses, and our writers and poets for financial support for this project for the village. We have great hope in our people. Addres: P.O. Box 1014, Beer al-Sabei'.

'It is important to have a public library, particularly for the youngsters. We must make sure that our young people do not waste their lives, especially now that the drug problem has reached our village. It has not reached the proportions that it has in places like Yaffa and 'Acca, but we now do have a couple of villagers who have become drug pushers.'

He stopped talking and turned the radio on to listen to the news in Arabic. After it was over, he said:

'I'm off to measure the doors of the old clinic. We're going to put in metal doors to make sure no one will come and burn our books.' And with a wry smile, he walked off into the distance.

The children returned from school. They too had changed: they were a year older, and that much taller. But Abeer's rule of tyranny remained unchanged. She threw her satchel on the porch, and ran to the back garden where her mother was sitting under the shade of an olive tree, chopping molokhia.

'What's for lunch?' asked the child.

'Molokhia.'

'I want chicken and chips,' Abeer ordered.

'You will have chicken, but we don't have chips today.'

'Why not? I want chips.'

Fatma ignored her. Abeer continued to nag, but finally tired of it when she realized her mother would not give in. She ran off in search of a more pliable target.

Mona, one of Fatma's sisters, arrived. She was a kindergarten teacher, and unlike Fatma she was not wearing the traditional Bedouin dress, but Western clothes and a headscarf. She had come to pick up her six-month-old baby. Usually it was her mother who took care of the child while she was at work, but Salma had gone to Gaza to visit a relative who had arrived from Jordan; so it was Fatma who baby-sat instead.

'Abeer has been doing very well in school. She is very bright and ambitious,' she said to Fatma.

Fatma smiled serenely, with pride. 'I wonder how long it will be before we start building our new permanent homes,' she said.

'I should think at least two or three months, that is if the authorities don't find endless excuses to delay us. You never know with these people; they may even change their minds altogether.'

They were both quiet for a while. Their thoughts were interrupted by the arrival of Nidal, Fatma's eldest son. He started mending the tyre of his bicycle.

Mona sighed and said: 'We are in limbo in every possible way. We don't have the same rights as the Jewish Israeli citizens, and the Jews don't consider us Arabs. On the other hand, some Arabs consider all Bedouins traitors because there are a few Bedouins who are in fact traitors: they join the Israeli army.' She looked angrily around her. 'Do you know that in the north the school inspectors are classified as Arabs, but here in the south, they are classified as Bedouin. I once said to the authorities: "What do you think we are? We are Arabs too, you know." '

Nidal remarked quietly: 'I'm going to be a teacher when I grow up. They have forbidden my father to teach, so I shall do it for him.'

His aunt continued: 'The world doesn't really know what our life is like. People outside are totally unaware of the injustices we suffer and the oppressive system we live under.'

She suddenly looked at her watch and said that she had to rush home to make lunch for her family.

Fatma got up and walked towards the kitchen, but she was distracted by the 'mad woman of Laqqiya'. She was middle aged, held a packet of cigarettes in her hand, and was pacing back and forth in front of the garden.

'She claims she knew Gamal Abdel Nasser,' said Fatma. 'She also claims that she was once married to Gadaffi. I used to take pity on her, and occasionally I used to let her spend the night here. But she began to drive me crazy too. She used to spend the night smoking, and talking to herself in a loud voice. So I finally had to tell her not to come here any more. She also gossips a great deal: false and harmful gossip.'

The 'mad woman of Laqqiya' stopped pacing, and walked away.

Fatma put the tray on the sitting-room floor, while Orouba brought the mattresses in from the porch.

'Why don't we have lunch outside?' said Amer, who had just returned from measuring the doors of the old clinic.

'Because it's too hot, and there are too many flies,' replied Fatma.

Everyone settled down on the mattresses and began eating lunch. Abeer fingered all of the chicken pieces, until her father told her to stop.

'Tomorrow is the last day of school,' she announced, but no one took any notice.

'Another change which has taken place is that I'm out of work,' Amer said. 'But then it gives me the chance to devote more time to the club and to setting up the library. I was kicked out of my job about eight months ago because I'm actively involved in developing awareness about our cause, and I'm outspoken. For example, at a meeting of the Jabha (Democratic Front for Peace and Equality), among other subjects we discussed racism. I was one of the people who gave a lecture on racism and the occupation. I spoke out strongly against them both. Shortly after that, I was called in by the Israeli security service. They interrogated me, and insulted me. They accused me of being a terrorist; they said that I was nothing but dirt, that I was a nonentity. I was expecting them to lock me up again, but in the end they didn't.

'At the moment I'm collecting unemployment benefit. But I've just been asked by the unemployment office to attend a meeting. They want to examine my case to see whether to continue to give me unemployment benefit.' He smiled mockingly, and then said: 'Who knows, they may be kind enough to find me another job.

'I'm also having problems with members of the Bene Shamon council. They don't want us to have a summer camp at the club. They claim that the one to be held in the school is enough, but I'm objecting strongly. The school summer camp will be supervised by a Jew, while the summer camp at the club will be supervised by me and other members of the club. This of course means that we will be able to give lectures on identity, sing Palestinian songs, discuss the intifada, etc., all of which won't be allowed in the school summer camp. One of the aims of the council is to try to influence the children to accept their policies.

'My other objection is that it isn't fair on the children to spend all year in school, and then have the summer camp there as well, where it would be associated with teachers, lessons, and authority. At least the club is a different environment. It's a place where they can enjoy themselves, and where they will learn about their cause. I'm determined to have a summer camp at the club whether the council likes it or not.'

It was time to go to the club.

The playground was the same, but there were changes inside. The room which was once used as a kindergarten had the kitchen added to it, and had been turned into a place for gymnastics, karate, and body building. There was also a training course for kindergarten teachers in progress.

'We have a new teacher to train them. She is a Palestinian who studied in America, and who lived there for many years before coming here. She is good. A non-governmental organization is also going to help us set up income-generating activities for women such as sewing and weaving. Weaving will not only produce an income, but it will re-introduce our heritage to the young women of today who have not learnt how to weave our beautiful traditional rugs.'

Hanging on one of the walls of the sports room was a poster of a Palestinian in the West Bank on which was written: *Down with occupation.* And on the walls of all the rooms were handwritten sayings and poems about equality, justice, and the homeland. They were more hard hitting than what had existed the previous year, and there were many more of them:

> *If the olives remembered who planted them*
> *The oil would turn to tears.* (Mahmoud Darwish)

> *We want peace for us and for all the children of the world. It is in all our interest to rid ourselves forever of violence, wars, and enmity between nations; and to replace them with equality, prosperity and peace.*

> *Freedom is not just the right of some individuals, or of a few nations, but it is the right of the whole world. It is my right, your right, the right of all people to be free of hunger, illness, ignorance, and exploitation. Freedom encompasses justice, and justice frees mankind from oppression: oppression of the strong against the weak; the able against the disabled; the old against the young; white against black; men against women; and the ruler against the ruled.*

'I try to make sure that the youngsters take an interest in these posters,' remarked Amer.

He began to weed the garden; he did it with great care, for the garden was like his child. After a while he stopped and rubbed the sweat from his forehead. He gazed at the boys who were playing football.

'The other day the club invited a young Jewish football team from Beer al-Sabei' to play against our team,' he said, sitting down on a step. 'We have a bigger football ground at the edge of the village, but of course it's nothing like the luxurious ones the Jews have. Can you imagine, when they came over they were actually surprised to discover that we were human beings, and that we could even play football.

'Before the game, I gave them a lecture about racism. What I tried to put across to them was that equality was a right and not a privilege. They seemed to take an interest, and they listened. But their friendly attitude changed after the game because our team won. They insulted us: they called us animals, savages, and other such names.'

He smiled and shook his head. 'But we did not give up. We invited another Jewish team, this time they were boy scouts. Once again we won the match, but the boy scouts were better behaved than the other lot. They accepted our victory without acrimony. We want to show these people that we are just as capable as they are. We want to show them that we too are human beings, and that we too have rights.

'The intifada has affected us in more than one way. It has developed the awareness of the Palestinians who were politically ignorant; it has intensified our struggle for our rights; and it has even affected tribal procedures for resolving conflicts.

'The other day, not far from here, a boy from the village was accidentally killed on the road by a driver who was also from Laqqiya. They were from different clans. Normally, the offender and his family would have had to leave the village. A jaha would have mediated between the two families until some sort of settlement was reached, after which the family would have been allowed to return to the village. However, in this case the boy's family told the jaha that their problems were small in comparison with the way the Jews were treating the people in the West Bank and Gaza, and that they did not want the driver and his family to leave the village, and nor did they want a settlement. But while both families were happy to leave it at that, of course the driver had to appear in court.

'Another case involved two teenagers from the village, both again from different clans. The boys had a fight, and one accidentally killed the other. Although the offender was held in custody by the police, his family left the village as tribal law dictated. But then the victim's family rejected the traditional procedure of reconciliation, and asked them, through the jaha, to return. They said that while they mourned the death of their son, their grief could not be greater than that of the hundreds of parents who had lost their sons in the intifada.

'People are beginning to be more aware of their political and social situation. They realize that to make traditional tribal demands for compensation is both negative and against their interests. It only serves the interests of the Israelis because they would like to see us in a state of conflict; they want us to be divided.'

The evening brought a pleasant breeze. Amer sat quietly on the porch engrossed in his thoughts. Fatma brought out an album of family photographs. There was a black-and-white photograph of her and Amer taken shortly after they were married.

'It was the tradition, and it still is, to marry one's cousin,' explained Fatma. 'I was happy when my family chose Amer because we loved one another.' And she smiled tenderly at her husband.

Amer grinned, and then looked at his watch. 'I must go. I have a meeting with some members of the club. We are going to discuss further renovations we want to make to the club, and we're going to examine a list of volunteers to choose a suitable person to teach English. We are also going to finalize the logo we are putting on the T-shirts we're giving the children who are going to attend the summer camp. The logo is to commemorate the caricaturist Naji al-Ali. There will be a picture of one of his main caricatures, and then below it will be written in both Arabic and Hebrew, *Yes to peace. No to racism.*

Amer told Fatma not to expect him for supper as the meeting was likely to be a long one. She and the children remained on the porch waiting for the electricity to come on. A figure clad in the Islamic dress of the fundamentalists passed by and greeted Fatma. When she was out of earshot, Fatma said:

'The Islamic fundamentalists say that it is a sin to wear the traditional Palestinian dress, and that one should only wear the Islamic dress they wear.'

She shook her head disapprovingly and continued: 'To be a practising Muslim is a good thing, but to be a fanatic is meaningless and destructive. On my wedding day I wore a Western wedding dress. It was one of my aunt's, who insisted that I wore it. She lived in Jordan and had modern ideas. I was one of the first women to wear such a wedding dress, and I was severely criticized for not wearing a Palestinian wedding dress. But in everyday life I've always worn the Palestinian dress, and I shall go on wearing it. It covers me up as well as what the

fundamentalists wear today. One of my brothers is a fundamentalist, and so is his wife. I don't think he will talk to you
because you're a woman, but I'm sure you can talk to his wife.'

The children jumped up and rushed indoors, for the
electricity had come on. They immediately turned on the
television and watched a programme in Hebrew. Fatma went to
prepare the supper and, to Abeer's delight, her mother had
made chips. After supper, Fatma sat with the children to watch
television. She told them to turn it on to an Arabic programme
as she did not understand Hebrew. The only Arabic channel
they could get was from Jordan, and King Hussein was giving a
speech.

'This is boring,' complained Orouba, and promptly turned it
back to the Israeli channel.

'Turn it back to Jordan. Boring or not, at least I can
understand the language,' her mother said angrily.

They obeyed her, and then left the room to find another form
of entertainment. But the electricity was cut off earlier than
usual and, as there was nothing else to do, everyone went to
bed.

Fatma woke up at 6.00, swept the kitchen, and prepared
breakfast.

'I came in very late last night,' said Amer. 'The meeting went
on for a very long time; we had a heated argument about the
logo. One of the men at the meeting said that we should not use
Hebrew on the T-shirts. I replied: "In that case tear up your
identity card since it's written in Hebrew. If you're going to be
fanatical about it, you'll be as destructive as the right-wing
Jews. What you suggest is unrealistic and counter-productive.
We are struggling for our rights, but we also have to accept the
fact that we must live and deal with the Jews. There are some
Jews who are aware of our grievances, and they want to
understand our cause. We must win them over."

'He really made me very angry. Does he think by refusing to
use Hebrew on the T-shirts he will start a revolution which will
change our situation? Fanaticism of any kind is destructive. We
now have the Islamic movements, and unfortunately they did
well in the last elections. They won in various villages, and in
Umm al-Fahem, one of the largest Arab towns. They carry out

voluntary work, such as road construction, cleaning up the streets, and so on, just like the Jabha and Abna' al-Balad. However, the main difference is that they do it all in the name of religion. They tell the people who join the movement that they will be rewarded in heaven.

'When the fundamentalists won the elections, the authorities thought that they were going to be a bigger threat than the other parties. But now they welcome them because they have discovered that many fundamentalists refuse to join the demonstrations other parties hold; they do not join in the struggle. And why should they when they're told that they will eventually find happiness in heaven? It makes their problems on earth more bearable. I think many of those who join the movement don't really understand what is happening in the country.'

Amer stopped talking and listened to the news.

Outside, there was the early morning hustle and bustle of people going off to work. Some of the women came out to hang their washing in the sun, or to air their mattresses, bed covers and rugs. Men from Gaza arrived in their vans to sell their produce. They drove slowly through the village shouting through a loudspeaker:

'Fresh molokhia, cucumbers, green peppers, aubergines!'

Others sold mats, pots and pans.

Amer finished his breakfast and went off to Beer al-Sabei'.

Hoda, Fatma's fundamentalist sister-in-law who is also her cousin, teaches in the primary school. She is in her late twenties, and has a three-year-old son. Her house consists of one bedroom, a sitting-room, kitchen and bathroom.

Hoda's son was asleep on the sofa in the sitting-room. 'He's not feeling well,' she remarked, as she placed some cold drinks on the table.

She asked if Fatma and her family were well, and then after a brief silence said: 'You know, I wasn't brought up here. I was brought up in Jordan. My father was involved in the struggle of 1948 and, since then, the Israelis have not allowed him to return.

'I graduated from the Institute of Education in Jordan, and then was more or less immediately married off to Fatma's brother, who is also my cousin. At first, I didn't want to marry him because he lived here; I didn't want to leave my family, or Jordan. I kept refusing him, but then I gave in because of family pressure. It's not easy for a girl in our society to oppose her family. When I came over here, I found life difficult. To begin with, we had a hard time persuading the authorities to let me stay here with my husband, and then it was not easy to adjust to a lower standard of living than I was used to in Jordan. I'm getting used to it though; I've been here for four years now.

'I was brought up to be a good Muslim. But it's only recently that I have become part of the Islamic movement. The victory of the movement in the elections means that many people finally realize that it is the only real Palestinian nationalist movement. It's our only hope and salvation in both the '48 region, and in the West Bank and Gaza. It also shows that many of us have not adopted Jewish values and culture.

'Palestine and the Islamic movement are indivisible. When we have a Palestinian state in the West Bank and Gaza, it will be based on an Islamic constitution because the majority are Muslims. If we have a genuine and proper Muslim state then the Christians will be treated equally and justly. But to have a real Muslim state, at least 75 per cent of the people have to change; they have to practise real Islam. At the moment, many people are practising it superficially. Proper Islam will solve all our problems: political, economic and social.

'There is a conflict at the moment between the ideologies of the PLO and those of the Islamic movement. The mistake the fundamentalists make is that they want to *impose* an Islamic state. This just produces a negative reaction; you can't impose an Islamic state if the majority of the people are unwilling to have it. You have to win them over first, and then teach them to become good Muslims. On the other hand, if we have a secular state there will be chaos because it will not have a solid Islamic base. It is easier to use Islam to solve our social problems than it is to create a genuine Islamic state. People's deep-rooted secular attitudes have to change first; it is a complicated process.

'I try in my own way to change people's attitudes by teaching Islam to young girls and to women. I hold classes twice a week in the mosque. At the moment I'm teaching 40 young girls and 15 women: their ages vary from 12 years to 45. The young ones are the best students; they are even wearing the proper Islamic dress. They are also much more aware than the older ones that the Islamic movement is our only hope for obtaining justice and equality. The older women are not really interested in the Islamic movement. They are too frightened and inhibited to become involved. Many of the older people, especially those who have been badly treated by the Jews, do not speak about the Palestinian cause. They are terrified of the authorities. However, my generation is not afraid to talk openly about the Palestinian cause, and about the Islamic movement. Unfortunately, not all of the young girls in the village attend my course. There are still many who wear Western clothes, and who are not interested in becoming true Muslims. But one day all this will change.'

Nidal and Esam were lying on the porch, when a loud shriek came from the kitchen. They jumped up: 'Mother, mother, what is it!' they shouted as they ran towards her.

It was a gecko scurrying across the wall of the kitchen. The boys smiled and chased it out with a broom.

'It's harmless,' said Nidal.

'I can't stand these things,' replied his mother.

She finished preparing lunch, and just as she was setting it on the floor of the sitting-room Amer and his younger brother Mohammad arrived.

Mohammad also works as a caretaker at the University of Beer al-Sabei', and he is the coach of the village football team.

As he began eating, he said: 'You know that some of the Jews want the Palestinians from the West Bank and Gaza who work in Israel to wear badges so that they can be easily identified. Well, some of the left-wing Jewish students at the university said that if this were to happen, then they too would wear badges stating where they and their families originally came from.'

'The authorities are using all kinds of methods to try to destroy us,' said Amer. 'In the West Bank and Gaza, they are killing Palestinians every day; and here, they're trying to destroy our identity by their educational system, by forbidding us to teach our culture and heritage, and by banning us from certain jobs. They even go as far as dividing us into Muslims, Christians, Druze and Bedouins, which is a distortion of reality. We are all Palestinians, historically and nationally. Whatever happens, the Jews will never destroy us or our identity. One day there will be a Palestinian state in the West Bank and Gaza. I wouldn't move there because this is where I've lived all my life; this is my home and my land. But, on the other hand, they might force me to leave because of my political activities.'

It was time for the news. More Palestinians had been killed in the West Bank. Fatma sighed wearily and said:

'What kind of world do we live in? There's so much suffering and so much killing. What kind of history is mankind leaving behind?'

BIBLIOGRAPHY

El-Asmar, Fouzi. 1978. *To Be An Arab in Israel*. Beirut, the Institution of Palestine Studies.

——. 1986. *Through the Hebrew Looking Glass: Arab Stereotypes in Children's Literature*. London, Zed Books.

Edge, Simon. 1988. *The Arabs of 1948: The Situation of the Palestinian Citizens of Israel*. London, Council for the Advancement of Arab–British Understanding (Briefing no. 22).

Elrazik, Adnan Abd, Amin, Riyad and Davis, Uri. 1978. 'Problems of Palestinians in Israel: land, work, education', in *Journal of Palestine Studies*, vol. 7, no. 3.

Falah, Ghazi. Winter 1989. 'Israeli state policy toward Bedouin sedentarization in the Negev', in *Journal of Palestine Studies*, vol. 18, no. 2.

Habiby, Emile. 1985. *The Secret Life of Saeed the Pessoptimist*. London, Zed Books.

Haidar, Aziz and Zureik, Elia. 1987. 'The Palestinians seen through the Israeli cultural paradigm', in *Journal of Palestine Studies*, vol. 16, no. 3.

al-Haj, Majid and Rosenfeld, Henry. 1988. *Arab Local Government in Israel*. Tel Aviv, the International Center for Peace in the Middle East.

Jiryis, Sabri. 1976. *The Arabs in Israel*. New York, Monthly Press Review.

——. 1979. 'The Arabs in Israel, 1973–79', in *Journal of Palestine Studies*, vol. 8, no. 4.

Khalidi, Raja. 1984. 'The Arab economy in Israel: dependency or development?', in *Journal of Palestine Studies*, vol. 13, no. 3.

——. 1988. *The Arab Economy in Israel: the Dynamics of a Region's Development*. London, Croom Helm.

Khalidi, Walid. 1985. *Before Their Diaspora: a Photographic History of the Palestinians 1876–1948*. Washington DC, Institute for Palestine Studies.

Makhoul, Najwa. 1982. 'Changes in the employment structure of Arabs in Israel', in *Journal of Palestine Studies*, vol. 11, no. 3.

Mar'i, Sami. 1978. *Arab Education in Israel*. Syracuse, Syracuse University Press.

——. 1985. 'The future of Palestinian Arab education in Israel', in *Journal of Palestine Studies*, vol. 14, no. 2.

McDowall, David. 1989. *Palestine and Israel: the Uprising and Beyond*. London, I.B. Tauris.

Nakhleh, Khalil. 'Anthropological and sociological studies on the Arabs in Israel: a critique', in *Journal of Palestine Studies*, vol. 6, no. 4.

Nakkara, Hanna Dib. 1985. 'Israeli land seizure under various defense and emergency regulations', in *Journal of Palestine Studies*, vol. 14, no. 2.

Rouhana, Nadim. 1989. 'The political transformation of the Palestinians in Israel: from acquiescence to challenge', in *Journal of Palestine Studies*, vol. 18, no. 3.

Sayigh, Rosemary. 1979. *Palestinians: from Peasants to Revolutionaries*. London, Zed Books.

Shammas, Anton. 1988. *Arabesques*. London, Viking.

Smith, Pamela Ann. 1984. *Palestine and the Palestinians: 1876–1983*. Beckenham, Kent, Croom Helm.

Touma, Emile. 1985. 'The political coming-of-age of the "national minority" ', in *Journal of Palestine Studies*, vol. 14, no. 2.

Zayyad, Tawfiq. 1976. 'The fate of the Arabs in Israel', in *Journal of Palestine Studies*, vol. 6, no. 1.

Zureik, Elia. 1976. 'Transformation of class structure among the Arabs in Israel: from peasantry to proletariat', in *Journal of Palestine Studies*, vol. 6, no. 1.

——. 1979. *The Palestinians in Israel: a Study in Internal Colonialism*. London, Routledge & Kegan Paul.

Periodicals

al-Bayader al-Siyassi
al-Fajr (English-language weekly)
al-Ittihad (Arab-language daily)

The Jerusalem Post (English-language weekly)
Journal of Palestine Studies
Middle East International (English-language fortnightly)
Tanmiya (quarterly newsletter on Palestinian development issues published since 1985 by Welfare Association, Geneva)

Index

205

Miari, Muhammad, 16, 25, 94
Middle East International, 58
Minister of Arab Affairs, 131
Ministry of Education, 113, 131
Ministry of Housing, 166, 175, 189
Morocco, 159
Moroccan Jew, 107, 159
Moughar, 87
Muawiya, 54
Muslim Initiative Association, 47–8
Muslim League, 19, 94
Muslim club, 173
Musmus, 48–9
   Al-Amal al-Tatawe (Voluntary
    Work Association), 48–9, 93

Nahf, 37
Nakhleh, Khalil, 90
Nakkara, Hanna, 31–2
Nasser, Gamal Abdel, 4, 6, 78,
    105–6, 164, 173, 192
The Nation, 154
National Religious Party, 33
Nazareth, (al-Nasra), 4–5, 7, 9,
    13–14, 21–2, 26, 33, 34, 37, 39,
    47, 49, 65, 70–1, 75–7, 91, 138,
    144, 161
   Democratic Front, 7
   Graduates' League, 59
Negev (Naqab), 54, 80–2, 84–5,
    178, 183
New York, 151
New York Review of Books, 29
New York Times, 27, 35, 95, 96
Nidal, municipality worker, 11
Northern District, 34
Norway, 153

Olmert, Ehud, 27
Orthodox club, 173

Palestine Liberation Organization
   (PLO), 16, 24–5, 91–2, 96,
    112, 117, 131, 136, 169, 171,
    178, 199
   Non-Governmental organizations
    on question of, 16
Palestinian state, 16–17, 24–5, 29,
    96, 120–1, 131, 136, 155,
    177–8, 199, 201
Paris, 151
Poland, 159
Peled, Matti, 16
Petach Tikva, 83
Prague, 134
Prisoners' Friends Association
   (PFA), 75–6
Progressive List for Peace (PLP),
    16, 18–19, 21–3, 25, 94

Al-Qabas, 14
Quaker, 107

Rabin, Yitzhak, 13, 17
Rahat, 80–2, 84
Rakah, 7, 12–13
   see also Communist Party;
    Democratic Front
Rama, 33, 40
Ramleh, 26, 42, 44, 47, 63, 158
   Rabitat al-Jamiyyin, 44
Ramadan, *see* festivals
Al-Raya, 12, 21, 86
Reches, Eli, 27
Red Cross, 159, 181
Regional Committee of Heads of
    Arab Local Councils, 14–16,
    19, 29, 39, 57, 59, 69, 72, 77,
    79, 95, 131
Research Centre for Arab Heritage,
    76
Romania, 133
Romanian Jew, 184
Rouhana, Nadim, 14, 17, 23–4,
    28–9, 89
Russia, 134

Sabra, 184
Safad, 33, 54
Sakhneen, 13, 21, 79, 150
Sanduq al Marda, 184
Sane', 181
Sephardim, 26
Shafa Amr, 53
Shamir, Yitzhak, 27, 129
Shammas, Anton, 29, 97